THE
BASEBALL
BOOK OF
WHY

THE BASEBALL BOOK OF WHY

Dan Schlossberg

**With a Foreword by
Bob Feller**

JONATHAN DAVID PUBLISHERS, INC.
MIDDLE VILLAGE, NY 11379

THE BASEBALL BOOK OF WHY

JONATHAN DAVID PUBLISHERS, INC.
68-22 Eliot Avenue
Middle Village, New York 11379

10 9 8 7 6 5 4 3 2

Library of Congress Cataloging in Publication Data

Schlossberg, Dan, 1948-
    The baseball book of why.

    Includes index.
    1. Baseball—United States—Miscellanea.   I. Title.
GV863.A1S35   1984   796.357'0973   83-26137
ISBN 0-8246-0298-6

Printed in the United States of America

This book is dedicated to baseball, the only sport worthy of the title "America's national game," and its unique meaning in my life. I am eternally grateful to everyone who has tolerated my passion for the game and enabled this dream to reach reality. With special thanks to:

Both my parents, Ezra and Miriam, for their love and encouragement

All my devoted friends in the Dialogue leadership group

Samantha, my lovely daughter and budding All-Star pitcher

Each of the young women who gave their time, affection, and support

Beauty in soul—greater even than beauty in sport

Atlanta and its Braves, my favorite team

Laughter, the spice of life, which helps lift the spirit

Love, the greatest motivating force I know.

Contents

Acknowledgments

The author extends heartfelt thanks to those friends and colleagues whose generous contributions helped make this book possible: collectors Barry Halper and Bill Jacobowitz of Livingston, New Jersey; sportscasters Ed Lucas of Jersey City, New Jersey, and Kevin Barnes of Atlanta; the media relations directors of the 26 teams, with special mention for Katy Feeney of the National League, Phyllis Merhige of the American League, Rick Cerrone of the Commissioner's Office, and Vince Nauss, who has moved from the Commissioner's Office to the Philadelphia Phillies; and SABR (Society for American Baseball Research) members Kit Crissey, Bob Davids, and Cliff Kachline.

Thanks also to John J. McGee, a SABR member from Reading, Pennsylvania, who provided materials for a similar book he planned to author but whose interests took him elsewhere because he learned there is more to life than baseball.

Appreciation is extended to the editors of *The Sporting News, Sport,* and *Baseball Digest,* whose publications served as valuable sources of questions and answers, and to four SABR periodicals: *Baseball Historical Review* (1981–82), *Baseball Research Journal* (1976–77–80–81–82),

Minor League Baseball Stars (1978), and *Great Hitting Pitchers* (1979).

Chief reference books for this volume were *The Sports Encyclopedia: Baseball* (New York: Grosset & Dunlap, 1982), by David S. Neft, Richard M. Cohen, and Jordan A. Deutsch; *The Sporting News Official Baseball Record Book* (St. Louis: The Sporting News, 1982), edited by Craig Carter; *High & Inside: the Complete Guide to Baseball Slang* (New York: Warner Books, 1980), by Joseph McBride; *The Ballparks* (New York: Hawthorn Books, 1975), by Bill Shannon and George Kalinsky; *Invisible Men* (New York: Atheneum, 1983), by Donn Rogosin; and *The Sporting News Baseball Trivia Book* (St. Louis: The Sporting News, 1983), co-edited by Joe Hoppel and Craig Carter).

Foreword

It was dark, windy, and wet on the fantail of the Queen Elizabeth II in October 1981 as we listened to a Miami radio station broadcasting the play-by-play of the World Series between the Los Angeles Dodgers and the New York Yankees.

My wife Anne, Dan Schlossberg, and other interested people gathered by my small battery-powered radio that was just audible enough to hear about 90 percent of the action.

We were on our way at 26 knots from St. Thomas to Bermuda and it was about 1:00 a.m. The ship's passenger radio was silent, but we could not wait until morning to know the results of the game. A few late deck-walkers joined us. "What are you doing here at this hour? What's happening?" they asked. "The World Series is happening," we responded.

The strollers stopped to listen in. They wanted to know why we would brave the salty sea breeze and intermittent static to hear a faraway baseball game.

Why baseball? Because it's a fascinating game, a challenge, an enterprise that has meant so much to millions of Americans—and particularly to me, as a player, coach, broadcaster, and fan.

I'll never forget my first contact with professional baseball—in 1928, when I was 10 years old. Babe Ruth and Lou
Gehrig came to Des Moines with their barnstorming teams
and my father took me to see them. They were selling
autographed balls for $5 apiece to raise money for the
crippled children's hospital in Des Moines. I bought a ball
with money I earned from catching gophers; for every pair of
gopher claws, we got a dime in bounty at the county
treasurer's office. I got my 50 gophers in a couple of weeks
and was able to get the ball. I still have that ball and it's
probably my most prized trophy—more than anything I ever
earned myself.

That "gopher ball" symbolizes what baseball means to
me: a game rich in tradition as well as sentimentality. No-
where is that meaning so obvious as in the pages that follow.

Ever since Fanny Brice, in the famous comedy show
Baby Snooks said, "Why, Daddy?" the American baseball
fan has been asking the same question. Even Abbott and
Costello, in their hilarious baseball routine *Who's on First*
had a leftfielder named Why.

Dan Schlossberg has written *The Baseball Book of
Why*—which could be a million pages long—so I will only say
that the question "Why?" is more important than ever.

When a manager, coach, parent, or teacher tells his
charges to do something, they no longer do it (unless they
are Marine privates). Today, everyone wants to know
"Why?" You must explain. You don't say, "Because I'm the
boss" or "Because I'm in charge." You are expected to
explain why.

Why does a baseball manager use a lefthanded pitcher
against a righthanded hitter and vice versa? It is because of
the size and shape of the ballpark, the way the wind is
blowing (in, out, or across), and on and on. Maybe the
manager is playing percentages, following a hunch, or perhaps over-managing.

Why do the players call the ball an "apple," an error a
"boot" or "kick," an easy-to-hit pitcher a "cousin," a good
curve a "hook," a bad arm a "putty arm," a short single over

the infield a "Texas Leaguer"? And why is a hitter who doesn't get a hit said to be wearing a "horse collar"?

I doubt if other languages or dialects have as much slang as we do when it comes to our national pastime—but slang seems preferable to correct English as a form of expression because it commands so much attention.

The origin of baseball terminology has always held a special fascination for me. But I was just as interested in the rest of this book. I was curious to know how many "whys" of baseball Dan Schlossberg could answer. If anyone can answer, Dan can—as this book will show—though some answers are certain to remain controversial forever.

With a little thought, you can figure out why a "round-house" is a curveball and a "butterfly" is a knuckleball, but why is a "traffic cop" a line drive, a "nothing ball" a batting practice pitch, a "Baltimore chop" a ball that bounces high in front of the plate, a "fishing trip" a swing at a bad pitch, and a "Dick Smith" a loner?

Dan Schlossberg knows—as he shows not only in this book but also in his marvelous earlier volume, *The Baseball Catalog*. In addition to being a friend and a fine writer, Dan is an enthusiastic fan, diligent researcher, and student of baseball history.

As a result, the pages that follow provide many hours of entertainment for both avid and casual followers of the game. That's not surprising in a book compiled by an authority who knows just about everything involving our Great American pastime.

Enjoy. I know you will.

BOB FELLER

Gates Mills, Ohio

Introduction

During the 1982 World Series, I was asked to give a breakfast talk to the Men's Club of the Glen Rock, New Jersey, Jewish Center. The subject matter was left up to me, so I decided to focus on humorous anecdotes—anything to keep a Sunday morning audience awake.

I could have just as easily settled on the question-and-answer format that dominates this book. Curiosity has piqued not only the interest of cats but also of baseball fans—starting at an early age. Adults as well as children seem to have an endless supply of questions starting with the word "why."

In some ways, writing this book reminded me of going on a long drive with my 12-year-old daughter Samantha. Maybe she's outgrown it a little bit, but she still seems to question almost everything—as any writer's offspring should. *Why* are we going? *Why* are we going today instead of tomorrow? *Why* did you get me up so early? *Why* do I have to go to bed so early tonight? *Why* are we driving instead of flying? *Why* can't we stop for lunch? *Why* do we have to miss *Happy Days?*

Such questions can drive a dad to distraction—and conceiving other "why" questions for a baseball book can be an equally mind-wrenching assignment. But researching the answers turned out to be as enjoyable as formulating the questions. Surrounding the rabid baseball fan with newspapers, magazines, research journals, and books laden with history and statistics must be something like putting a wino in a well-stocked wine cellar. In a word, it's heaven.

The purpose of this book is twofold: to entertain and to enlighten. As Bob Feller notes in his Foreword, *The Baseball Book of Why* could be longer than it is. The charm of the game, with a heritage that dates back more than a century, evokes thousands of questions. A separate book of "why" questions could be written on each topic.

The book makes no attempt to cover every development in baseball history, but strives instead to convey the spirit of a game that has captured the imagination of Americans, not to mention foreign fans, for more than 100 years.

That imagination has been fueled by real-life heroes who have assumed legendary status with the passage of time. Babe Ruth, for example, is regarded not only as a star rightfielder for the New York Yankees but also as a Paul Bunyon figure, a larger-than-life giant who made headlines with his camel-hair coat, eating habits, and hospital visits as well as his batting prowess.

No one disputes the fact that Ruth hit 714 lifetime home runs, second only to Hank Aaron among baseball's great sluggers, but there is considerable dispute over other early records. Before the advent of the electronic age, spearheaded by radio and the subsequent development of television, reporting and record-keeping were sometimes sloppy and occasionally exaggerated for effect. That problem is reflected in conflicting statistics from the early days of baseball.

With the "facts" often presented differently in various sources, I had a choice: find a third source and go with the majority opinion (if two of three sources were in agreement) or use my judgment as to which source was the most reliable (sometimes three sources presented three different versions of the same event, such as the confusing finish of the "Merkle's boner" game in 1908).

Because of my membership in the Society for American Baseball Research (SABR) and my high regard for the research methods employed by that body of historians, writers, and advocates of the game, the context of this book often reflects the published findings of SABR—even when those findings conflict with such traditional sources as *The Sporting News* or the baseball encyclopedias.

More than anything else, members of SABR are devoted fans of the game. My intent in writing this book is to share that love of baseball with others through a unique format unlike any presented previously. That prospect explains *why* so much time and energy was devoted to the research and writing of this book.

Dan Schlossberg

Passaic, New Jersey
January 1984

Chapter 1

HISTORICAL ROOTS

Introduction

To some, it is a sport. To others, it is a business. To Bill Klem the great Hall of Fame umpire, baseball was a religion.

Professional baseball has thrived for more than a century, establishing itself as "America's national pastime" without question. Fans continue to turn out in such record numbers that only horse racing (with betting the biggest incentive) attracts a larger national audience.

But baseball is far more than a spectator sport; it is also a sport in which more than 20 million amateurs participate. The enjoyment of baseball stems from the unbridled enthusiasm of spectators and participants of all ages. That enthusiasm began before the Civil War.

According to legend, Abner Doubleday "invented" baseball in Cooperstown, New York in 1839—though most historians believe Doubleday was a West Point plebe that year and never set foot in Cooperstown. The Doubleday legend was still the primary reason that the National Baseball Hall of Fame and Museum opened in Cooperstown in 1939, a century after the initial game was supposedly played.

Ironically, the Hall of Fame itself contains a plaque referring to Alexander Cartwright, rather than Doubleday, as "the father of modern baseball."

It was Cartwright, a New York bank teller, who wrote the first rules and organized the first game—played on June 19, 1846, at the Elysian Fields of Hoboken, New Jersey. The New York Nine embarrassed Cartwright's New York Knickerbockers, 23–1.

By 1849, the Knicks appeared in uniforms for the first time (previous games were played in street clothes). Eight years later, the first league was organized, with the Fashion Race Course in Jamaica, New York, declared the official site for all games. Although only New York teams were league members, the fledgling circuit bore the audacious name of the National Association of Baseball Clubs. Teams helped meet their expenses with proceeds from the 50-cent admission charged to spectators.

Players were not paid, however, until 1869, when former cricket star Harry Wright gathered nine top players for his Cincinnati Red Stockings. Cincinnati won 69 games without a loss (there was one tie) and forged a 130-game winning streak that lasted until June 14, 1870. The team was so popular that President Ulysses S. Grant received members at the White House.

The Red Stockings were part of the first professional league, the National Association of Professional Baseball Players, formed in 1871. But constant franchise and player movement, plus the unsavory influence of gamblers, doomed the new venture. Several club owners picked up the remains to form the infant National League in 1876.

The National League's eight clubs played 70-game seasons in their early years, then increased the format to 112 contests by 1884 and 126 two years later. By 1901, when the American League began play, both major circuits were playing 140 games. The season was lengthened to 154 games in 1904 and to 162 with expansion to 10-team leagues in 1961–62. Divisional play began in 1969, when each league expanded to 12 teams. The American League added two clubs in 1977 but maintained the 162-game schedule length.

Other "major" leagues have come and gone since the National League started play in 1876. The American Association, the Union Association, the Players League, and the Federal League all sought big-league status at one time or another, but most lasted only a season or two.

The American League, easily the most successful of early National League rivals, won a place in the major-league system in 1903, when a document known as the National Agreement was drawn up and ratified in Cincinnati (a previous National Agreement, signed in 1883, made peace between the National League and American Association, then a major league). The 1903 Agreement created a reserve rule to prevent rival clubs from raiding each other's rosters and also protected the territory and independence of minor-league teams. With the National Agreement in force, there were no changes in the baseball map between 1903 and 1953.

Baseball officials have always worked to keep accurate records. Batting averages were introduced in 1871 and won-lost records for pitchers in 1877, but records of complete games were not kept until National League executive John Heydler began the practice in 1909.

Three years later, Heydler introduced the concept of rating pitchers by calculating a new statistic known as earned run average. Neither league tabulated runs batted in officially until 1920, though the *Chicago Tribune* began keeping track of runs batted in during the 1880 campaign.

Today, statistics are a vital part of the game. When batters appear on national television, their batting averages, home run totals, and runs batted in tallies—often calculated up-to-the-minute by computer—are flashed on screen.

Long-distance radio reception and cable television have made it easier to follow baseball through live broadcasts—a practice that began in 1921 when Pittsburgh station KDKA broadcast a game between the Pirates and the Philadelphia Phillies.

The love affair between Americans and their favorite game endures and gathers strength with time. Baseball began before the Civil War and has since become firmly entrenched as an integral ingredient of Americana. This chapter explores those historical roots and their evolution.

Why can't modern statistics be compared with early National League statistics?

The National League began play in 1876 but constant changes in rules and customs rendered early records virtually meaningless. Well into the 1880s, for example, batters "ordered" their pitches and runners were permitted to interfere with fielders trying to make plays. Pitchers were required to throw underhand and faced other restrictions that stayed in force until 1884. The distance from pitcher to batter moved from 45 to 50 feet and eventually to the current 60 feet, 6 inches (in 1893). With old pitching distances closer to home, pitchers worked more and won more. Old Hoss Radbourn had a 60-12 mark for Providence of the National League in 1884. Strikes were not charged on fouls until 1895 (a foul tip caught after two strikes was not considered a strikeout until 1903) and stolen bases were not credited as they are today until 1898. Changing schedule lengths also made it difficult to compare statistics. Teams played 70-game slates in 1876, then 112 in 1884, and 126 in 1886. At the century's turn, the schedule jumped to 140 games, to 154 in 1904, and to 162 in 1961.

Why was a pitcher once able to win 70 games in a season?

In the early days of baseball, teams carried only a few pitchers. The best ones worked as often as they were physically able. Jim Galvin of the 1878 Buffalo Bisons pitched in 101 games (league and nonleague), completed 96, and posted a composite record of 72-25, with three ties. He won 10 of 15 from National League clubs and threw a total of 17 shutouts. Because boxscores of the day don't reflect innings pitched, Galvin's workhorse efforts can't be pinpointed precisely, but it is estimated that he worked at least 895 innings and possibly as many as 905. Buffalo, then in the International Association, played a total of 116 games in 1878.

(The modern major-league record for single season victories is 41, by Jack Chesbro of the 1904 New York Highlanders. Prior to the century's change, Hoss Radbourn enjoyed a 60-win season for Providence of the National League, but pitching rules were changed substantially in 1893, 10 years after Radbourn's feat.)

Why did baseball introduce the reserve clause?

The old reserve clause—which bound a player to a club until it sold, traded, or released him—was created on September 29, 1879, at a National League meeting in Buffalo, New York. A. H. Soden, owner of the Boston franchise, suggested a clause which permitted clubs to hold five players "in reserve" as protection against raids from other teams. In the early years, players considered it an honor to be included among the five protected players because those five were supposed to be the best on each club. Later players equated the reserve clause with slavery, binding them to one club and hindering their potential career development (a bench-warmer for one club might be a starter for another).

Why was an early baseball executive called the "Bismarck of Baseball"?

National League president Abraham Mills earned the title the "Bismarck of Baseball" in 1883, when he signed the first National Agreement, a peace pact with the American Association, then a major league. The agreement established an 11-player reserve list, guaranteed territorial rights, set minimum salaries at $1,000, and even created a postseason series between league champions, a forerunner of the modern World Series. Bismarck was a German leader whose expert diplomacy helped keep Europe at peace during the same period.

Why did major-league baseball players once form their own league?

In 1890, many major-leaguers revolted when club owners announced a salary ceiling of $2,500 per year, with a strong reserve clause that bound players to their teams unless sold, traded, or released. The players, led by John Montgomery Ward, found financial backing, opened ball parks, and provided such stiff competition for fan attention that the American Association, then a major league, went under and the senior National League was severely damaged. Owners led by Al Spalding managed to buy out Players League backers shortly after the 1890 campaign, forcing the players back into the National League fold. With the American Association eliminated, the National League expanded to 12 clubs in 1892 in order to absorb all available talent (the National League returned to its eight-club format by the turn-of-the-century).

Why did baseball play a split season in 1892?

Since the National League was the only major circuit operating in 1892, league executives decided to pattern their season after a successful Eastern League (minor league) experiment of 1891: the first half of the season would end on July 15 and the second in late October—with the schedule expanded from 140 to 154 games. Boston, the first-half winner, defeated Cleveland, the second-half winner, in five straight playoff games (best-of-nine format), but fan interest was so limited that the format was dropped. Fan interest increased in 1893, however, when an increase in the pitching distance from 50 feet to 60 feet, 6 inches produced games with greater offensive production (ostensibly because batters had more time to judge incoming pitches).

Why did the National League dismiss the American League as an upstart unlikely to succeed?

Before the American League was created just after the turn of the century, the National League (nee 1876) had withstood several challenges from would-be "major" leagues. Because it believed the American was nothing more than another interloper, the National League resented the American League for raiding its rosters and copying its style of play (some 110 of the American League's 185 players in the initial 1901 campaign had prior National League experience).

The American League first surfaced as the American Association in 1900, but changed its name on November 14, 1900. Initial American League members were Baltimore, Buffalo, Chicago, Cleveland, Detroit, Milwaukee, Philadelphia, and Washington. By 1903, Boston had replaced Buffalo, Milwaukee had moved to St. Louis, and Baltimore had moved to New York.

American League founders were convinced it would survive because of its twin goals: (1) to foster honest competition without the reserve rule and (2) to lure big crowds with low ticket prices.

Within two years, National League owners conceded that the junior circuit was worthy of recognition as a major league. A National Agreement, drawn up in January 1903 and ratified in Cincinnati, provided National League recognition of the American, created a tightened reserve rule to prevent roster raiding between leagues, and established a post-season World Series between league champions.

Why was the date of the last game played by the New York Highlanders important in baseball history?

The New York Highlanders, predecessors of the New York Yankees, played their last game on October 5, 1912.

The date was memorable for several reasons: the Highlanders played in Hilltop Park, closing out their stay in that stadium with an 8-6 win over Washington. The same day, the Brooklyn Dodgers played their last game in Washington Park, beating the New York Giants, 1-0. The next year, the Highlanders—with the new name of Yankees—became tenants of the Giants in the Polo Grounds, while the Dodgers moved to Ebbets Field.

Why did the 1919 World Series become known as "the Black Sox Scandal"?

After the Cincinnati Reds defeated the favored Chicago White Sox, five games to three, in the 1919 World Series, fans speculated that the rigorous American League pennant race had worn out the White Sox. The following September, however, they learned that seven Chicago players had allegedly agreed to accept $100,000 from gamblers for "throwing" the Fall Classic—prompting the "Black Sox" tag to represent the shame of the men involved. The seven players—Ed Cicotte, Shoeless Joe Jackson, Lefty Williams, Chick Gandil, Swede Risberg, Fred McMullin, and Happy Felsch—were unmasked when Cicotte and Jackson confessed the conspiracy to a Chicago grand jury. An eighth player, Buck Weaver, did not participate but did conceal his knowledge of the fix, prompting Chicago owner Charles Comiskey to suspend him along with the seven conspirators. (Three National League players—Heinie Zimmerman, Hal Chase, and Lee Magee—had been banned after the 1919 season for throwing games.) All those involved in the Black Sox scandal were permanently banned from baseball—even though they were acquitted in their second court trial (the first ended in a mistrial when evidence disappeared).

Why did Organized Baseball decide to appoint a Commissioner?

The Commissioner of Baseball, elected to a seven-year term by the major-league owners, is the chief executive of the game. He settles disputes, disciplines players and owners, and uses his powers to make decisions that he considers to be "in the best interests of the game."

Before the advent of the Commissioner system, league presidents acted arbitrarily in their own interests instead of the best interests of the game. Each answered only to his own league's club owners, and battles between the leagues were frequent. Following the Black Sox Scandal of 1919, however, owners from both the National League and the American League agreed that a strong executive was needed to govern the game impartially and provide stability as the sport recovered from the attempted World Series fix.

Judge Kenesaw Mountain Landis agreed to become Commissioner only after he was granted the autocratic powers needed to restore the integrity of the game. Landis, whose term lasted from January 12, 1921 until his death in 1944, was given authority to protect the best interests of the game by (1) investigating and punishing acts detrimental to the game, (2) resolving inter-league disputes, (3) handling serious labor-management problems, and (4) enforcing the five documents governing the game: the Major League Agreement, the Major League Rules, the Major-Minor League Agreement, the Major-Minor League Rules, and the National Association Rules (governing minor league baseball).

Why was a tripleheader played in 1920?

In the last week of the 1920 season, first place was already decided, with the Brooklyn Robins certain to be National League champions. The New York Giants were locked into second place. But the fourth-place Pittsburgh

Pirates had a chance to catch the third-place Cincinnati Reds and earn a slice of the World Series money pool (which was divided among the top three finishers under the 154-game schedule format).

Cincinnati was slated to play three games against Pittsburgh before both clubs ended the season with single games against other opponents. Four Pirate wins, coupled with four Red losses, would give Pittsburgh third place. But a Friday rainout dampened Pirate hopes.

Resourceful Pirate owner Barney Dreyfuss then suggested the Saturday doubleheader be changed into a tripleheader. Cincinnati manager Pat Moran refused but Dreyfuss got National League president John Heydler to overrule him—an easy decision since there had been baseball precedent (in 1890, Pittsburgh swept Brooklyn in a tripleheader and, six years later, Baltimore swept Louisville). Unfortunately for Dreyfuss and his charges, the Reds won the first two games to clinch third place. Pittsburgh won the third game, which was shortened to six innings because of darkness.

Why was the period before 1920 known as the "dead-ball era"?

When Babe Ruth joined the New York Yankees via purchase from the Boston Red Sox in 1920, he electrified the baseball world with 54 home runs and 137 runs batted in and an .847 slugging percentage (no one else hit more than 19 homers).

That same season, the Black Sox scandal (involving the fixing of the 1919 World Series by members of the Chicago White Sox) convinced baseball club owners that they needed to present a new image of the game to keep fans coming through the turnstiles. They decided they could best woo back disenchanted fans by promoting such long-ball heroics as Ruth was espousing.

Rules-makers mandated tighter winding of the ball; outlawed such trick deliveries as the spitball, emery ball, and shine ball; and ordered umpires to keep fresh, white balls (for better visibility) in play.

Prior to Babe Ruth's one-man power show in 1920, teams had emphasized speed, hit-and-run plays, bunts, and other strategies that produced one run at a time. The ball had a different core from the lively ball now in use (a cushioned cork center was introduced in 1926). It moved more slowly, seldom took high bounces, and rarely reached the deepest part of the outfield.

Heavier bats were used to push, rather than drive, the ball, and pitchers took short strides, emphasizing control rather than strikeouts. Pitchers let batters hit the ball and hoped fielders would catch it, thus saving wear-and-tear on their arms. Home runs were so rare that in 1902 National League home run leader Tommy Leach failed to hit even one outside of the park. All six of his homers were hit inside-the-park.

Why did the art of base-stealing decline once the lively ball era began?

Base thievery declined when managers saw the power of Babe Ruth, who could accomplish more with one swing than any base-stealer. Ty Cobb had established the single-season steal mark of 96 (since broken) in 1915. By the time Ruth's Yankee career began to pick up momentum five years later, however, emphasis on the steal had waned. Even Cobb changed his game; he never stole more than 28 bases in the 10 years he played after 1918. By 1938, National League leader Stan Hack had only 16 stolen bases. As late as 1950, American League leader Dom DiMaggio had just 15 steals.

Renewed emphasis on stealing began with the breaking of the color line in 1947, when players like Jackie Robinson and later Willie Mays proved the value of power plus speed. Luis Aparicio and Maury Wills showed that teams could win with pitching, defense, and speed at the expense of power, helping the art of stealing to make a strong comeback after years of dormancy. Wills broke Cobb's one-season standard before Lou Brock established season and career marks for steals. Rickey Henderson reached a new single-season mark with 130 in 1982.

Why were night games first scheduled?

The original intent behind night baseball—once dubbed "madness under moonlight" by skeptics—was to create a novelty which would bring fans to the ballpark. But night ball also appealed to large masses of workers who sought entertainment to fill their free time rather than entertainment that conflicted with their job.

The Cincinnati Reds installed $50,000 lights at Crosley Field in 1935 and played the first major-league night game, against the Philadelphia Phillies, on May 24, 1935. The Reds won, 2-1, before 20,422 fans and played a half-dozen other night contests that year.

Minor-league clubs in Des Moines, Iowa, and Independence, Kansas, had played the first professional baseball night games in 1930, but amateur teams in Massachusetts met in 1880 and again in 1923 (with new General Electric equipment used for the latter game).

Why were night games banned in 1943?

Wartime blackout restrictions, plus the need to conserve energy, were the primary factors in the year-long blackout of night baseball. During the war, many clubs started games at three or four o'clock in the afternoon to accommodate changing shifts of workers at defense plants.

Why was the All-Star Game scrubbed in 1945?

Although baseball executives insisted wartime travel restrictions forced cancellation of the 1945 All-Star Game, it is also true that the game was scrubbed because most of the game's best players were in military, rather than baseball, uniforms. A two-day series of exhibition games to raise money for war relief was substituted for the traditional All-Star Game.

Why did baseball continue during World War II?

Although most of the game's top stars were serving their country during World War II, baseball continued. In his famous "green light letter," President Franklin D. Roosevelt wrote Baseball Commissioner Kenesaw Mountain Landis in January 1942 that baseball was a morale-booster which provided much-needed entertainment during the bleak war years. So the game continued—even though more than 200 draft-board rejects had to be recruited for big-league jobs.

Why did ball clubs stop traveling by train?

Even before big-league baseball expanded west of St. Louis in 1958, speed had become important in traveling from one point to the next. As air travel became increasingly safe, teams looked to it for efficient travel. The first professional team to fly was the Hollywood Stars of the Pacific Coast League, in 1928. The Cincinnati Reds were the first to fly in the majors when they flew from Cincinnati to Chicago for a three-game series on June 8–10, 1934. But it took more than a dozen years before the New York Yankees became the first team to use air travel extensively. As late as 1961, Boston Red Sox slugger Jackie Jensen refused to fly with the club. Wracked with a fear of flying, Jensen drove or took the train while his teammates flew. On one occasion, he drove 850 miles from Boston to Detroit, then played a game the following day.

Why did doubleheader frequency decrease after World War II?

As the popularity of doubleheaders declined with baseball fans, teams began to schedule them less frequently. Club management, hoping to gain separate admission for as many different home dates as possible, tired of giving two-games-for-one, but other factors also interfered: an increase in game length caused by emphasis on relief pitchers and pinch-hitters, emphasis on night play which would make doubleheaders last too long for most fans, rival forms of entertainment that seemed preferable to six or seven hours at a ballpark, and broadcast time considerations. Twin bills also take their toll on participants, as well as spectators.

Modern teams schedule few, if any, doubleheaders, preferring to play twin bills only as makeups of previous rainouts. That attitude is a far cry from early-century teams, which depended on Sunday doubleheaders for their largest crowds and—on rare occasions—even played tripleheaders (the last was in 1920).

Why did the Continental League force the Major Leagues to expand?

In 1960, Branch Rickey disclosed his intention to establish a third major league, the Continental League. Rickey believed his league would thrive because certain proposed franchises—especially those in New York and Houston—would fill baseball voids in those cities, attracting instant followings. Major-league executives, recognizing Rickey's record of success, agreed to keep Rickey out of Houston and other lucrative virgin territory. Expansion was the direct result. The American and National leagues agreed to expand in 1961–62, absorbing New York, Houston, and other proposed Continental League cities. Rickey subsequently abandoned his plans for the new venture.

Why did expansion clubs complain about the high price of players in the expansion drafts?

As a general rule, most of the available "talent" was not worth the price: $75,000 each to the new American League teams of 1961 and $75,000 each (plus four others at $125,000 each) for the new National League clubs of 1962. By the 1968 expansion drafts, the prices had gone up to $175,000 for American League draftees and $200,000 for National League draftees, but the method of selection was changed so that existing clubs could protect only 15 players from their 40-man rosters in the initial round of the 1968 draft (more players were protected in subsequent rounds). The American League charged new teams $175,000 for each player selected in the 1976 expansion draft. Not surprisingly, all 10 expansion teams finished at, or near, the bottom in their first year, with all losing at least 91 games. The worst entry was the New York Mets, with a 40–120 record that included 44 losses by the two "best" starters, Roger Craig and Al Jackson.

Why did the Major Leagues decide to play a 162-game schedule?

When baseball first expanded in 1961–62, the American and National Leagues had to decide on a new schedule since the old 154-game format (used when the leagues had eight teams each) did not work out mathematically. At first, they decided on a 153-game slate (17 games against each rival) but then changed their minds because a 162-game schedule would allow an equal number of home and road games (not to mention added revenue) which a 153-game format would not. The American League was the first to try the 162-game schedule because its 1961 expansion was a year ahead of the National League's.

Why was the first year of expansion considered a vintage year for hitters?

In 1961, the first year of expansion baseball, the quality of pitching was obviously diluted around the American League. With the Washington Senators (second edition) and Los Angeles Angels joining the league, swelling membership to 10 clubs, there simply wasn't enough good pitching to go around. As a result, Roger Maris enjoyed the only 40-homer season of his career—he hit a record 61 home runs—and Mickey Mantle hit a career high of 54. In addition, American League batting king Norm Cash experienced his only .300 campaign. Cash, who played from 1958 to 1974, never hit higher than .286 in a season with the sole exception of the .361 mark he posted in 1961.

Why did baseball create a special draft for amateur players?

As a means of ending bidding wars for top young talent, a draft of free agent amateurs was inaugurated on June 9, 1965. Such bidding wars not only had caused huge bonuses to be given to unproven amateurs, but had also enabled the richest teams to corner the market on top talent. With the advent of the amateur drafts, held each January and June, teams are able to select negotiating rights to top players in reverse order of the previous year's standings. This system helps weaker teams become stronger, thereby giving baseball better competitive balance. Among No. 1 amateur draft choices who reached the majors are Rick Monday (the top draft pick in 1965) and Bob Horner.

Chapter 2

RULES

Introduction

Baseball is a game that is easy for the casual fan to understand but complex enough to provide ample ammunition for the second-guesser. It is a game played by rules that have evolved over more than a century of trial and error. And it is a game governed by officials whose knowledge of those rules must be tempered with shrewd interpretation, personal judgment, and ironclad consistency.

To some observers, baseball may seem like a simple game: nine men on a side, nine innings, a diamond-shaped infield cornered by three bases and home plate, three outs per inning, and limits of four balls and three strikes on each batter. But veteran National League umpire Paul Pryor insists the game is much more intricate than that.

"Most fans go out to the ballpark to enjoy themselves," he says, "but I bet they don't know one rule out of 20. When clubs sell season tickets, they should give the fans rule books so they can follow the game more closely."

Any discussion of rules changes through the years would require an entire book of its own. Early in National League history, pitchers stood only 45 feet from home plate (instead of the current 60 feet, 6 inches) and catchers stood 20 feet behind it (instead of immediately behind the batter).

Pitchers were required to throw underhand to make it easier for hitters, who were also allowed to "order" whatever pitches they wanted (high ball, low ball, fastball, slow ball, etc.). It took nine pitches (instead of four) to get a base on balls, but also four strikes (instead of three) to strike out. One season, walks even counted as hits—inflating batting averages dramatically.

Game rules are enforced by umpires—the policemen of the sport. They must not only know the rules but also know how to make their decisions stick, how to handle the thankless aspects of their jobs, and how to make snap judgments on close plays.

"You're only as good as your last call," insists Bill Haller, who joined the American League umpiring staff in 1963. "You can call 100 in a row right, but miss that last one and that's the one they'll remember."

Bill Klem, who said he never missed a call in his heart, was so good at umpiring that he stayed on the job a record 35 years and went on to the Hall of Fame after retiring. Four other umpires are also enshrined in Cooperstown.

There are 56 umpiring berths in the Major Leagues today but it often takes a dozen or more years of minor-league apprenticeship before the best young umpires can move up—even though four arbiters work modern big-league games.

By the time they reach the majors, young umpires know baseball rules thoroughly. This chapter is designed to help the reader understand the reasons behind the rules as well as the duties of the men charged with enforcing them.

Why are umpires called "the men in blue"?

Umpires have worn navy blue garb throughout much of baseball history, although umpires' clothing has been modified in recent years (American League arbiters now wear red blazers, for example). The tradition of wearing blue began in 1882, when the American Association, then a major league, hired the first full-time umpiring staff and outfitted the officials in blue jackets and hats.

Why does the home-plate umpire stand behind the catcher?

In the early days of baseball, only one umpire was assigned per game. Some umpires stood behind the pitcher, others behind the catcher. In 1888, an arbiter named John Gaffney decided to position himself behind the catcher with no one on base, but to move behind the pitcher—for a better view of the strike zone, as well as all four bases—with runners on. The league liked the idea and recommended that all its arbiters follow suit. The Gaffney style is still followed in those high school games where only one umpire officiates.

Why do four umpires work major-league games?

Until 1920, only one umpire officiated at each major-league game. But a single umpire, stationed behind home plate, had difficulty seeing close calls on the bases and judging where hard-hit drives landed along the foul lines. Two-umpire teams began working in 1920, with crews expanded to three in 1930 and to four in 1952, with one ump at home, one behind second, and one for each of the foul lines near first and third.

Six umpires presently officiate at World Series games but as late as 1909, when the Pittsburgh Pirates played the Detroit Tigers, only two were assigned. Four umpires—two from each league—were assigned to this Series, but they worked in alternating pairs.

With umpires Bill Klem and Billy Evans sitting in the stands, Max Carey of Pittsburgh hit the ball over the fence. It was not an automatic home run because a special ground rule, agreed to by both teams, set aside a certain area for automatic doubles. Neither Klem nor Evans could tell where the ball hit, and the on-duty umpires were equally uncertain. So the four arbiters, accompanied by two puzzled team managers, marched to the approximate area and let the crowd convince them that the ball was actually a two-base hit. Evans, upset that fans had served as unofficial umpires, wired American League president Ban Johnson, who decided all four arbiters should work the balance of the Series. Four umpires continued to handle World Series play until the total was increased to six in 1947.

Why do umpires use hand signals to signify strike calls?

The practice of umpires using hand signals for strikes is generally believed to have started around the turn-of-the-century, when a deaf-mute named William (Dummy) Hoy asked the home plate umpire to raise his right hand to signify a strike. Hoy couldn't hear the call but he could see the hand go up. Hand signals also enable the scorer, the media, and the spectators to keep up-to-date in the ball-and-strike count on the batter.

The first arbiter to use exaggerated gestures for strike calls was Bill Klem, whose 35-year career as an umpire began in 1905, three years after Dummy Hoy left the majors. Klem, a member of the Baseball Hall of Fame, developed his style while taking leisurely horseback rides in the seashore pines near Lakewood, New Jersey.

Why do umpires use whisk brooms to dust the plate?

Until 1904, umpires commonly used long-handled brooms to dust off home plate, then tossed the brooms aside until the next time they were needed. In 1904, Jack McCarthy, an outfielder for the Chicago Cubs, suffered an ankle injury when he accidentally stepped on a broom while trying to score from third base. National League president H. C. Pulliam immediately ordered umpires to switch to whisk brooms and store them in their pockets when not in use. The American League issued a similar edict.

Why are umpires in charge of baseballs for major-league games?

Prior to 1906, the home team's manager was in charge of supplying fresh game balls. But he didn't always fulfill that obligation fairly. Sometimes, balls were doctored (frozen, scuffed, or discolored) to help the home club—or thwart the opposition. When complaints became too frequent, the leagues placed control of game balls in the hands of the umpires.

Why do umpires rub mud on game balls prior to each contest?

In 1937, an umpire named Harry Geisel complained that new balls were too slick. Lena Blackburne, coaching for the Philadelphia Athletics, rubbed some balls with silt from a stream near his South Jersey home and Geisel liked the results. The mud had a cold-cream texture and neither darkened nor scratched the ball. In less than a year, word spread all the way to American League headquarters, where league president Will Harridge ordered all umpires to apply Blackburne's mud before games (a 20-minute job). The National League and several Triple-A circuits immediately followed suit—putting Blackburne in business as the supplier of baseball mud. His family maintains that business today.

Why do umpires interpret the strike zone differently?

Technically, the strike zone is that area between the batter's armpits and knee tops through which a pitched baseball, thrown over the 17-inch span of home plate, must pass. Such a pitch is called a strike if, in the umpire's judgment, the ball is over the plate and in the armpits-to-kneetops zone with the batter in his natural batting stance. Some batters crouch, others stand straight, and some hit from a deep crouch—causing the umpire to adjust the strike zone for each hitter.

Another reason for various interpretations is the equipment that umpires wear. Some wear the cumbersome balloon chest protector which makes it difficult to squat and forces the arbiter to look over the catcher's head at the pitch. Others (including the current majority) wear inside (under the coat) protectors and peer over the catcher's shoulder. Each group gets a different view—those with inside protectors see low strikes very well, while those with balloon protectors see high strikes very well.

Why was Hank Aaron once called out for hitting a home run?

On August 18, 1965, Hank Aaron's shot onto the roof of Sportsman's Park, St. Louis, was ruled an out by umpire Chris Pelekoudas. Pelekoudas made the call on an appeal from Cardinal catcher Bob Uecker, who pointed out that Aaron's back foot had been out of the batter's box when he took his stance. The rules dictate that the batter must remain in the box until the pitcher delivers the ball, but that the umpire is not obligated to cite the infraction unless the opposing team appeals.

Why is the "phantom double play" often over-looked by the umpire?

On the phantom double play, the pivot man—either the second baseman or the shortstop—does not actually step on second base as he takes the throw from his fellow infielder before completing the play by throwing to first. If he does step on the bag, he may not have the ball in his possession at the precise moment his foot is on the base. Umpires will credit the phantom force-out at second if the attempt is reasonably close—primarily because they realize the pivot man must leap to avoid the oncoming runner or risk amputation.

Just as the phantom double play is tolerated, so is a runner's hard slide *at the fielder*—even if the fielder is several steps off the base. Technically, runners are supposed to slide into the *base,* not into the *infielder* making the play. Since baserunners are seldom called out for interference ("breaking up the double play" is considered part of the game), infielders are allowed the phantom double play as compensation.

Why did an umpire once eject occupants of the press box?

When he was a 19-year-old umpire in the Northern League in the '50s, Bruce Froemming—who later moved up to the National League—cleared the press box when those seated there became too vocal in their salty abuse of the arbiters. Froemming, then in his first year as an official, had overruled his partner on a close play at second, setting off wagging tongues for the second straight night. Froemming had warned the writers the previous day; this time, he acted. When they refused to go, he pulled both St. Cloud and Duluth off the field, threatening to forfeit the game to the visitors if the writers didn't clear out in 10 minutes. The president of the Duluth team finally prevailed upon the press to vacate so that he wouldn't have to refund the money of the fans.

Why is an umpire in two Halls of Fame?

Cal Hubbard spent 16 years as an American League umpire (1936–51) before becoming supervisor of umpires. He was good at his job, attracting the attention of Hall of Fame electors who elected him to the Baseball Hall of Fame in 1976. Hubbard previously had won enshrinement in the Pro Football Hall of Fame for his National Football League play as a lineman in nine seasons (1927–33 and 1935–36). He is the only man inducted into both Halls of Fame.

Why are coaches required to stand inside specially marked boxes?

Before 1888, coaches and managers roamed up and down the field behind the foul lines in a concerted effort to rile the opposition. Although the fans loved to hear the constant heckling and jockeying—some of which was rather personal—rules-makers considered taking the coaches off the field. Realizing such action might hamper attendance, they decided instead to create "coaching lines," or boxes, behind first and third bases. Coaches must restrict themselves to these areas.

Why do four pitched balls constitute a walk?

Baseball arrived at the current four-ball formula by trial and error. Before 1889, it took five balls to draw a walk. As a result, there were fewer walks and hits, more strikeouts, and less scoring. With the implementation of the four-ball walk, more hits and walks were produced, putting more runners on the bases, improving the liveliness of games, and creating more scoring opportunities—all of which helped attract more fans.

Why was the distance from pitching rubber to home plate fixed at 60 feet, 6 inches?

Baseball's pitching distance has changed several times since the first rules were mapped for the game in 1845. The distance was 45 feet until 1881, then 50 feet until 1893, when the distance was fixed at 60 feet, 0 inches. But the surveyor misread the "0" as a "6" and the mistake was never rectified.(Pitching distance was 51½ feet in the Players League, a major league which existed only for the 1890 season.)

Why was pinch-hitting impossible in the early years of baseball?

Before 1891, baseball rules prohibited the introduction of substitute batters (except under emergency conditions such as injury). Even after that provision was revoked, managers seldom relied on pinch-hitters. It wasn't until 1908 that Dode Criss of the St. Louis Browns became the first frequent pinch-hitter, with 12 hits in 41 emergency swings.

Although the advent of the designated hitter in 1973 reduced the role of pinch-hitters in the American League, they continued to thrive in the National, which did not adopt the DH (permitting a regular batting replacement for the pitcher).

In 1976, Jose Morales of the Montreal Expos had more pinch-hit appearances (82), at-bats (78), and hits (25) in a season than any previous player. He had a pinch-hitting average of .320, matching the lifetime pinch-hitting mark of Tommy Davis, who ranks first in that department.

Ed Kranepool hit .486 as a pinch-hitter in 1974, Smead Jolley pinch-hit .467 in 1931, and Frenchy Bordagaray pinch-hit .465 in 1938.

Why did existing rules regarding foul bunts help Wee Willie Keeler compile a record hitting streak?

Before Pete Rose tied his record in 1978, Wee Willie Keeler had compiled the longest hitting streak in National League history: 44 games. Keeler accomplished the feat between April 22 and June 18, 1897. The 5-4, 145-pound outfielder of the Baltimore Orioles, then a National League team managed by Ned Hanlon, made expert use of a prevailing rule that a foul bunt on a third strike was not a strikeout (though it is under modern rules). Keeler, a great bat control artist, was able to bunt dozens of two-strike pitches foul until he found one to his liking.

Keeler also perfected the "Baltimore chop," a high-bounding ball that gave infielders fits because batters often reached base before they could field it. Using the bunt and the Baltimore chop to collect dozens of infield hits, Keeler bragged to a sportswriter that he "hit 'em where they ain't"—meaning that he sent balls between fielders to get his hits. Keeler is one of five original Orioles to make the Hall of Fame (managers John McGraw and Wilbert Robinson and players Hugh Jennings and Joe Kelley are the others).

Why can't owners own more than one team?

Baseball thrives on competitive balance. In 1899, the Robison family owned both the St. Louis and the Cleveland clubs of the National League but shifted most of Cleveland's stars to St. Louis, so weakening the Spiders that they finished with a won-lost record of 20–134, a .130 "winning" percentage that ranks as the worst ever recorded in the majors. They had to play most of their games on the road because they were afraid of their own fans. The player moves helped the Robison team in St. Louis, which went from last in the 12-team National League in 1898 to fifth the following year. Baseball subsequently passed a rule prohibiting ownership of more than one major-league team.

Why does the ball remain in play when it strikes an umpire?

Years ago, a ball that hit an umpire was a "do-over." As a result, infielders made umpires their target when they couldn't throw out a runner. Umpires tired of having the ball thrown at them and the current ruling resulted.

Why do baseball rules require that bases be run in one direction only?

Herman (Germany) Schaefer of the Washington Senators, who played early in the century, liked to rattle the opposition any way he could. In one game, he was on first with a teammate on third when he stole second, hoping to draw a throw that would allow the lead runner to score. The catcher held the ball, so Schaefer "stole back to first" on the next pitch and decided to try his steal of second again. As a direct result of his antics, baseball rules now preclude runners from running the bases in reverse order.

Why was the foul-strike rule instituted?

Before the turn of the century, foul balls were not counted as strikes. Clever hitters could wear out rival pitchers by deliberately hitting pitches foul. Frustrated hurlers would eventually serve up "fat" pitches which the batters would transform into solid hits. In 1901, Philadelphia Phillies leadoff hitter Roy Thomas proved so adept at causing delays by hitting fouls that the rules-makers decided to count all fouls as strikes except in third-strike situations. Many early-century players continued to hit deliberate fouls despite the rule change. One later player who became a master of the practice was Luke Appling, who played from 1930 to 1950.

Why is "Merkle's boner" considered the most famous rules violation in the history of baseball?

On September 24, 1908, the New York Giants and Chicago Cubs were among three teams fighting for the National League pennant. Chicago and New York, playing each other, were tied 1–1 in the bottom of the ninth when the Giants put Moose McCormick on third and Fred Merkle on first with two outs. Al Bridwell singled to center, scoring McCormick with the apparent winning run, but Merkle stopped short of second and headed for the clubhouse. The Cubs noticed and screamed for the ball, knowing they could touch second for a force, ending the inning and nullifying the tie-breaking run. Giants' pitcher Joe (Iron Man) McGinnity, sensing the potential disaster, bolted onto the field, seized the ball, and threw it into the crowd. But umpire Hank O'Day ruled Merkle out because of interference by McGinnity, forcing the game to end in a 1–1 tie.

The game had to be replayed when the Cubs and Giants ended the season with identical 98–55 records. Chicago won the replay and the pennant. An interesting footnote to the original game: "Merkle's boner" cost Christy Mathewson a chance to become the winningest pitcher in National League history. Matty ended his career with 373 wins, a total later equalled by Grover Cleveland Alexander. The Giant great would have had one more win if not for Fred Merkle.

Why was Babe Ruth deprived of a home run on a ball that cleared the fence?

On September 8, 1918, when Babe Ruth was a pitcher for the Boston Red Sox, he came to bat with a man on first base in the bottom of the ninth and the score tied. Ruth deposited the ball over the fence, winning the game against Cleveland, but was only credited with a triple. Under prevailing rules, once the winning run scored, the game was automatically over, so Ruth could get no more than three bases on his apparent homer. The rule has since been amended. If a game-winning hit does not leave the playing field, the batter is credited with as many bases as he can get before the winning run scores, but he is credited with a home run if the game-winning hit leaves the playing field—regardless of the number of men on base.

Why did an appeal play once save a no-hitter that seemed lost?

Near the end of the 1923 season, Boston Red Sox pitcher Howard Ehmke lost his no-hitter against the Philadelphia Athletics when rival pitcher Slim Harriss hit an apparent double off the right field fence. But Harriss failed to touch first and was ruled out when the Red Sox appealed, saving the no-hitter for Ehmke.

Why was the spitball officially banned in 1920?

The spitball—so named because the pitcher applies spit or another slippery substance to the ball—is a pitch that sinks sharply as it nears home plate. The ban on the spitter—which also applied to such other unorthodox deliveries as the shine ball and the emery ball—was part of a sweeping reform effort to "clean up baseball" in the wake of the Black Sox Scandal of 1919 (the alleged conspiracy of eight White Sox to throw the 1919 World Series to the Reds). When news of the scandal hit, the very survival of the game was threatened. Resulting reforms included the creation of the Commissioner's job as well as the bans on trick pitches.

Some historians note that the spitball was actually barred in an effort to give batters a better break; owners agreed that the best defense from customer criticism was good offense on the field. Babe Ruth quickly proved their point with his booming bat—even though he had to face a handful of pitchers who were allowed to continue using the spitball (and other tricky serves) after 1920. Pitchers throwing pitches outlawed by the reform legislation were permitted to continue using such pitches until they left the game.

Why did Burleigh Grimes throw legal spitballs 14 years after the pitch was banned?

Of the 17 spitball pitchers allowed to keep throwing the slippery pitch after the spitball was banned (on February 10, 1920), Burleigh Grimes lasted the longest. He made his last appearance for the Pittsburgh Pirates, working against the Brooklyn Dodgers, on September 20, 1934. He fanned the last man he faced in the one inning he worked that day. The spitball was banned in the wake of the 1919 Black Sox scandal as baseball sought to clean up its image in the eyes of the general public.

Why is it unfair to compare home run totals before 1930 with those after that year?

In 1930, baseball rules were changed to prohibit balls that bounced over fences from being automatic home runs; batters were awarded two bases on such hits. When Hank Aaron mounted his challenge to Babe Ruth's home run record during the '70s, researchers learned that none of Babe Ruth's lifetime 714 home runs would have been an automatic double; all cleared the fence in the air or were inside-the-park home runs.

Why did a base-running blunder cost Lou Gehrig a home run crown?

In 1931, Lou Gehrig tied Babe Ruth for American League home run leadership (46 each) because of a base-running blunder by Yankee teammate Lyn Lary. On April 26, Gehrig homered in Washington against Firpo Marberry, star Senator reliever, but Lary—the runner on first—thought the ball had been caught in center field for the third out. After rounding third, Lary proceeded directly into the dugout. Gehrig, head down in his home run trot, was called out at home (for passing Lary at third) and the Yankees lost the game, 9–7.

Why did stalling tactics by an opponent cost Joe Medwick a home run crown?

Joe Medwick, then with the St. Louis Cardinals, shared the 1937 National League home run crown with Mel Ott of the New York Giants (each with 31). Medwick would have had 32, enough to win the crown outright, if not for stalling tactics by the Philadelphia Phillies in a late-season game. Medwick's homer had given the Cardinals a 3–0 lead in the nightcap of a doubleheader that had been delayed by rain. Trailing, and sensing that it might be hard to squeeze in the required five innings to make the game official (there were no lights), Philadelphia manager Jimmy Wilson began his stalling tactics. After ignoring several warnings from umpire Bill Klem, Wilson watched his team forfeit the game to St. Louis. In the record books, the game appears as a 9–0 victory for St. Louis—but no home run for Medwick as individual records in a forfeit count only if five innings have elapsed. Medwick had no choice other than to settle for a home run tie with Mel Ott.

Why did a Red Sox hitter once get a triple on a foul ball?

In 1947, Jake Jones, batting with two outs and no one on base in the sixth inning, hit a roller outside the third base line that looked like it might go fair. St. Louis pitcher Fred

Sanford, realizing Jones would have a sure infield hit if that happened, threw his glove at the ball in an attempt to keep it foul. When glove and ball met, existing rules gave Jones an automatic triple. In 1954, that rule was changed to apply only to fair balls.

Why did Warren Spahn pitch a complete game without a win or a loss?

In his rookie season with the Boston Braves in 1942, future Hall of Fame lefthander Warren Spahn was on the mound in the nightcap of a September 26 doubleheader when hundreds of young fans spilled onto the field. Although he was trailing, 5–2, when the fracas erupted in the eighth inning, Spahn avoided what seemed like a sure loss when umpire Ziggy Sears forfeited the game to the Braves. Since forfeits are recorded as 9–0 victories without winning or losing pitchers, Spahn got credit for a complete game but finished the year with a record of 0–0 in four appearances.

Why was a future basketball star ejected from a baseball game he wasn't in?

Bill Sharman, later a basketball superstar with the Boston Celtics, was sitting on the Brooklyn Dodgers bench on September 27, 1951, when home plate umpire Frank Dascoli ejected pitcher Preacher Roe, catcher Roy Campanella, and the entire bench in the wake of a disputed play at home. Sharman, a rookie up for a September look-see, never got into a game for Brooklyn—leaving the ejection as his sole achievement in the Major Leagues.

Why did existing rules deprive Ted Williams of a batting crown he deserved?

In 1954, prevailing rules mandated that qualifiers for the

batting championship receive a minimum of 400 *official at-bats* (walks, sacrifices, and hit-by-pitches not included). Williams, whose .345 batting average for the Boston Red Sox was four points higher than the .341 mark recorded by Bobby Avila of the Cleveland Indians, was denied the title because he walked 136 times, was hit by a pitch once, and had three sacrifice flies—limiting his official at-bats to 386. In 1956, eligibility rules were changed to reflect *total plate appearances*, rather than official at-bats.

The formula used to determine the minimum number of plate appearances required to be eligible for the batting crown is the number of games scheduled multiplied by 3.1 (the average number of at-bats per game). Under the 154-game format of 1954, 477 plate appearances were required (Williams qualified); under the current 162-game schedule, 502 appearances are needed. Williams in 1954 became the only man in baseball history to have fewer than 400 official at-bats but more than 502 plate appearances.

Why do players no longer leave their gloves on the field when sides change during a game?

A baseball rule passed in 1954 eliminated the practice of leaving gloves on the field. Balls sometimes hit the gloves—which were usually in fair territory—and athletes sometimes tripped over them, creating potentially dangerous situations.

Why did the Major Leagues adopt a special rule governing bonuses?

Teams once used bonus money to sign highly-touted amateur free agents. But bidding wars resulted for the best players, so the majors passed a rule (in 1947) that teams had to keep "bonus babies" on the major-league roster for two years or risk losing them to rivals on waivers. The dollar limit on "bonus babies" was set at $4,000 and increased to $6,000 in 1952, when the bonus rule was reinstated after a two-year suspension. Bonus restrictions ended in 1957.

The first bona fide "bonus baby" was Dick Wakefield, signed off the University of Michigan campus by the Detroit Tigers in 1941. He was inked for $51,000. Wakefield was an outfielder who hit .293 in 9 seasons.

Why did a batter hit by a Don Drysdale pitch fail to reach base?

On May 31, 1968, Don Drysdale, the star righthander of the Los Angeles Dodgers, seemed certain to record his fifth straight shutout when he took a 3–0 lead against San Francisco into the ninth inning at Dodger Stadium. But Willie McCovey walked, Jim Ray Hart singled, and Dave Marshall walked, loading the bases with none out in the visitors' ninth.

With a 2–2 count on catcher Dick Dietz, an inside slider nicked the batter's arm, apparently ending the 44-inning scoreless streak. But umpire Harry Wendelstedt called Dietz back, citing Rule 6.08b(2), which prohibits a batter from taking a base if he makes no effort to avoid a pitched ball. In such a case, the pitch is ruled a ball. Dietz hit two fouls on the 3–2 count, then lofted a short fly to left—not far enough to score a run. Pinch-hitter Ty Cline grounded into a force at home and Jack Hiatt popped to first baseman Wes Parker, keeping Drysdale's streak intact. Drysdale went on to break Walter Johnson's record of 56 consecutive scoreless innings, reaching 58 2/3 innings before his string was broken.

Why did the save become an unofficial baseball statistic?

By 1960, most major-league managers had begun to

depend heavily upon relief pitchers. Because of improved power production caused by the lively ball, plus coast-to-coast travel conditions and the dominance of night play, most starters had become unable to go the distance and retain their effectiveness, creating the need for late-inning relief.

The Sporting News, the St. Louis sports weekly, began awarding "saves" to relievers in 1960 and the Major Leagues made the concept an official statistic nine years later. The definition has evolved over the years, however.

In 1984, a pitcher could receive a save if he (1) is the finishing pitcher but not the winning pitcher in a game won by his club and (2) either pitches effectively for three innings (regardless of the score); enters the game with the potential tying run on base, at bat, or on deck; or enters with a lead of no more than three runs and pitches at least one inning. The save is a good indicator of relief pitching excellence, especially since it is often difficult to determine the effectiveness of a relief specialist from his won-lost record.

Why don't pitchers bat in American League games?

Although some pitchers are excellent hitters (Babe Ruth began as a pitcher), most are almost "automatic outs" at the plate. Example: Bob Buhl of the Milwaukee Braves once went 0-for-70 in a season. The American League, thinking increased offense would increase revenue from ticket sales, adopted the designated hitter (DH) rule after eight of the twelve clubs in the loop lost money during the 1972 campaign (nine teams drew less than a million fans that year). The rule allows a specified player to take the batting turn of the weakest hitter (usually the pitcher) without otherwise entering the contest or forcing the man he hits for out of the lineup.

The DH rule allowed the American League to boost its overall league batting average from .239 in 1972 (the last year pitchers batted) to .258 in the first three years of the designated hitter. Although the American League immediately began to outscore the National (where pitchers continued to bat), overall league averages were almost identical as long as three years after the DH was implemented. In 1975, National League teams combined for a .257 average, while American League clubs hit .258. In 1982, the American League's composite average was up to .264, while the National League mark was .258.

Why is the designated hitter used in alternate years of World Series play?

After the American League introduced the designated hitter in 1973, its pitchers no longer batted. American League managers subsequently complained that playing under National League rules—where pitchers bat—in the World Series is unfair. Commissioner Bowie Kuhn, seeking to mollify both sides, ruled that the DH would be used in alternating years, starting in 1976.

Why did the designated hitter rule fail when it was first suggested?

The designated hitter was originally the brainchild of National League president John Heydler, a one-time umpire who created the concept in 1928. At the time, neither National League owners nor American League owners wanted to change the game so radically. By the early 1970s, however, American League attendance had fallen in direct proportion to declining offense. The designated hitter, adopted in 1972, helped reverse both trends.

Why do some pitchers dislike the designated hitter rule?

Many pitchers like to take their turns at bat—and some

are quite good at the plate. In the American League, the designated hitter rule, initiated in 1973, deprives them of that opportunity.

Had the designated hitter rule been in effect earlier this century, Babe Ruth, George Sisler, and Stan Musial might have floundered in oblivion; all became famous after their hitting overshadowed their pitching.

Although most pitchers throughout baseball history have been virtual automatic outs at the plate, the only *player* to hit two grand-slams in one game in National League history was a pitcher: Tony Cloninger of the Atlanta Braves. On July 3, 1966, Cloninger hit two home runs with the bases filled, plus an RBI single, as the Braves blasted the San Francisco Giants, 17-3.

Even Cloninger's performance pales when contrasted with the minor-league slugging record compiled on June 5, 1914, by pitcher John Gantley of Opelika, Alabama in the Georgia-Alabama League. All Gantley did that day was hit three grand-slams and knock in seven other runs in a 19-1 rout over Talladega, Alabama. Not bad for a day's work: three homers, 19 runs batted in, and one run allowed as a winning pitcher!

In 1983, several National League pitchers excelled at bat, making the most of opportunities they would not have had in the American League. Among the best-hitting pitchers were Steve Carlton of the Philadelphia Phillies, Rick Rhoden of the Pittsburgh Pirates, Walt Terrell of the New York Mets, and Fernando Valenzuela of the Los Angeles Dodgers.

Why did an American League pitcher hit a home run two seasons after the introduction of the designated hitter?

The designated hitter rule—providing a hitter designated to hit for the weakest hitter in the lineup (invariably the pitcher) without defensive replacement of the weak hitter—was instituted by the American League in 1973. Because it was never used by the National League, where pitchers still bat for themselves, the DH rule is used only in alternating World Series meetings between league champions (a practice launched by Baseball Commissioner Bowie Kuhn in 1976). From 1973 through 1975, American League pitchers routinely batted in World Series play. That made it possible for one of them to hit a home run—and Ken Holtzman of the Oakland Athletics did just that, connecting against the Los Angeles Dodgers during the 1974 Fall Classic. (The last home run by an American League pitcher during the regular season was produced by Baltimore's Roric Harrison on October 3, 1972.)

Why did a designated hitter help the National League win a World Series?

In 1976, the designated hitter rule was used in a World Series for the first time, following an edict from Baseball Commissioner Bowie Kuhn that the DH would be used in alternating years. Dan Driessen of the Cincinnati Reds was the first National League designated hitter—and he responded with a .357 batting average that helped the Reds sweep the New York Yankees in four straight games.

Why was Tim McCarver once credited with a three-run single?

Catching for the Philadelphia Phillies on July 4, 1976, Tim McCarver pounded Pirate pitcher Larry Demery for a grand-slam homer in the second inning. But he kept his eye on the ball instead of on the basepaths. Rounding first, he inadvertently passed teammate Garry Maddox, who had retreated to first to tag the bag in case the long drive was caught. Ed Vargo, the umpire at second, ruled McCarver out for passing Maddox but allowed all three base-runners to score. The catcher's "home run" had turned into an over-the-fence single.

Why is a pitcher required to throw four wide pitches when walking a batter intentionally instead of being allowed to grant the batter an automatic walk?

From time to time, proponents of speeding up baseball games have suggested that a batter being intentionally passed be awarded first base without any pitches thrown to him. The proposal has always been rejected—for several reasons. For one thing, a batter can swing at any thrown pitch—even if it is considerably wide of the plate. In addition, there is always the possibility that the pitcher will make a wild pitch while attempting an intentional walk. There are numerous cases of batters getting key hits on deliberate balls that were thrown too close to the plate.

Hitters, as well as pitchers, must pay attention during apparent "intentional" walks. In the 1972 World Series, Oakland Athletics relief pitcher Rollie Fingers embarrassed Cincinnati Reds slugger Johnny Bench when he indicated he was about to issue an intentional walk with a 3-2 count. Fingers huddled with his catcher, told the receiver to jump out as if to receive a ball outside the strike zone, then zipped the third strike over the plate—catching the Cincy slugger by surprise.

Why does the catcher jump out to catch each pitch when a hitter is being intentionally walked?

Baseball rules stipulate that the catcher must be in the catcher's box when the pitcher begins his windup. In early baseball history, the catcher was permitted to stand wide of the plate during an intentional pass, but this practice was voided.

Why is it possible for a pitcher to strike out more than three men in one inning?

Baseball rules stipulate that a strikeout pitch must be caught by the catcher before it touches the ground. If the catcher fails to hold onto the third strike, the batter can run to first base. If he makes it before the ball arrives, he's safe—even though the pitcher is credited with a strikeout (a wild pitch or passed ball is also charged). Many pitchers have fanned four batters in one inning, but knuckleballer Joe Niekro of the Houston Astros once whiffed *five*. It happened during a 1977 spring exhibition game, when Cliff Johnson, an iron-gloved catcher, was having as much trouble holding onto the elusive knuckler as the batters were trying to hit it. Phil Niekro, brother of Joe Niekro, is one of those who have fanned four in an inning during the regular season. Phil Niekro also throws the knuckleball.

Why are some no-hitters less than nine innings long?

As long as a game is official *and the pitcher has not yielded a hit,* the hurler receives credit for a no-hitter. Abbreviated no-hitters have been recorded some 19 times in this century. On October 5, 1907, Rube Vickers of the Philadelphia Athletics pitched 12 innings of four-hit relief in the opener of a doubleheader against the Washington Senators, started the second game, *and pitched five perfect innings* before darkness halted play.

Mike McCormick, a lefthander with the San Francisco Giants, also got credit for a shortened no-hitter, against the Philadelphia Phillies on June 12, 1959, even though he gave up an infield hit to Richie Ashburn in the sixth. Rain washed out the top of the sixth, the score reverted back to the previous full inning, and McCormick was credited with a fluke no-hitter. On August 6, 1967, Dean Chance of the

Minnesota Twins pitched five hitless innings against the California Angels and saw his 2–0 lead stand up when rain washed out the rest of the contest (Chance pitched a nine-inning no-hitter later that season).

On four separate occasions, abbreviated no-hitters were credited to pitchers when games were stopped early to allow clubs to catch trains for other towns. That can't happen in the jet age—but the natural elements can combine to create unusual footnotes in the long history of the game.

Why has baseball changed the sacrifice fly rule so often?

Under current rules, a sacrifice fly occurs when, with less than two out, a runner tags up and scores after a fly ball is caught. The batter is credited with a run batted in and no time at bat. The sacrifice fly rule is probably the most-changed rule in the history of the game. It has been in and out of the rule book more times than baseball historians like to remember.

Between 1894 and 1908, there was no sacrifice fly rule, and sacrifice hits were limited to bunts. From 1908 to 1925, a sacrifice (no time-at-bat) was credited to anyone whose fly ball allowed a base-runner to score after the catch. From 1926 through 1930, any fly ball that advanced runners was scored as a sacrifice—even if those runners didn't score. When the collective big-league batting average swelled to .290 in 1930, officials killed the average-inflating sacrifice fly rule, keeping it inactive until 1939. In that year, the 1908 interpretation of the sacrifice fly was resurrected, only to be banned again in 1940 and lie dormant until 1954. During the years sacrifice flies were not scored as sacrifice hits, players whose fly balls scored runners received credit for runs batted in but were also charged with official (hitless) at-bats.

Why are restrictions placed on rookie status?

There are two primary reasons why it is important to know whether a player has rookie status (less than 130 at-bats, 50 innings pitched, or 45 days on a major-league roster prior to September 1).

Those reasons are (1) players need six official seasons of major-league service before they become eligible for free agency and (2) the Rookie-of-the-Year Award, created in 1947, carries considerable prestige.

Many players get brief tastes of major-league life in September but retain their rookie status the following season.

Why is it illegal for pine tar to extend more than 18 inches from the handle of a bat?

Because pine tar is a dark, sticky substance that would discolor any ball it touched, Rule 1.10 (b) of the Official Baseball Rules prohibits application of pine tar—normally used to give batters a better grip—beyond 18 inches from the bat handle. Bats in violation should be removed, according to the rule. Rule 6.06 (d) mandates that any batter whose bat has been altered in a way that would improve the distance factor or flight of the ball must be called out and ejected from the game.

Interpretation of these seemingly contradictory rules has varied through the years. In 1975, Ted Simmons, then with the St. Louis Cardinals, was called out after hitting a home run because an umpire noticed he had roughened the surface of his bat with a nail. That same year, John Mayberry of the Kansas City Royals homered twice to lead an 11-inning, 8–7 victory over the California Angels—even though the umpires admitted the pine tar on his bat extended beyond the permissible 18 inches (Angel manager Dick Williams brought the bat to the umpires' dressing room after the game).

The late Thurman Munson was called out after producing an RBI single for the New York Yankees in the first inning of a 1975 game against the Minnesota Twins (Twins manager Frank Quilici was upheld in his protest about excessive pine tar) but a Yankee home run by Graig Nettles a year earlier—the only run in a 1-0 victory over the Detroit Tigers—stood even though home plate umpire Lou DiMuro later nullified a Nettles single after his cork-filled bat broke open.

Because excessive pine tar does not have the same effect as a bat doctored with cork, tacks, nails, or other roughening substances, American League President Lee MacPhail overruled umpires who nullified a two-run, ninth-inning home run by George Brett of the Kansas City Royals on July 24, 1983.

Brett's two-out home run in the top of the ninth had given the Royals a 5-4 lead but home plate umpire Tim McClelland—upholding the protest of Yankee manager Billy Martin—ruled Brett out, ostensibly ending the game, after examining his bat.

The Royals protested and MacPhail agreed, ruling on July 28 that the game would have to be resumed at point of interruption with the Royals ahead, 5-4. Kansas City eventually won the game by that score.

MacPhail, in his first decision overruling an umpiring crew in his 10-year tenure as league president, stated that the rules should be clarified so that there would be no doubt about future incidents involving excessive pine tar or doctoring of a bat. The bat, not the player, should be removed in cases of excessive pine tar, he said, with player removal appropriate only when the bat is deliberately altered to change the distance or flight of the ball.

Why can a pitcher win an ERA crown if he leaves his league in mid-season?

Pitchers must work one inning per game scheduled (162 innings under the current scheduling format) to be eligible for the ERA (earned run average) championship. In 1983, lefthander Rick Honeycutt worked 174 2/3 innings for the Texas Rangers before his August trade to the Los Angeles Dodgers. Although he was out of the league, Honeycutt still won the ERA crown of the American League with a 2.42 mark. He had a 14–8 record at Texas, then went 2–3 for Los Angeles.

Why is it possible for a team to get six hits in an inning without scoring?

The scenario is simple: the first three batters reach base on infield singles. Then the runners on second and third are picked off. The next two batters hit infield singles, reloading the bases. The next batter hits a ball that strikes a base runner; the runner is out but the batter receives credit for a hit. That makes six hits but no runs for the inning.

Why are players paid only for the first four games of the World Series?

The players' share of the World Series money pie covers only the first four games to guarantee the integrity of the Fall Classic. If the player pool were extended beyond four games—the minimum number needed for a sweep—it would be theoretically possible for players of both teams to conspire in a plot to extend the World Series to a full seven games, thereby adding to the size of the player pot. Funds produced by World Series games five, six, and seven are utilized for operating expenses of the Commissioner's office and the leagues.

Chapter 3

EQUIPMENT

Introduction

Baseball players—sandlot or professional—need certain basic equipment. Sandlot players might make do with bat, ball, and glove, but more serious ball players need to invest in spiked shoes, uniforms, hats, catching gear, helmets, and perhaps warm-up jackets or sweaters.

The evolution of baseball equipment is one of the most interesting aspects of the game's history. Early professional players—hoping to emphasize their masculinity—didn't wear gloves at all, resorting to hand protection only after a series of injuries left little choice. Early mitts offered scant protection because of their small size, exposed fingers, and inadequate padding.

Chest protectors, shin guards, and helmets were introduced much later—with umpiring equipment also relatively slow in development.

Bats used by major-leaguers are carefully molded to meet specific requirements—a tradition that is almost as old as the game itself. The weight, length, grip, and even color of a bat concern professional players, but the most important element of bat selection is wood texture. Many players personally choose the wood for their bats; Ted Williams spent hours looking through timber stacks for a narrow grain, while Al Simmons preferred a wider grain.

Considerable care also goes into the making of baseballs. Balls have been "dead" and "lively," white and colored, horsehide and cowhide. Ball size was standardized as long ago as 1872, but its composition has undergone severe modifications over the years. The biggest change was the 1926 introduction of the cushioned cork center, causing a transition from the "dead-ball era" of hit-and-run plays, bunts, and sprayed hits by hitters choking up on the bat to an era of home runs and long balls by batters swinging from their heels. The new center of the baseball changed batters' focus from place-hitting to pull-hitting.

More recently, the baseball went from horsehide to cowhide, white uniforms burst into a rainbow of color, and form-fitting double-knits replaced baggy wool flannels.

As competing companies seek major-league markets for their products, new ideas are introduced—accelerating the evolution of baseball equipment. This chapter examines and explains that evolution.

Why is the most famous baseball bat called a Louisville Slugger?

The name "Louisville Slugger" stems from a 19th-century bat order placed by Pete Browning, star slugger for a Louisville nine called "The Eclipse," with 18-year-old Bud Hillerich. The day after the order was filled, Browning went 3-for-3 with the new bat and quickly spread the word. The simple wood-turning shop of J. F. Hillerich became a bat-making plant. That company, which later won international acclaim as Hillerich & Bradsby, has since moved eight miles from Louisville, Kentucky, to Jeffersonville, Indiana. Its basic bat-turning process in the six-and-a-half acre complex has changed little from those early years. No two bats are exactly alike; they differ in weight, balance, length, and shape of barrel and handle.

Why do players believe the trademark of a bat should be facing away from the ball?

It's generally understood in baseball that a bat is least likely to break if held so that the trademark is topside—thus allowing the ball to hit the cross-grain of the wood. Not all players subscribe to the theory, however. Once, while batting against the Dodgers, Hank Aaron rotated the bat in his hands until it felt comfortable, then stepped in to hit with the trademark facing the wrong way. This was pointed out to him by catcher John Roseboro. Aaron had a ready response: "I didn't come up here to read," he said.

Why did Wee Willie Keeler use such a short bat?

Willie Keeler, a place hitter whose career predated the 20th century, stood only 5 feet 4½ inches tall and weighed 140 pounds. By using a bat only 30½ inches in length— believed to be the shortest in baseball history—he was able to wield exceptional bat control. This enabled him to place the ball between the fielders, prompting the famous baseball saying, "Wee Willie Keeler hit 'em where they ain't."

Why did Al Simmons swing such a long bat?

Al Simmons, Hall of Fame slugger for the Philadelphia Athletics and other clubs, needed a long bat because of his unusual "foot in the bucket" stance, which moved him away from the plate as he swung. Simmons used a war club 38 inches in length, longest in baseball history.

Why do weights and lengths vary from bat to bat?

Players have peculiar demands concerning the bats they

use. Babe Ruth usually used a 44-ounce bat that measured 35½ inches in length, but used others as well—including one massive club that weighed 54 ounces. Edd Roush, who used a 46-ounce bat, claimed he liked it because he was used to hauling heavy objects as a country farm boy who arose every morning at 4:30. Most modern players prefer lighter bats to the "wagon tongues" used by Roush and other earlier athletes.

The majority of the bats now in use are made from strands of straight ash from Pennsylvania, New York's Adirondack Mountains, and other forests in the northeast. Ash is known for its resiliency and driving power and has been a favorite for years. Hickory and wood known as "Cuban timber" have fallen into disuse because they are too dense to facilitate the process of making baseball bats. Both Hillerich & Bradsby and the Adirondack Company—the leaders in supplying bats for big-leaguers—employ "wood scouts" who judge and purchase bat-making timber. Hillerich & Bradsby turns out more than three million bats per year—including custom-made models for major-league clients.

Why did Babe Ruth have an impact on the manufacture of baseball bats?

Prior to the 1919 baseball season, Babe Ruth, then a pitcher-outfielder with the Boston Red Sox, told Hillerich & Bradsby, bat manufacturers in Louisville, Kentucky, to make him a bat with a narrow handle and a knob—the first time that concept had been ordered. The R43 model used by Ruth that year produced 29 home runs, best in the majors, and sparked a flurry of interest from other players—revolutionizing the bat-making industry. Hillerich & Bradsby, marking its 100th anniversary in 1984, now makes 20,000 Louisville Sluggers, all made-to-order, for major-league players each season.

Why was a cow bone once an important piece of equipment?

Teams once catered to hitters by nailing a cow's shin-bone onto a piece of wood and tying it near the bat rack. Players came out early to rub their bats against the bone—a wood-sealing process which made bats harder and less likely to break.

Why did old-time players use fewer bats than modern athletes?

Because of endorsements and mass manufacture of baseball bats, current players have dozens of personalized, made-to-order bats at their disposal. They go from one to another with little hesitation. Old-timers, however, preferred to rely on favorite weapons even when they started to split. Although it was illegal, many players hammered nails into splitting bats and hid the evidence by coloring the entire barrel, including the nail-holes. Umpires seldom noticed.

Why do baseball bats break more easily today?

Because most players use lighter bats (30 or 31 ounces) than their predecessors of 40 years ago, who often used 40-ounce models, bats are more likely to break when stung by hopping fastballs. Handles on lighter bats are thinner and more fragile than those of heavier clubs.

Other contributing factors to modern bat fragility include the following: (1) the ball is more lively; (2) pitchers are always fresh (live-armed) because of the dependence on relief pitching; (3) modern pitchers are generally bigger, stronger, and faster than early-century counterparts; and (4) hitters today swing more from the heels and, as a result, do not make good bat-to-ball contact.

Why do players take special care of their personal bats?

To keep bats in prime condition, players treat them with tobacco juice, pine tar, oil, and special sprays. Some smooth the surface by rubbing Coke bottles against the wood. Ty Cobb, owner of a record .367 lifetime batting average (1905–28), used Nerve navycut, an especially juicy chewing tobacco, in an effort to keep dampness out of the wood of his bats. Cobb rubbed his bats for hours with the hollowed-out thigh of a steer in his zeal to create potent war clubs for his attacks on enemy pitchers. Years after Cobb retired, the bone he used was still chained to a table in the Detroit clubhouse.

Why are baseballs changed frequently during games?

Until Ray Chapman of the Cleveland Indians was killed by a pitch from Carl Mays of the New York Yankees in 1920, balls were rarely changed during games. After the Chapman tragedy, umpires were determined to maintain maximum visibility for batters to avoid other accidents. Nicked, scratched, or dirty balls now come out quickly—a far cry from early-century games, when one ball might have lasted for the full nine innings. Another reason balls are thrown out quickly is that nicked, scratched, or scuffed baseballs give pitchers an unfair advantage because (1) they behave unpredictably on their way to home plate and (2) they often don't carry for distance if hit.

Why was "the rabbit ball" toned down after the 1930 season?

During the 1930 season, six of the eight National League teams hit .300 and the other two hit .280 or better. The pennant-winning St. Louis Cardinals had 11 .300 hitters and the New York Giants had a record team batting average of .319. There was too much offense everywhere; the National League produced a composite .303 batting average, while American League clubs combined for a .288 mark. After the season ended, baseball moguls—seeking a restoration of offensive and defensive balance—"dejuiced" the ball.

Why did the covering of the baseball change from horsehide to cowhide?

Until 1974, baseballs were covered with horsehide. The Spalding Sporting Goods Company, which manufactured major-league balls at the time, and made the switch from horsehide to cowhide, gave two reasons for the change: a shortage of quality horsehide and the lower price of cowhide. Although Rawlings replaced Spalding as the supplier of major-league baseballs in 1977, company spokesman Frank Torre, a former major-league player, insisted that the change in companies did not interfere with the quality of the ball.

Rawlings manufactures its balls in Haiti but uses American materials, machinery, supervision, and quality control. After some "start-up problems" with the Rawlings cowhide ball in 1977 (players said it was soft and ripped easily), there have been few complaints about baseball quality from professional players.

Why does the curveball curve?

The curveball is a study in aerodynamics. When the ball is gripped with the thumb touching the seam at the bottom and the second finger guiding the third finger on top, the rotation of the thrown ball will catch the air currents and arc across the plate. Candy Cummings threw the first curveball in 1864 but, six years later, skeptics had to be convinced the ball actually curved. The National Bureau of Standards has since determined that a ball curves no more than 17½ inches.

Why did early players shun the use of fielder's gloves?

The first professional players thought wearing fielder's gloves was "unmanly" and didn't want to risk the wrath of rivals or jeering spectators. Charles Waitt (pronounced White), first baseman with a pre-National League team in New England, is believed to have been the first player to wear a mitt (in 1875). In 1883, after Providence shortstop Arthur Irwin broke a finger on his gloveless left hand, he wore a buckskin driving glove, several sizes too large, with padding to cushion the impact of hard-hit balls or throws on his injured hand. When John Montgomery Ward, a star of the times, soon copied the concept, manufacturers began mass production.

The most innovative change in glove manufacturing came in 1919, when spitball pitcher Bill Doak of the St. Louis Cardinals persuaded the Rawlings Sporting Goods Company to produce the first gloves with natural deep pockets and greased inner palms. The Doak glove lasted 33 years after its initial appearance in 1920. In the 1950s, gloves with a multithonged web between thumb and forefinger proved very beneficial to fielders—helping fielding percentages zoom 20 points higher than they had been at the century's turn.

Why are the gloves of first basemen and catchers so large?

Because first basemen and catchers receive more throws than other players—and have to hang onto many balls thrown wildly—their mitts are necessarily larger than the gloves of other fielders. But those mitts have limits. Opponents complained when Hank Greenberg of the Detroit Tigers appeared at first base with a big, fish-net style mitt in the mid-30s. Rivals said the unusually large gear enabled Greenberg to get balls other first basemen missed. As a direct result, baseball passed a rule limiting the size of the first baseman's mitt to eight inches across and 12 inches lengthwise. Years later, similar restrictive legislation was passed for catchers' mitts after Baltimore Orioles manager Paul Richards devised a huge glove for Gus Triandos, charged with holding Hoyt Wilhelm's knuckleball. Current rules allow catcher's mitts to be no more than 38 inches in circumference nor more than 15½ inches from top to bottom.

Why do catchers wear so much extra protection?

Without adequate protection, catchers would be injured often—by wild pitches, thrown bats, and foul tips as well as trick pitches (like knuckleballs) that are sometimes as difficult to catch as they are to hit. The evolution of catcher's equipment has a long history. The first catcher's mask was worn by a Harvard receiver in 1875 after coach Fred Thayer ordered his catcher to stand immediately behind the plate (a practice foreign to the majors until 1893). Thayer cut up a fencer's mask for his reluctant backstop, but a tinsmith refined the invention by replacing the mesh with wide-spaced iron bars, the first "bird cage" mask. In 1885, both catchers and umpires wore the first chest protectors, though they were primitive by modern standards.

It wasn't until 1890 that Buck Ewing of the New York Giants used the first padded catcher's mitt. Even with padding, however, the Ewing mitt offered so little protection that more than a decade later, Ossie Schreckengost of the Philadelphia Athletics stuffed his glove with goose feathers to cushion the blow of Rube Waddell's fastball.

Other catchers used raw beefsteak to provide padding. Roger Bresnahan of the Giants wore the first shin guards in 1908 and appeared later that year with a plastic helmet and heavily-padded chest protector, completing the ensemble familiar to the modern catcher.

One thing Bresnahan did not wear was the dangling chin-guard, devised by Steve Yeager of the Los Angeles Dodgers in the late '70s after he was struck in the throat by a large piece of splintered bat.

Why is catching gear dubbed "the tools of ignorance"?

The first man to call catching gear "the tools of ignorance" was highly-educated Washington Senators receiver Muddy Ruel, an off-season attorney. Ruel reasoned that he didn't have to be as clever catching the ball as he did catching his opponents off guard in court. The "tools of ignorance" tag is especially misleading because many of baseball's brightest men were catchers, including Moe Berg, Mickey Cochrane, and Al Lopez. Cochrane and Lopez were among the many catchers who became standout managers.

Why do players wear spiked shoes?

Early baseball teams wore canvas (later leather) shoes with cleats. By 1888, spikes had come into general use in the majors. They enabled batters to dig in at home plate and gain traction on the bases. Heels and toeplates, first sold separately, were incorporated into the shoe in 1890. Old-stlye cleats contained 5 to 7 ounces of steel, but modern spikes are lighter, with each spike placed individually as opposed to the former single triangular unit. With the advent of artificial turf, big-leaguers now have two sets of shoes: the traditional spikes for grass and artificial turf shoes that contain multiple cleats and soles made of heat-resistant polyurethane. Adidas introduced white kangaroo leather shoes in 1967, sparking a color revolution that brought red, blue, brown, green, and other colored shoes to the major-league scene.

Why do batters wear helmets?

Safety is essential at bat, where hitters have only a split second to react to a tiny white sphere moving at speed approaching 100 miles per hour. Cleveland's Ray Chapman died as the result of head injuries incurred while facing Yankee submariner Carl Mays in 1920, and many others, including Hall of Famer Mickey Cochrane, have been seriously injured when hit in the head by pitches. Although Roger Bresnahan of the New York Giants is credited with inventing head protection for batters, the true inventor was the A. J. Reach Company, which created the Reach Pneumatic Batters' Head Protector early in this century. After Bresnahan was knocked unconscious by a pitched ball in 1907, Reach sent the receiver a sample piece of headgear and Bresnahan began wearing it—the first player to do so (many players of the time wore "protective" inserts inside their caps but they failed to provide much protection).

Although Bresnahan appeared with the Reach helmet in 1907—50 years before the American League became the first circuit to mandate the wearing of helmets for all players—it wasn't until 1950 that Cleveland engineers Ed Crick and Ralph Davis invented modern helmets of fiberglass and polyester resin (the same materials used to produce bulletproof items for the military). Branch Rickey, then Pittsburgh general manager, subsequently formed the American Baseball Cap Company, which distributed the new helmets. Players liked the new headgear, which came in three sizes and weighed only 6½ ounces. It is now a rule that batters wear batting helmets.

Why did ball clubs wear white at home and gray on the road?

Until major-league teams began to wear colored softball-type uniforms in the 1970s, it was traditional for the home team to wear white and the visiting team gray. That tradition began at the turn of the century when players had to cover laundry bills and were required to appear in clean uniforms at all times. Extra sets of uniforms at home alleviated the problem of clean whites, but road trips were another story. Connie Mack, running the Philadelphia Athletics, noticed that his charges played hard, aggressive baseball before the home fans but often refused to slide for fear of dirtying their white uniforms away from home. Mack therefore decided to come up with gray uniforms for road games, figuring that dirt wouldn't be so obvious on road grays. The idea took hold and the white-at-home, gray-on-the-road tradition was born.

Why did baseball pants once have wide belt loops?

The double-knit uniforms now used by most major-league clubs have stretch-top pants instead of belts. Before the advent of double knits in the '70s, however, baseball pants had very wide loops—a tailoring custom that began in 1876, the first season of the National League. Cap Anson, first baseman for Chicago, was trying to get back to the bag for a throw when he was grabbed by Boston base runner Mike Kelly around the belt. Kelly managed to get all the way to third before Anson recovered the ball. The angry Anson convinced a sporting goods firm to design pants with belt loops so wide that there wouldn't be enough belt-leather showing for an opponent to grab.

Why did players dislike the old flannel uniforms?

Because eight-ounce flannel uniforms absorbed their weight in sweat and shrank after laundering, players once began their season with uniforms that were deliberately one size too large—giving them a sloppy look that they accepted only because they didn't know any better. After the advent of form-fitting double knits, pioneered by the Pittsburgh Pirates in 1971, players pushed to have the cooler modern fibers adopted in place of the bulky flannels. Other clubs copied the Pittsburgh lead and began outfitting their players in the new uniforms, which featured pullover rather than buttoned jerseys and stretch-top rather than belted pants.

Why were colored stockings such an important part of early baseball uniforms?

In the absence of player numbers, scorecards, and public address systems, baseball management of the last century felt fans could identify players best by color code. At its 1881 winter meetings, the National League voted to have its clubs wear stockings of different colors: Cleveland was to wear dark blue, Providence light blue, Worcester brown, Buffalo gray, Troy green, Boston red, and Detroit yellow. Position players had to wear shirts, belts, and caps in the following colors: catchers scarlet, first basemen scarlet-and-white, second baseman orange-and-blue, third basemen blue-and-white, shortstops maroon, left fielders white, center fielders red-and-black, right fielders gray, and substitutes green-and-brown. Pants and—believe it or not—ties were universally white.

The confusing plan was an extension of the color scheme used by the Chicago White Stockings in 1876, the National League's inaugural season. Chicago had a different colored hat for each player, including a red, white, and blue cap for pitcher-manager Al Spalding.

Why did early ball players seldom wear glasses?

In the early part of the century, managers believed bespectacled players had inferior eyesight. The idea that corrective lenses could make weak eyes just as effective as perfectly normal eyes was just not widely accepted. William Henry White, who won 227 games as a pitcher for three National League clubs from 1877 to 1886, was the only "four-eyed" major-leaguer until 1915, when "Specs" Meadows joined the St. Louis Cardinals. The first fielder with glasses was George (Specs) Toporcer, an infielder who joined St. Louis six years later. The first catcher to wear glasses, Clint (Scrap Iron) Courtney of the St. Louis Browns, lasted 11 seasons in the big leagues (1951–61). Glasses are hardly controversial in modern baseball—especially since bespectacled sluggers Dick Allen, Reggie Jackson, and Jeff Burroughs won successive Most Valuable Player awards in the American League from 1972 to 1974. Even umpires wear glasses on occasion—though they usually prefer contacts in an effort to be less obvious about their defective eyes. Larry Goetz, who served 22 years as an arbiter in the National League, is a bespectacled umpire of recent vintage.

Why do umpires need so much special equipment?

In addition to the mask, chest protector, and shin guards, umpires depend on ball-and-strike indicators to keep track of the count; whisk brooms to dust off home plate; and mound measuring sticks to make sure pitching mounds conform with baseball rules. Mounds must be sloped one inch per foot, and must be uniform with the warm-up mounds in the same ballpark. Mounds must rise no more than 10 inches from ground level and be no larger than 18 feet in diameter.

Why don't umpires of both leagues use the same chest protectors?

National League umpires have been using inside (under the coat) protectors for years, while American League arbiters have the option. of using either inside or outside (balloon) protectors. Those who use the outside protector insist it offers better protection from injury caused by foul tips. This is probably true, but use of the outside protector also restricts the view on low pitches, accounting for different interpretations of the strike zone in each league. Leagues provide umpires with pants, hats, and shirts every year and coats every other year. Umpires buy their own masks, shin guards, whisk brooms, and indicators.

Chapter 4

BALLPARKS

Introduction

The first game of baseball, as we now know it, was played in an open area called the Elysian Fields, in Hoboken, New Jersey, on June 19, 1846. But it wasn't until 1862 that the first real ballpark—Union Grounds in Brooklyn—was opened (admission was 10 cents).

Early stadiums were made of wood and had limited seating capacities. Often, there were no outfield fences and only a rope barrier (to ward off freeloaders) at the ballpark property line. Horseless carriages (succeeding horse-drawn carriages) often parked deep in the outfield after entering through a special gate. On days when spectator turnout exceeded seating capacity, fans stood (or sat) behind roped-off sections of outfield—creating the need for special ground rules to govern balls that disappeared into the crowd.

Early parks were an obvious fire hazard because of their wood construction, and a number of parks fell victim to flames. Concrete-and-steel stadiums began to spring up early in the century, erasing the memory of such wooden ballparks as Robison Field, St. Louis, which housed the last big-league game in a park of wooden construction on June 6, 1920.

After leaving Robison Field, the St. Louis Browns be-

came tenants of the St. Louis Cardinals at Sportsman's Park
(renamed Busch Stadium in 1953). Sportsman's Park was
first used during the National League's inaugural 1876 season and remained in continuous use until May 8, 1966
(except between 1878 and 1884, when the city was without a
team).

The first of the "modern" ballparks, Sportsman's Park
also lasted longer than any other early stadium because it
was reinforced with concrete and steel in 1908.

Eighteen of the 26 major-league parks now in use were
built in 1960 or later. Chicago's Comiskey Park, opened in
1910, is the oldest in continuous service, followed by
Boston's Fenway Park and Detroit's Tiger Stadium (both
1912) and Wrigley Field, opened for the Chicago franchise of
the ill-fated Federal League in 1914.

Fenway Park, which holds just over 33,000 fans, is the
smallest of the active parks, while Cleveland's Municipal
Stadium, with a capacity of 78,000, is the largest. All 26 are
vast improvements over the first ballparks—and some are
as much symbols of the future as early parks were symbols
of the past.

The first domed stadium opened in Houston in 1965,
followed by Seattle's Kingdome in 1977 and the Hubert H.
Humphrey Metrodome in Minneapolis in 1982. Other parks
are expected to add coverings in the near future. Domed
stadiums precluded weather-caused postponements (with
several exceptions) and introduced an element that
changed the game dramatically: artificial grass.

With or without domes, no two major-league parks are
alike. Batted balls consistently carry well in Atlanta and
Philadelphia, but wind conditions play an important role
during the all-daylight games in Wrigley Field. Home runs
are seldom hit in St. Louis and righthanded hitters have to
overcome deep power-alleys in Yankee Stadium's left-center field. Righties have fun in Fenway—just as lefthanded
hitters enjoy Yankee Stadium, Tiger Stadium, and the Metrodome.

Like players, managers, and owners, ballparks have

their own personalities. This chapter provides a peek at some of them.

Why aren't the outfield dimensions of all major-league parks the same size?

The first baseball parks—built before automobile ownership became commonplace—were erected within city limits so that fans could get there on local streetcar lines. The shape of these parks was often determined by existing apartment houses and businesses. It is for this reason that such older parks as Wrigley Field, home of the Chicago Cubs, and Fenway Park, home of the Boston Red Sox, seem so confined. Wrigley has little in the way of foul territory, while Fenway features its close left field fence. As population centers shifted to suburbia in the 1950s, new ballparks were constructed close to where people lived. With more land available, parks became more spacious and more uniformly geometric. Although no baseball rule mandates exactly what size a park should be, the minimum distance from home plate to the closest outfield fence has been written into the rules. *(See next question.)*

Why did baseball establish minimum distances to the outfield fences?

Before 1884, there were no rules regulating the distance from home plate to the outfield fences. In fact, some parks had no fences at all—merely deep boundaries where patrons could park horses and buggies. The first distance rule, passed in 1884, mandated a 210-foot distance from home to the nearest fence. The Chicago White Stockings of the National League played in a park with a fence just 196 feet from home and balls hit over that barrier were automatic doubles rather than home runs.

In 1925, the minimum home run distance was set at 250

feet, though existing parks with shorter dimensions were exempted. By 1959, standards for minimum boundaries in new parks were set at 325 feet down the lines and 400 to center field, though some exemptions were allowed (the Seattle Kingdome is the prime example). Establishment of minimum requirements for outfield fence distances was made in the interest of maintaining uniform standards. Keeping fences too close to home would "cheapen" the game in the minds of many fans—something baseball operators hoped to avoid.

Why do ballparks have a screen behind home plate?

In 1879, Providence of the National League decided it was tired of fans suing the ball club when they were hit by foul balls. To prevent future incidents, Providence erected a wire mesh screen in front of the grandstand. Other clubs liked the idea and followed suit. Prior to the erection of the screen, the seats directly behind home plate had been called "slaughter pens" because of the great number of injuries suffered by fans seated there.

Why do ballparks have "warning tracks" in the outfield?

Although some ballparks—notably Cincinnati's Crosley Field—had outfield inclines to warn outfielders they were nearing barriers, most teams made no effort to protect their flychasers until Pete Reiser was seriously injured crashing into an Ebbets Field wall in Brooklyn in 1947. Reiser, injured earlier in St. Louis in a similar manner, was out long enough to convince the Dodgers that walls should be padded to protect players from future mishaps. Not long after the Dodgers added the padding, narrow cinder "warning tracks" appeared in Wrigley Field (Chicago), Shibe Park

(Philadelphia), and Braves Field (Boston). Today, all 26 major-league parks feature dirt "warning tracks" to alert outfielders they are approaching walls.

Why do grounds keepers play such an important role in a team's success?

There are many legal tricks grounds keepers can employ to help the home team win. They can water the base paths or slope the foul lines to thwart a bunt-and-steal team, let the grass grow long to compensate for a slow-footed third baseman who can't reach hard-hit grounders, or take extra time in placing or replacing a tarpaulin during rain delays. It was once common practice to place the visitors' dugout in line with the hot afternoon sun (night ball has largely neutralized that tactic). Grounds keepers pay special attention to the batter's box, pitcher's mound, and the baselines. Pitchers have their own preferences about the height and texture of dirt on the mound.

The legendary Connie Mack, a major-league manager for 50 years, used a variety of grounds keeping tricks to thwart his rivals. For example, he kept his pitching mound 20 inches high for ace pitchers Lefty Grove, George Earnshaw, Chief Bender, and Eddie Plank.

Other teams used different ploys. When Ty Cobb played for Detroit, opposing teams kept their grass cut short so his bunts and infield hits would reach infielders more quickly. Years later, the Washington Senators and Cleveland Indians made life easier for their own third basemen, Harmon Killebrew and Al Rosen, respectively, by letting their infield grass grow long to slow balls down. Grounds keepers in Philadelphia probably enabled Richie Ashburn to win the 1955 National League batting title by deliberately keeping the third base foul line inclined slightly to prevent his bunts from rolling foul. St. Louis manager Eddie Stanky was among those who led the vocal protest against "Ashburn's

Ridge." Stanky tried to stomp down the incline with his spikes before games in Philadelphia.

Why did a grounds keeper once live in a ballpark?

During the '30s New York Giants owner Horace Stoneham enticed Marty Schwab, head grounds keeper of the Brooklyn Dodgers, to work for the Giants by building an apartment for the Schwab family inside the Polo Grounds. The Schwabs lived under Section 31 in left field—the only grounds keeping family to live and work in the same place.

Why did the St. Louis grounds keeper keep a pet goat?

Bill Stockstick, long-time grounds keeper at Sportsman's Park (later Busch Stadium) in St. Louis, used his pet goat to help trim the outfield grass during the '40s.

Why are sliding pits no longer used by ball clubs?

Sliding pits—rectangular pits filled with loose dirt for the purpose of spring training sliding practice—went the way of the medicine ball and the spittoon because (1) the pits failed to provide realism in training runners and (2) the development of quilted pants permitted painless and stainless sliding practice on the outfield grass. When players slid in the pits, they came to sudden stops—uncharacteristic of the experiences encountered on the base paths during actual games. Without proper protection for grass sliding practice, athletes were liable to acquire painful "strawberries" and to stain uniform pants.

Why did the New York Giants once play on Staten Island?

The New York Giants of 1889 had to vacate their original stadium, the Polo Grounds at 110th Street, when the city-owned park was designated for demolition because it stood in the way of street improvements. Although the team was baseball's best in 1888, it opened the 1889 season on Staten Island—the least populated and most remote of New York City's five boroughs—at the St. George Grounds, originally built for the New York Metropolitans of the American Association (the Metropolitans suspended play after the 1887 campaign). Visiting teams hated St. George Grounds because it flooded so frequently that wooden boards had to be spread over the outfield to provide stability for fielders. Staten Island provided sanctuary for the Giants for 25 games in 1889 until the new Polo Grounds at 155th Street was ready later that year.

Why did the Players League revolt prove beneficial to the New York Giants of the National League?

After serious labor-management disputes sparked a revolt by major-league players prior to the 1890 season, dozens of top stars launched the Players League—an attempt to set up a third "major" league to go with the existing National League and American Association. The Players League only lasted for the 1890 season, but it so weakened the other two circuits that the American Association folded and the National League barely managed to survive, even after the Players League jumpers returned.

Although the Players League lasted only one year, initial plans were considerably more grandiose. Backers built many new ballparks, some of them better than existing big-league parks. One such example was the New York Players League stadium, built so close to the home park of the New

York Giants that Mike Tiernan's home run on May 12, 1890, actually sailed from one park into the other—prompting cheers from fans at both fields. The superior Players League park was purchased by the Giants after the Players League collapsed. Dubbed "the new Polo Grounds," the park hosted the Giants continuously (except for a three-month hiatus caused by fire in 1911) from 1891 to 1957.

Why was the New York Giants' park called the Polo Gounds?

Since polo was never played at the Polo Grounds, the home park of the New York Giants (and later New York Mets), the name is indeed unusual. Actually, the *original* Polo Grounds at 110th Street *was* built on grounds once used for polo matches. When the team relocated, first to 155th Street in 1889 and then to 157th Street in 1891 (that park burned and was reconstructed in 1911), it simply kept the name of the original stadium.

Why was major-league baseball once played in Fort Wayne, Indiana?

Fort Wayne was one of several neutral sites utilized by major-league teams located in cities that banned Sunday baseball. During its first two seasons in 1876 and 1877, the National League threatened to expel players or teams who played on Sunday. It wasn't until 1892 that the league staged its first recognized Sunday game.

Still, Sunday ball did not come to New York until 1917 and was not universally accepted in the majors until the mid-1930s. To get around Sunday blue laws, teams sometimes shifted to neutral sites to take advantage of potentially lucrative Sunday gates.

In 1902–03, the Cleveland Indians played Sunday games

in Canton, Columbus, and Dayton, Ohio, as well as Fort Wayne, Indiana. The Detroit Tigers played in Columbus and Toledo, Ohio, and Grand Rapids, Michigan. And the Boston Braves played a "home" game in Providence, Rhode Island.

Why did Boston's teams switch home fields for World Series games?

In 1914, when the "miracle" Boston Braves won the National League pennant, they played their home games at the South End Grounds. Fenway Park, which had opened in 1912 and was home to the Red Sox, had a bigger capacity, so the Braves opted to play their home World Series games there. In 1915 and 1916, the American League championship went to the Red Sox, who deemed Fenway Park too small to accommodate their faithful fans. So the Sox asked the Braves for permission to play in the new Braves Field, which had 4,300 more seats than Fenway.

Why is Fenway Park considered a nightmare for pitchers?

Fenway Park's short dimensions, particularly in left field (where a 37-foot-high wall sits 315 feet from home), pose grave difficulties for lefthanded hurlers facing righthanded lineups. It isn't easy for righties either, but southpaws generally have a harder time because of the proximity to the plate of the left-field wall, also known as "the Green Monster." High-scoring games are common in Fenway. In 1923, the Sox lost 24-4 to the New York Yankees. Seventeen years later, Boston won by the same score, routing the Washington Senators. In 1950, Boston defeated the St. Louis Browns, 20-4 and 29-4 in consecutive games. They scored a record 17 runs in an inning against the Detroit Tigers in 1953, winning 23-3. In 1978, the Bosox were victims of a "pop fly home run" by Bucky Dent that reversed a Red Sox lead and gave the New York Yankees the victory in a sudden-death divisional playoff game. The ball just cleared the top of the wall.

Why was a portion of Braves Field called "the Jury Box"?

When the Braves played in Boston (prior to 1953), their stadium contained a boxed section of bleachers separate from the main grandstand. Because it reminded observers of the courtroom arrangement for jury trials, the area was dubbed "the Jury Box" by writers covering the team.

Why was Braves Field conducive to inside-the-park home runs?

From its opening in August 1915 until its alteration before the 1928 season, Braves Field in Boston was probably baseball's best park for producing inside-the-park homers (where the hitter manages to circle all the bases with the ball in play). On April 19, 1922, when distances from home plate to the outfield fences were 402 feet in left, 520 feet in center, and 365 feet in right, the New York Giants managed four of them—including a pair by George Kelly. In 1927, the team moved the outfield fences in to accommodate its long-ball sluggers, but players could still take advantage of the spacious dimensions in right-center field, where it was possible for balls to roll more than 500 feet to the flagpole.

Why has the incidence of inside-the-park home runs declined?

The percentage of home runs hit inside-the-park has dropped from 35 percent at the turn of the century to less than one percent today. Wholesale construction of new symmetrical parks, with standardized field dimensions and accessible outfield fences, has cut down the number of inside-the-park home runs so drastically that this type of four-base hit now ranks with the steal of home as the most unusual play in the game. When Willie Wilson of the Kansas City Royals hit five inside-the-park homers (and one over-the-fence homer) in 1979, it represented nearly one-sixth of the major-league total (31) of inside-the-park home runs that year.

Why is Yankee Stadium called "the House that Ruth Built"?

After Babe Ruth became a member of the Yankees in 1920, New York fans flocked to Yankee games at the Polo Grounds in record numbers. The 1920 Yankees drew 1,289,422, then a major league record, and were told by the landlord New York Giants—envious of their tenants' success—to find a new home. Colonel Jacob Ruppert, co-owner of the Yankees, purchased a Bronx lumberyard across the Harlem River from the Polo Grounds. There he built Yankee Stadium—largely on the proceeds the team made from Babe Ruth's popularity. When Yankee Stadium opened on April 18, 1923, the crowd inside the park was given as 74,217, though it was probably even larger. Thousands more were turned away at the gates. Naturally, it was Ruth's three-run homer that made the difference in the Yankees' 4-1 victory over the Boston Red Sox, Ruth's old team.

Why did the Polo Grounds have a monument in center field?

On May 30, 1921, the New York Giants unveiled a center field plaque honoring the memory of infielder Eddie Grant, who was killed in action a month before the end of World

War I (on October 5, 1918). Grant, who was 35 when he died, had played 10 years in the majors, finishing with the Giants after previous stints with the Indians, Phillies, and Reds. Ironically, Grant had retired from baseball before the war in order to pursue a career as a lawyer. Grant held an undergraduate degree from Harvard University.

Why did the Phillies play in an American League park?

On May 14, 1927, part of the grandstand at Baker Bowl, home of the National League Philadelphia Phillies, collapsed, forcing the team to switch several games to Shibe Park, home of the American League Philadelphia Athletics. The Phils became permanent residents of Shibe Park in 1938 when the 18,800 capacity of Baker Bowl was deemed too small by management. The last game at Baker Bowl was played on June 30, 1938, against the New York Giants. To share Shibe Park with the A's, the Phils paid $25,000 in annual rental plus $15,000 yearly taxes to the city and $5,000 grounds keeping costs. They remained in the stadium, later known as Connie Mack Stadium, until Veterans Stadium opened in 1971. Baker Bowl was destroyed in 1950, the same year the "Philadelphia Whiz Kids," a National League team in a former American League park, won the pennant.

Why did the Indians have two home fields at the same time?

The Cleveland Indians moved into Municipal Stadium, their present home, on July 31, 1932. In 1934, however, the team returned to League Park because of lease problems with the City of Cleveland. From 1934 to 1946, most Indian games were played at League Park, with Municipal Stadium's larger capacity utilized for weekend and holiday contests. Bill Veeck finally engineered a long-term lease for

Municipal Stadium in 1947. Municipal Stadium was the only new park built between the construction of Yankee Stadium (1923) and that of Milwaukee County Stadium (1953).

Why did a major-league outfielder once make 44 assists in a season?

Chuck Klein of the Philadelphia Phillies established the season record for assists by an outfielder in 1930 because his club's pitching staff was so bad (6.71 team earned run average) that enemy sluggers kept rattling the tin fences at Baker Bowl (where the Phils played until 1938). With the right-field fence just 280 feet from home plate, Klein was frequently close enough to the infield to make plays on runners at first base—as well as at second and third.

Led by Klein's .386 batting average, 40 homers, and 170 runs batted in in 156 games, the 1930 Phillies hit .315 as a team. But their offense wasn't enough to offset their porous pitching and the club finished dead last, 40 games behind the St. Louis Cardinals.

Why did Larry MacPhail vote against installing lights in Cincinnati?

Although Cincinnati Reds' general manager Larry Mac-Phail had lobbied loud and long for permission to install light towers at Crosley Field, the home of the Reds, in the '30s he wound up voting against the measure when recalcitrant National League executives vetoed his plan to stage a series of night exhibition games against American League clubs. MacPhail had hoped to pay off the cost of erecting the lights with the gate receipts secured from the exhibitions. Despite MacPhail's "no" vote, the Cincinnati board of directors voted to go ahead with stadium lights—a move initially designed to draw fans (and make money) in the National League's smallest city.

Why was night ball in Cincinnati not a "first" for Organized Baseball?

Although the Cincinnati Reds defeated the Philadelphia Phillies, 2–1, in the first major-league night game on May 24, 1935, Crosley Field was not the first professional stadium to host baseball after dark. The first night game in professional baseball occurred in 1930, when Independence, Kansas, of the Western Association lost to Muskogee, 13–3, under a primitive lighting system. Des Moines followed suit and fans were so taken with the "madness under moonlight" that it played another night game the following day. Team president E. Lee Keyser said night ball would be the salvation of the minors because it attracted families and working people who could not attend weekday daylight games. The same logic was applied to night games in the majors years later.

Why was a section of Forbes Field called Greenberg Gardens?

When Hank Greenberg joined the Pirates in 1947, Pittsburgh executives wanted to make it easier for the aging slugger to reach the outfield fence. So they erected a shorter fence inside the existing barrier, and the area in between became known as "Greenberg Gardens." Greenberg retired after hitting 25 home runs in his one season with the Pirates, but Ralph Kiner, another righthanded power-hitter, continued to use the new dimensions with regularity. To suit the new slugger, followers of the team changed the name from Greenberg Gardens to Kiner's Korner. Years later, Kiner used Kiner's Korner as the name of his postgame interview show following broadcasts of New York Mets' baseball.

Why were their home parks considered disadvantageous for Joe DiMaggio and Ted Williams?

Joe DiMaggio, a righthanded hitter with great power to left field, played half his games in Yankee Stadium—a park with an inviting right field fence but a long left-center field power alley. Ted Williams, on the other hand, was a lefthanded hitter with great power to right field. Unfortunately for Williams, his Boston Red Sox played half their games in a stadium with a short left field but longer right field. Most baseball historians believe that a DiMaggio-Williams trade—which nearly happened in 1949—might have allowed both men to challenge the single-season and career home run records. Williams managed to hit 521 career homers anyway, while DiMaggio concluded his career with 361.

Why was Washington's Griffith Stadium regarded as a graveyard for power-hitters?

Only the strongest sluggers were able to reach the fences at Griffith Stadium (350 feet to left, 380 to the left-center power alley, 401 to center, 373 to right-center, and 320 down the right-field line). During the 1945 season, the entire Washington team—weakened by wartime military calls—hit just one home run there, an inside-the-park blast by Joe Kuhel. In 19 seasons as a Senator, Sam Rice *never* hit a ball over the fence; his nine "home" homers were all inside-the-park jobs. Muscular Harmon Killebrew, however, was undaunted by the park. Killebrew managed to tie Cleveland's Rocky Colavito for the American League home run crown in 1959, when both hit 42.

Why was center field such a difficult home run target at the old Polo Grounds?

The distance from home plate to the center field bleachers at the Polo Grounds stood at 475 feet (it was further to the inset clubhouse) after remodeling of the park in 1923. Joe Adcock, first baseman of the Milwaukee Braves, became the first man to homer into those bleachers on April 29, 1953 (Jim Hearn of the Giants was his victim). The only other players to deposit balls into center field at the Polo Grounds did it on successive nights against the New York Mets. Lou Brock, then with the Chicago Cubs, found the range on June 17, 1962, against Al Jackson, while Hank Aaron hit a grand-slam off Jay Hook on June 18.

Why did the last game played at Griffith Stadium pit the new Senators against the old Senators?

Griffith Stadium opened in 1911 as the home of the Washington Senators and remained in use as the home of the second-edition Senators after the team owned by the Griffith family became the Minnesota Twins in 1961. The new Senators, an expansion team that later became the Texas Rangers, spent their inaugural 1961 season in Griffith Stadium while D.C. Stadium (also known as Robert F. Kennedy Stadium) was being built. On September 21, 1961, the Senators played their last home game at the old park. The visiting club, the Minnesota Twins, had been the Washington Senators the year before.

Why was it difficult to play the outfield at Ebbets Field?

Ebbets Field, home of the Brooklyn Dodgers from 1913 to 1957, had a real personality. Balls frequently took unexpected bounces off outfield walls in Brooklyn—particularly in right field, where the concave barrier extended only 297 feet down the line. Outfielders had to guess how they would field caroms and often guessed wrong, turning singles into extra-base hits that deflated the egos of visiting pitchers. Carl Furillo, the rifle-armed Dodger rightfielder of the '50s, was a master at "reading" the wall.

Why did the Brooklyn Dodgers play some games in New Jersey?

To emphasize their unhappiness with ancient Ebbets Field (and their desire for city aid in refurbishing it or constructing a new park), the Brooklyn Dodgers played 14 games in Jersey City, New Jersey, in 1956 and 1957. Roosevelt Stadium hosted these National League games. Unfortunately for Brooklyn fans, New York City fathers failed to act on a new ballpark—occasioning the 1958 transfer to Los Angeles.

Why did the Dodgers leave Brooklyn?

Walter O'Malley, who owned the club in the '50s, was unsuccessful in his bids to get a new ballpark built for his team. The Brooklyn Dodgers drew well in Ebbets Field but both ballpark and neighborhood were decaying, forcing O'Malley to search for greener pastures. Persuading the New York Giants to join him in flight to California, O'Malley was rewarded when the Los Angeles Dodgers immediately drew well in their new surroundings. Dodger Stadium, opened in 1962, attracted more than three million customers—a major-league record—in 1978 and several subsequent seasons.

Why were "Moon Shots" beneficial to the Los Angeles Dodgers?

During their first four years in Los Angeles, the Dodgers

played in the Los Angeles Coliseum, a converted football field, while waiting for Dodger Stadium to be built. The 250-foot left-field wall (with its 42-foot screen to make it "semilegitimate") proved very inviting to righthanded batters. The power alley in right-center, however, was 440 feet away—making life tough for such lefthanded hitters as Duke Snider.

One southpaw swinger who prospered at the Coliseum was Wally Moon, a former St. Louis Cardinals outfielder with a penchant for hitting to the opposite field. In the first 10 home games of the 1961 season, Moon golfed balls over the screen six times—prompting writers inspired by the first manned American space capsule to dub the blasts "Moon Shots." Moon finished the year with 17 home runs.

Why wasn't Crosley Field demolished after the Reds left?

After the Cincinnati Reds moved from Crosley Field to Riverfront Stadium in June 1970, a Kentucky farmer purchased the old park and had it rebuilt, piece by piece, on his property.

Why do some ballparks have artificial turf?

Artificial turf provides "true" bounces for the baseball, permits hard-hit grounders to rocket through the infield, allows fleet base runners to get excellent traction on the base paths, reduces rain delays and postponements because of easy water removal, requires less maintenance than natural grass, and gives ballparks sweeping green expanses often more vivid than natural turf.

On the minus side, however, baseball doctors believe the artificial surface shortens the careers of players because its texture places chronic strain on backs, knees, and feet. Athletes coming off artificial turf often suffer pain in the ankles and shins. Most artificial surfaces are rock-hard, without the "give" of natural grass-and-soil fields.

The first major-league field with artificial turf was the Houston Astrodome, which opened with natural grass in 1965 and installed AstroTurf shortly thereafter. Five other National League teams and four American League teams had artificial surfaces by the time the 1984 season opened (Cincinnati, Pittsburgh, St. Louis, Philadelphia, and Montreal of the senior circuit, plus Seattle, Kansas City, Toronto, and Minnesota of the junior).

Artificial fields are coveted by the management of teams which emphasize speed and defense—and rarely by teams which accentuate long-ball production (unless they operate in domed ballparks). In 1982, the St. Louis Cardinals became World Champions when they used the artificial turf of Busch Memorial Stadium to parlay a combination of speed (best-in-baseball 200 stolen bases) and defense into a winning weapon that compensated for lack of power (worst-in-baseball 67 home runs).

Why did Mike Schmidt lose a home run to the Houston Astrodome?

On June 10, 1974, Mike Schmidt of the Philadelphia Phillies connected with a Claude Osteen pitch, sending it high and far into the outfield. The shot seemed certain to become a tape-measure home run—but a speaker hanging 117 feet over center field, 329 feet from home plate, deflected the ball. According to stadium ground rules, the ball was in play. Two base runners stopped in their tracks and Schmidt wound up with a long single—probably the longest in baseball history.

Why were games postponed at indoor ballparks?

Since the first covered stadium (the Houston Astrodome) opened in 1965, two contests scheduled to be played indoors have been postponed. On June 15, 1976, when torrential rains flooded Houston with up to 10 inches of water, the umpires, fans, and most ballpark personnel couldn't get to the Astrodome. Although the Houston Astros and Pittsburgh Pirates somehow managed to show up, they had to settle for baseball's first "rain-in."

A second postponement at a domed stadium occurred on April 14, 1983, when a 10-inch spring snowstorm prevented the California Angels from landing at the Minneapolis-St. Paul airport for their game against the Minnesota Twins at the Hubert H. Humphrey Metrodome that night. The Angels were rerouted to Chicago, where they stayed overnight.

Why did the Yankees once play in Shea Stadium?

Although Shea Stadium is known as the home of the National League's New York Mets, the New York Yankees played there as tenants of the Mets in 1974 and 1975, while Yankee Stadium (opened in 1923) was undergoing modernization. Ironically, the Yankees had previously been tenants of the Polo Grounds (the *first* home of the Mets) when that field was the home park of the New York Giants. The Yankees built their own park and moved out of the Polo Grounds after they began spinning the turnstiles at a pace that far exceeded the box office business of the Giants. The Mets, who began play in 1962, occupied the Polo Grounds for two seasons while Shea Stadium was being built. The site of the Polo Grounds, across the Harlem River from Yankee Stadium, is now occupied by a low-income housing project.

Why does Wrigley Field host only day games?

Wrigley Field, home park of the Chicago Cubs since

1914, has never had lights. Talk of installing lights from time to time has upset neighborhood residents who believe the advent of night baseball would prompt an influx of undesirables. The team came closest to adding lights in 1942, when owner Phil Wrigley went so far as to order the light towers. Before he could install them, however, Wrigley realized there was a greater need; he donated the structures to a nearby shipyard to help in the war effort.

Why is it possible to hit 315-foot home runs down the 325-foot right-field foul line in Detroit?

Although the distance from home plate to the right-field fence at Tiger Stadium is listed as 325 feet, the upper deck overhangs the field by 10 feet. Fly balls which graze the upper deck automatically become home runs.

Why is Atlanta-Fulton County Stadium called "the Launching Pad"?

Atlanta-Fulton County Stadium, known as the easiest home run touch in the National League, was branded "the Launching Pad" shortly after the Braves fled south from Milwaukee in 1966. Pat Jarvis, one-time ace pitcher of the Braves, is responsible for the tag. During a team bus trip, he told newly-arrived hurlers, "There it is, boys. Welcome to the Launching Pad. You might as well get used to it—the ball really jumps out of here." Atlanta's altitude—1,050 feet above sea level (highest in the majors)—might have something to do with the high annual home run totals, but the cozy dimensions (330 feet down the lines) and short outfield fences (six feet high) are other key factors.

Why is the home park of the Minnesota Twins known as "the Homerdome"?

When the Minnesota Twins began play in the 54,000-seat Hubert H. Humphrey Metrodome in 1982, they quickly discovered that the air jets used to keep the roof inflated provided atmospheric conditions conducive to the long ball. With balls flying over the domed park's fences in record numbers, writers tagged the park "the Homerdome." There were 191 home runs hit in the domed park in '82; only Tiger Stadium (208) was more conducive to the long-ball among the 14 American League fields.

Chapter 5

TEAMS

Introduction

Through most of this century, baseball has had 16 major-league teams, eight in the American League and eight in the National. Expansion changed the map, starting in 1961, to the present configuration of 26 clubs (14 in the American League and 12 in the National League). East and West divisional winners meet in a best-of-five League Championship Series to determine pennant-winners who, in turn, play a best-of-seven World Series.

Baseball history is filled with great performances—by both individuals and teams. A collection of stars on one club may not guarantee a first-place finish, but just the right blend of talent—coupled with adequate reserve strength to compensate for illness or injury—often proves a potent formula for success. The St. Louis Cardinals became 1982 World Champions, for example, even though they ranked last in the majors with 67 home runs. The team they defeated, the Milwaukee Brewers, ranked first with 216 home runs.

Success seems to come more easily for some teams than others. The New York Yankees, with 33 overall pennants (twice five in a row), hold major-league records in those categories. The Dodgers, starting with the 1890 Brooklyn edition, hold the National League mark with 19 flags (17 since 1900).

Philadelphia fans have suffered while those in New York have prospered. The Phillies, with 24 cellar finishes, and the Athletics, who migrated to Kansas City and later Oakland, hold records for most times finished last. The A's were rock-bottom 18 times in the Quaker City and seven more times since departing for Missouri in 1955.

The Phils also hold the record for the longest losing streak since 1900 (23 games in 1961). They were one loss short of the all-time record, 24 straight setbacks suffered by the 1899 Cleveland Spiders of the National League. The Spiders went 20–134 that year, recording a .130 "winning percentage" that ranks as the worst in baseball history.

While some teams plunge into ice-cold conditions, others explode with hot surges. The New York Giants of John McGraw compiled the longest winning streak on record— 26 straight (with one tie) in 1916.

More intriguing, perhaps, than the record-setting teams are the great "comeback" teams of baseball history. Probably the first "miracle" team was the 1914 Boston Braves, a franchise that made such a midseason reversal that the "miracle" tag is often synonymous with the year and team involved.

The Braves were 15 games out of first place and last in the National League standings on July 4 when their fortunes began to change. By August 23, they had forged a first-place tie. Boston won 34 of its last 44 to clinch the flag with a 10½-game bulge and went on to sweep the favored Philadelphia Athletics in the World Series—the first Series sweep in Fall Classic history.

Another famous miracle team was the New York Giants of 1951. On August 11, the Giants trailed the Brooklyn Dodgers by 13½ games. From that point on, New York went 39–8 down the stretch, forcing an end-of-season tie broken by Bobby Thomson's ninth-inning homer in the final playoff game. That team's performance has come to be known as "the little miracle of Coogan's Bluff."

Bucky Dent, light-hitting shortstop of the New York Yankees, also delivered a pennant-winning playoff homer.

His fly ball into the left field screen of Boston's Fenway Park capped a Yankee comeback that erased Boston's 14-game lead of July 19.

The bottom line here is obvious: baseball is full of surprises. One-time National League president Harry Pulliam was well aware of that factor; he kept a placard on his desk that read, "Take nothing for granted in baseball."

Teams change players, managers, owners, and even cities with surprising frequency. When a fan favorite is traded, fan loyalty rarely goes with him. Casey Stengel, beloved outfielder of the Brooklyn Dodgers early in the century, was booed when he returned to Ebbets Field in the uniform of the Pittsburgh Pirates.

Rooting requires loyalty through good times and bad, but team identification gives baseball roots by making fans feel like part of a team. Avid baseball buffs refer to their teams as "we" rather than "they" and teams relish the unswerving support of the faithful.

This chapter looks at some of baseball's famous teams and explains their places in the game's colorful history. It involves the men who play, the men who supervise their play, and the ordinary and extraordinary happenings that have shaped pennant races as well as championship games.

Why were Philadelphia and New York once thrown out of the National League?

During the league's very first season, in 1876, the Philadelphia Athletics and New York Mutuals refused to make their final western road trips. Both teams said they had lost money and didn't want to lose any more. At the winter meetings that year, National League owners expelled the two renegade teams, thereby losing the two largest cities in the circuit. But the bold action—approved by league president William Hulbert—made a strong positive impression on fans as well as officials (who wondered privately whether the league would survive). The National League did survive, operating as a six-club loop (without Philadelphia and New York) in 1877. The league expanded to eight members in 1879, but New York and Philadelphia did not return until 1884.

Why were the Phillies also known as "Quakers"?

After the Philadelphia Phillies opened their new park in 1895 the team played well, winning games in the manner of a well-oiled machine. The combination of success without controversy created a quiet confidence that reminded observers of the region's founding religious sect, the Quakers. Writers often referred to the club as "Quakers" and later, when red was introduced as a primary uniform color, as "Red Quakers."

Why does Indianapolis claim to be the site of the first night game?

On September 6, 1888, Indianapolis of the National League played baseball by gaslight against Chicago. Fielders had trouble on ground balls and fly balls could not be seen immediately upon leaving the bat. The experiment with gaslight, which had also included a practice game on August 22, was therefore abandoned.

Why did the Athletics have a white elephant as their team symbol?

In the first American League season in 1901, the Philadelphia Athletics were derisively called "the White Elephants" by their closest geographic rivals, the Baltimore Orioles, then managed by John McGraw. The A's won the 1902 pennant, however, and proudly adopted the derogatory label as a symbol of strength and supremacy. The tradition survived well past the transfer of the franchise to Kansas City in 1955.

Why were the White Sox once known as "the Hitless Wonders"?

The Chicago franchise won the American League pennant in 1906 but hit only six home runs in the process. During the "dead-ball era," prior to 1920, hitters choked up, sprayed balls to all fields, specialized in bunts and hit-and-run plays, and seldom drove balls over outfield fences. In 1907, the "Hitless Wonders" managed only *three* home runs! (The pennant-winning 1959 Chicago White Sox were also called "Hitless Wonders" because they ranked last in home runs (97) and sixth in batting (.250) among the eight American League teams.)

Why did a spitball cost the Chicago White Sox a pennant?

On October 2, 1908, the Chicago White Sox, Cleveland Indians, and Detroit Tigers were still fighting for the American League pennant. Ed Walsh, a 40-game winner for the White Sox, was matched against Cleveland's Addie Joss in a crucial game. Joss pitched a perfect game, beating Walsh, 1–0. Walsh yielded four hits and struck out 15, allowing only a single unearned run when a two-strike, two-out spitball broke off the glove of catcher Ossie Schreckengost in the third inning. That pitch allowed a runner on third to score the only run of the game. Detroit wound up first, Cleveland a half-game back, and Chicago one-and-a-half behind. Many experts insist the 1908 pennant race was the greatest in baseball history.

Why did the Detroit Tigers go on strike in 1912?

On May 15, 1912, Detroit's top star, Ty Cobb, received an indefinite suspension from the American League after he jumped into the stands to attack a heckler in New York. Cobb's teammates wired the league office that they would strike until he was reinstated. On May 18, when Cobb took the field with his teammates in Philadelphia, the umpires ordered him off. The rest of the Tigers went with him. Manager Hugh Jennings was prepared for this eventuality, however. He activated two coaches, recruited some semi-pros, including a future priest named Al Travers, and lost to the A's by a 24–2 score. Travers made $25 for his one-day career and earned his money by pitching the whole game and batting fourth. He allowed only 6 runs for the first 3 innings, but the A's then found the groove and peppered him with hits and runs for the rest of the way. American League executives subsequently ordered all striking Tigers back, threatening them with lifetime expulsion, and fining them $100 each. Cobb was reinstated on May 25 and asked to pay a $50 fine.

Why did poor defense cost the New York Giants the World Championship in 1912?

Although the New York Giants took a 2–1 lead in the top of the 10th inning in the eighth game of the 1912 World Series (one game was a tie), the Boston Red Sox rebounded for two runs when the New York defense collapsed.

Clyde Engle, leading off the Boston 10th, hit an easy fly to center field but Fred Snodgrass dropped it—an error later referred to as "the $12,000 Muff" because of the difference in winner's and loser's shares that fall. One out and one walk later, Tris Speaker hit a pop foul between home and first, but neither Fred Merkle, the first baseman, nor Chief Meyers, the catcher, went for the ball. Speaker then singled home

Engle with the tying run. Steve Yerkes, who had walked and advanced to third on Speaker's hit, brought home the World Championship when he scored on a sacrifice fly by Larry Gardner.

Why were the 1914 Boston Braves called the "miracle" Braves?

The Boston Braves were 11½ games out of first place in July 1914 and looked like anything but pennant-winners. Then they caught fire, winning 34 of their last 44 to finish first by 10 games. The Braves went on to sweep the favored Philadelphia Athletics in the 1914 World Series.

Why did Connie Mack break up the powerful Philadelphia Athletics?

Faced with player raids by the rival Federal League in 1914-15, Connie Mack, owner-manager of the Philadelphia Athletics, decided the sale of his stars to richer American League clubs would keep the league solvent (by keeping crowd-pleasing stars in familiar uniforms)—and save his A's from going broke. One of the stars sold by Philadelphia, second baseman Eddie Collins, immediately proved Mack's theory when he signed a five-year contract (unusual in a day when most players signed for a year at a time) and commanded an annual salary of $15,000, then considered to be big money. Mack's "fire sale" stripped the A's of contender status, but the team regrouped a decade later and regained championship form with the arrivals of Lefty Grove, Mickey Cochrane, and other fine young players.

The Great Depression prompted another "fire sale," however, as Mack disbanded the championship Athletic teams of 1929-30-31. He received more than $900,000 for Grove, Cochrane, Al Simmons, Mule Hass, and other stars.

But the sales plunged the team from the top to the bottom of the league, and the Athletics remained out of contention until Charlie Finley's young Oakland Athletics finished first in the American League West in 1971.

Why do the Yankees wear pinstripes?

Prior to the 1915 season, the uniforms of the New York American League club (known variously as Hilltoppers and Highlanders before adopting the Yankee nickname in 1913) featured drab flannels not very different from the uniforms of other clubs. After the 1914 season, management decided that the "dressed-for-success" look of Wall Street executives might also pay off on the baseball diamond. When the team took the field for the first game of the 1915 season, on April 22, Yankee players sported dark, thin vertical pinstripes on their home white uniforms. Although it took six years before the team won its first pennant, the Yankees went on to win more championships than any other team. Whether the pinstripes helped or not is subject to conjecture, but the tradition has survived nearly 70 years.

Why was the baseball schedule shortened the year after World War I ended?

In 1918, the last year of World War I, baseball had ended its season suddenly at the request of the U.S. War Department. With baseball ruled "non-essential" following a work-or-fight order by Provost Marshall General Crowder, baseball executives secured permission from Secretary of War Baker to continue the season until Labor Day. Play stopped September 2—long after teams began suffering losses because of draft, enlistment, and other military maneuvers. The first-place teams on September 2, the Boston Red Sox and Chicago Cubs, met in the earliest World Series on record.

Staggering from the war-marred year, baseball club owners were uncertain of the postwar economy and anticipated falling fan interest. So they sliced the schedule from 154 to 140 games (a format last used in 1903) for the 1919 season. Owner confidence returned with renewed fan enthusiasm, however, and the 154-game slate was restored in 1920.

Why did a pitcher bat sixth in the World Series?

In the fourth game of the 1918 World Series between the Boston Red Sox and the Chicago Cubs, the Boston pitcher—batting sixth—hit a two-run triple, grounded out, and delivered a sacrifice hit in a 3-2 victory. That pitcher, who moved to left field after yielding a single and walk to open the ninth, was named Babe Ruth.

Why did the Boston Red Sox sell Babe Ruth to the New York Yankees?

Boston Red Sox owner Harry Frazee was more interested in theater than baseball. His New York theatrical office was two doors from Yankee headquarters, so it wasn't surprising that eleven of his stars had donned pinstripes by 1923. The biggest sale involved Ruth, who had hit .322 with 29 home runs and 114 runs batted in for the Red Sox in 1919. Ruth also had an 8-5 pitching record and 2.98 earned run average that season. But, on January 3, 1920, the Bosox sent Ruth to the Yankees for the staggering (at the time) sum of $125,000. Ruth paid immediate dividends for New York—with 54 home runs in 1920 and 59 the following year. In 1927, he produced the only 60-home run season to be accomplished under the old 154-game schedule (pre-1961).

Why was the great batting order of the 1927 Yankees known as "Murderer's Row"?

An early baseball writer, drawing a parallel between slugging teams (with hitters who "kill" pitchers) and Death Row at the Tombs Prison in New York, first applied the "Murderer's Row" application to baseball in 1858. But the phrase took on more significance when Babe Ruth, Lou Gehrig, and several other feared sluggers pooled their resources to intimidate opponents in 1927—the year Ruth slammed 60 home runs in a 154-game schedule. Tony Lazzeri, Earle Combs, and Bob Meusel joined Ruth and Gehrig as .300 hitters, enabling the Yankees to lead the league with a .307 team average. The team also paced the circuit with 158 home runs, 1,644 hits, 975 runs scored, 908 runs batted in, and a .489 slugging average.

Why did a pebble help Washington win a World Series?

The 1924 World Series between the New York Giants and the Washington Senators ended when a 12th-inning grounder struck an infield pebble, bounding high over the head of third baseman Fred Lindstrom and allowing the winning run to score from second base. An error by New York catcher Hank Gowdy—who dropped a pop foul by Muddy Ruel—set the stage. Given another chance, Ruel doubled, then scored when Earl McNeely's grounder hit the pebble.

Why did baseball establish a June 15th deadline for waiver-free trades within each league?

At certain times during the year, trades are prohibited unless waivers are secured on the athletes involved. A team may place a player on waivers, allowing any interested club to pass on him (yielding the right to claim him) or to put in a claim for his contract. Once a waiver claim is made, the team asking waivers knows who has an interest in its player. It may then withdraw the player's name and initiate trade talks that may result in a "waiver deal." A team may not withdraw the name of a man who is on irrevocable waivers; any team claiming such a player need only pay the $20,000 waiver price for his contract.

The June 15th trading deadline was originally established after the 1922 season, when the New York Yankees acquired Joe Dugan from the Boston Red Sox in the latter stages of the pennant race. Dugan's play at third base enabled New York to squeak by the St. Louis Browns for the American League title, angering officials of both leagues. The June 15th deadline was the end result, though the rule actually did little to stymie the annual migration of veteran players to contenders in late summer. A "gentleman's agreement" among club owners has allowed quality players to change uniforms in August or September almost every year. The prevailing theory is that executives who "pass" on a waiver list player—thereby allowing his team to work out a postdeadline trade—will eventually benefit when other executives "pass" on the other team's player.

Why were the 1930–1932 New York Yankees regarded as baseball's most powerful team?

In addition to winning more pennants than any other club, the New York Yankees won with convincing style. For three straight years, 1930–32, the team scored more than 1,000 runs—an awesome feat accomplished by only three other teams (the 1930 St. Louis Cardinals, 1936 Yankees, and 1950 Boston Red Sox). The best of the 1,000-run teams was the 1931 Yankee club managed by Joe McCarthy. It scored 1,067 runs despite a meager-by-comparison home run total of 155. Big hitters on the team were Babe Ruth, Lou Gehrig, Tony Lazzeri, Joe Sewell, Earle Combs, Ben Chapman, Bill Dickey, and Lyn Lary. All but Lazzeri and Dickey scored at least 100 runs, led by Ruth's 163.

Why do Cubs' fans believe in "the goat curse of Wrigley Field"?

During the 1945 National League season, as the Chicago Cubs headed for the pennant, a fan brought his pet goat to every game. But the animal was barred during the World Series, angering its owner so much that he placed a hex on the club. The Cubs would never make the World Series again, he said. Through the 1983 season, the curse has held.

Why was Lefty Grove's 1933 shutout of the Yankees noteworthy?

In August 1933, Lefty Grove, the star lefthander of the Philadelphia Athletics, ended a record Yankee streak of 308 straight games without a shutout defeat. New York was not blanked at all in 1932 and almost made it through 1933 without the ignominy of a whitewash.

Why did the Phillies trade a Triple Crown winner?

In 1933, Chuck Klein of the Philadelphia Phillies led the National League with a .368 batting average, 28 home runs, and 120 runs batted in. But the financially-strapped team, seizing the opportunity to unload Klein's salary and add to the coffers at the same time, traded the Triple Crown winner to the Chicago Cubs for pitcher Ted Kleinhans, infielder Mark Koenig, outfielder Harvey Hendrick, and an estimated $65,000. That trade, completed on November 21, 1933, was the only one involving a player who had won a Triple Crown in the preceding season.

Why were the St. Louis Cardinals once called "the Gas House Gang"?

There are several differing versions of the "Gas House Gang" nickname—with the sole agreement being that it was first hung on the 1934 team that went on to become baseball's World Champions.

In one account, Dizzy Dean said of the team's fifth-place standing in June, "We'd be in first place if we were in the other league." Pepper Martin retorted, "They wouldn't let us in the other league. They'd say we were a lot of gas house ballplayers."

Martin was comparing the dirty uniforms of the Cards, an aggressive team on the bases, with the overalls worn by gas station (gas house) attendants.

Another account attributes the name to New York sportswriter Frank Graham, who compared the club's dirty livery with the wretched appearance of the populace in New York's rundown Gas House district.

It was Graham who referred to St. Louis in print as "The Gas House Gang"—a name that stuck right through the World Series against Detroit that fall.

Why were the Brooklyn Dodgers known to their fans as "Dem Bums"?

The Brooklyn Dodgers were inept during the '30s and often the source of frustration to their fans even during more successful seasons in the '40s and '50s. Fickle fans, with distinctive Brooklyn accents, hurled countless "Dem Bums" epithets at them from the confines of cozy Ebbets Field.

In time, the "Dem Bums" slogan became a trademark of

sorts for the ball club. Even the great Dodger teams of the late '40s and early '50s were associated with the saying.

The designation became so ingrained in the minds of the Brooklyn fans that Willard Mullins, in a famous *New York Daily News* front-page cartoon after the Dodgers had beaten the Yankees for their first World Championship, placed a headline over the top with the words "WHO'S A BUM?" in bold type.

Why did Ernie Lombardi "snooze" in the World Series?

In the 10th inning of Game 4 of the 1939 World Series between the Cincinnati Reds and New York Yankees, Cincinnati catcher Ernie Lombardi—attempting to catch a throw from right fielder Ival Goodman—was knocked cold in a collision with base runner Charlie Keller. While Lombardi was sprawled on the ground near home plate, Joe DiMaggio—who had hit the ball to Goodman—circled the bases to ice a three-run uprising that gave New York a 7–4 win and a World Series sweep.

Why did a passed ball result in a World Series defeat?

In the fourth game of the 1941 World Series between the Brooklyn Dodgers and New York Yankees, the Dodgers clung to a 4–3 lead in the ninth with two outs and nobody on base for New York. Tommy Henrich fanned—ostensibly the third out, ending the game—but Brooklyn receiver Mickey Owen missed the ball and Henrich reached first. Joe DiMaggio followed with a single, Charlie Keller doubled for two runs, Bill Dickey walked, and Joe Gordon doubled for two more runs. The Yankees won, 7–4, to take a three-to-one World Series lead. They became World Champions the next day.

Why were the Yankees of the '40s and '50s known as the "Bronx Bombers"?

Teams often have nicknames for their nicknames. The New York Yankees, whose stadium is situated in the Bronx, earned the nickname "Bronx Bombers" because of their tendency to rely on power for victory.

The club always seemed to have sluggers in the wings. Joe DiMaggio came up just as Lou Gehrig bowed out. Mickey Mantle succeeded DiMaggio. Bill Dickey, a Hall of Fame catcher, was succeeded by another in Yogi Berra.

The "Bronx Bombers" monicker was applied as long ago as the Roaring '20s, when Babe Ruth, Lou Gehrig, and other stalwarts in pinstripes combined to form a "Murderer's Row" that could spell death to enemy pitchers. The team was also known as "Ruppert's Rifles" because it represented the crack troops of owner Col. Jacob Ruppert.

Why was Larry MacPhail a controversial candidate for the Hall of Fame?

Larry MacPhail, the father of long-time American League president Lee MacPhail, was a dynamic but abrasive executive for several clubs, including the Cincinnati Reds, Brooklyn Dodgers, and New York Yankees in the '30s and '40s. At all three stops, MacPhail built a reputation as a financial wizard, ingenious promoter, and superb talent scout, but also as a battler—with commissioners, owners, managers, and players. Critics accused him of enjoying a martini as much as a home run. MacPhail, best remembered for bringing night baseball to the majors and broadcast baseball to New York, was a controversial candidate for Cooperstown because of his many detractors. But he won election anyway in 1978.

Why was Bill Veeck known as "the P.T. Barnum of Baseball"?

Bill Veeck was an innovative promoter who ran the Cleveland Indians, St. Louis Browns, and Chicago White Sox (twice) over a four-decade span after World War II. He believed in entertaining the fans with a variety of gimmicks—particularly when he ran losing teams with no pulling power of their own. Among other things, he sent a midget to bat in a major-league game, substituted 1,000 "grandstand managers" for his regular pilot, unveiled the first exploding scoreboard, dressed his team in shorts, installed an indoor shower in the center field bleachers, and brought black stars Larry Doby and Satchel Paige to the majors—integrating the American League. Known as a maverick, Veeck was unpopular among his more conservative colleagues, but succeeded through shrewd trades and clever promotions.

Why did the Tigers use a rookie pitcher to win a pennant?

On the final weekend of the 1940 season, the Detroit Tigers faced the Cleveland Indians in a three-game series. Detroit took a two-game lead into the weekend and would wrap up the pennant with one win in the series. With 27-game winner Bob Feller due to open for Cleveland, Detroit manager Del Baker decided to withhold his veteran pitchers for the second and third games. Rookie Floyd Giebell, up from Buffalo, got the assignment. Giebell had beaten the Philadelphia Athletics eight days earlier but had little big-league experience. Still, he outdueled Feller, 2–0, to clinch the pennant. Rudy York provided all the runs Giebell needed with a two-run homer off Feller. The Cleveland pitcher yielded just two other hits. While Feller would win many more games en route to 266 career wins, Giebell never again won in the majors.

Why did rival clubs deploy a radical shift against Ted Williams?

Ted Williams, a powerful lefthanded hitter for the Boston Red Sox, consistently hit the ball between first and second base. In an effort to neutralize the slugger's success against his club, Cleveland Indians player-manager Lou Boudreau conceived the "Williams shift" in 1946. When Williams came to bat, Boudreau stationed six fielders on the right side of the diamond. Only the leftfielder, playing deep shortstop, remained on the left side of second. The radical shift, unveiled on July 14, 1946, was copied with modification by other clubs.

Williams maintained he could have overcome the shift by bunting or slicing the ball to the opposite field, but such strategy would have reduced his power. Williams estimated that the shift probably cost him 20 to 30 points on his lifetime batting average of .344. Radical defenses had been tried before—often against lefthanded power hitters—but none attracted as much attention as the Ted Williams shift.

Why did the 1947 Pittsburgh Pirates have two defending home run champions on their roster?

Although the 1947 Pittsburgh Pirates finished last, locked in a seventh-place tie with the hapless Philadelphia Phillies, they were not totally boring to their fans—mainly because the club owned both home run kings of 1946. Ralph Kiner hit 23 homers, a meager total for a league leader, to pace National League sluggers in '46, then enjoyed a banner year with 51 circuit clouts in 1947. Pittsburgh also managed to obtain American League home run king Hank Greenberg from Detroit, where he had hit 44 homers and knocked in 127 runs—both league-leading statistics—at age 35 in 1946.

The Tigers, seeking to save some of Greenberg's enormous salary and hoping to inject more youth into their lineup, sent the slugger to Pittsburgh in a controversial waiver deal. He promptly hit 25 homers for the Pirates in 1947, his final season, and imparted valuable slugging tips to the young Kiner. Both men were righthanded hitters who benefitted from the club's new left field bullpen, which shortened the distance from home to the fence by 30 feet. The new section of Forbes Field was first called "Greenberg Gardens," then changed to "Kiner's Korner" a year later. The area was removed after Kiner was traded to the Chicago Cubs in 1953.

Why was renowned baseball executive Branch Rickey so tight with a dollar?

Rickey ran four different teams—the St. Louis Browns, the St. Louis Cardinals, the Brooklyn Dodgers, and the Pittsburgh Pirates—and always kept a tight reign on the purse-strings. His approach stemmed from his early days with the Cardinals, who were once so strapped for funds that they couldn't afford to go to spring training. The Cards of 1919 held "spring training" in snowbound St. Louis. The team had to wear its home uniforms on the road because it couldn't afford a separate set and Rickey even distributed his own salary to help meet the payroll. Memories of those days never left him. Actor Chuck Connors, who once played for Rickey in Brooklyn, said, "It was easy to figure out Mr. Rickey's thinking on contracts. He had both players and money and didn't like to see the two of them mix."

Why were the Phillies once known as the "Whiz Kids"?

The 1950 National League champion Philadelphia Phillies had a very young roster, prompting the nickname "Whiz Kids" from writers covering the club. The only regular over age 30 on the Philadelphia roster was bellwether reliever Jim Konstanty, who went on to win the National League's Most Valuable Player award with a 16-7 record and 22 saves (unofficial) in 74 appearances. Konstanty, a surprise starter in Game 1 of the World Series against the Yankees that fall, was 33 years old in 1950.

Why did the St. Louis Browns hire a psychologist?

Tired of finishing last, the St. Louis Browns (who became the Baltimore Orioles in 1954), hired New York psychologist Dr. David F. Tracy to work with their players in 1950. Dr. Tracy, who doubled as a hypnotist, came to the Browns after the team had recorded successive records of 59-95, 59-94, and 53-101. Unable to change the team's fortunes, Tracy was dismissed on May 31 when the last-place Browns had an 8-25 record.

Why did a team play different rivals on the same day?

The rare event of one team playing different rivals on the same day occurred twice within a three-year span in the 1950s. On September 13, 1951, Sportsman's Park in St. Louis was the scene of a day game between the Cardinals and the New York Giants (making up the previous night's rainout) and a regularly-scheduled night game between the Cardinals and the Boston Braves. (St. Louis won the day game, beating 20-game winner Sal Maglie, but lost at night to 20-game winner Warren Spahn.)

The Cardinals were again involved in unusual scheduling on September 25, 1954, when they were supposed to play a single game in Milwaukee against the Braves. Prior to that game, the Cincinnati Reds met the Braves in the conclusion of a game that had been protested by the Reds several days before. National League president Warren Giles ordered the game replayed from the point of protest—the ninth inning—and the Reds quickly erased an apparent 3–1 Milwaukee win by scoring two runs to tie. The Braves won in the home ninth, then went on to beat St. Louis in the scheduled game.

Why did the relocation of the Boston Braves trigger a wave of franchise shifting?

Between 1903 and 1953, there were no changes in the baseball map. Lou Perini, owner of the Boston Braves, ended that period of stability when he transferred his club to Milwaukee on March 18, 1953. The Braves, unable to compete with the Red Sox in Boston, had drawn only 281,278 fans in 1952—costing Perini $600,000. When the Braves drew 1,826,397 in their first year in Milwaukee, other struggling franchises found fresh sites: the St. Louis Browns became the Baltimore Orioles in 1954, the Philadelphia Athletics moved to Kansas City in 1955, the Brooklyn Dodgers went to Los Angeles, and the New York Giants to San Francisco after the 1957 season, and the Washington Senators (first edition) became the Minnesota Twins in 1961.

Why are several American League teams named for states instead of cities?

The Minnesota Twins, who transferred to the Twin Cities of Minneapolis-St. Paul from Washington after the 1960 season, became the first baseball team to identify with a state rather than a city. The Twins took the name "Minnesota" because they sought to honor both twin cities without offending either—though they initially played their games in suburban Bloomington.

The California Angels were the Los Angeles Angels

when they began life as a 1961 expansion team, but assumed a state identity after moving down the freeway to Anaheim.

The Texas Rangers adopted the "Texas" name for the same reasons as the Minnesota Twins. The Rangers, based in Arlington, but seeking fan support from all over the state, didn't wish to identify with a single community. Their nickname therefore honored the legendary lawmen of the Lone Star State instead of either host community, Dallas or Fort Worth.

Why did the Yankees trade Billy Martin?

On May 16, 1957, Billy Martin, second baseman of the New York Yankees, was celebrating his 29th birthday at New York's Copacabana nightclub with teammates Hank Bauer, Yogi Berra, Whitey Ford, Mickey Mantle, and Johnny Kucks. The baseball sextet became embroiled in a disturbance that resulted in the fining of all six players and the trade—a month later—of Martin to Kansas City. Martin, who later returned to the Yankees as manager, had been accused of being the instigator of the disturbance, though only Bauer was actually accused of striking a patron (he was later cleared).

Why did the New York Yankees feel they were deprived of a deserved World Championship in 1960?

Although the Pittsburgh Pirates won four games in the 1960 World Series against the New York Yankees, the American League champions felt they were the true World Champions. The Yankees won their games by scores of 16-3, 10-0, and 12-0, and outscored the Pirates, 55-27, in the seven games. New York also outhit Pittsburgh, 91-60. But the Pirates won the World Championship when Bill Mazeroski socked a leadoff homer in the home ninth of

Game 7, climaxing a 10–9 triumph. It was the only time in World Series history that a home run decided the World Championship.

Why was Frank Thomas a key man in New York baseball history?

Frank Thomas, who played first and third base as well as the outfield for several teams, was a member of the Pittsburgh Pirates when the New York Giants played their last game in the Polo Grounds before moving to San Francisco (on September 29, 1957). Thomas was also on hand for the return of baseball to New York, when he was with the original Mets for their home debut on April 11, 1962, against the St. Louis Cardinals. Thomas played first base for Pittsburgh and left field for the Mets in the historic games. No other player participated in both contests.

Why did baseball change the old format of two eight-team leagues?

Baseball team owners, always searching for new sources of revenue, realized that expansion would be beneficial because virgin territory could be exploited. In addition, expansion franchises plugged voids left by existing teams that shifted sites. In 1961, the American League expanded to 10 teams by creating the Los Angeles Angels and the second edition of the Washington Senators (replacing the team that became the Minnesota Twins the same year). The league increased to 12 clubs when the Seattle Pilots and Kansas City Royals (replacing the team that became the Oakland Athletics) were added in 1969, creating two six-team divisions. The Toronto Blue Jays and the Seattle Mariners (replacing the team—Pilots—that became the Milwaukee Brewers) swelled American League membership to 14 franchises in 1977.

National League expansion created the New York Mets and Houston Colts (now Astros) in 1962 and the San Diego Padres and Montreal Expos in 1969.

The move of the Seattle Pilots to Milwaukee in 1970 silenced pending litigation against baseball by the City of Milwaukee, which lost the National League Braves to Atlanta in 1966, but one city from the old 16-club format was left without a club. Washington lost its team for the second time when the Senators became the Texas Rangers in 1972.

Why did the Chicago White Sox play in Milwaukee?

Milwaukee lost its National League franchise to Atlanta after the 1965 season, creating a void in a city generally regarded as good baseball territory. The Chicago White Sox, hoping to create new fans in Wisconsin, played 20 home games in Milwaukee in 1968 and 1969 and might have continued the annual practice had the Seattle Pilots not become the Milwaukee Brewers in 1970.

Why did the Chicago Cubs operate without a manager for several years?

From 1961 to 65, the Chicago Cubs experimented with a rotating "Board of Coaches," with various head coaches in charge at different times during the season. The idea was the brainchild of club owner Phil Wrigley, a chewing-gum magnate who had tired of seeing his team lose the traditional way—with a single manager in charge. Ironically, the Cubs became respectable only after junking the coaching board and bringing Leo Durocher out of retirement in 1966.

Why was the Boston Red Sox pennant of 1967 called "the Impossible Dream"?

The Boston Red Sox overcame 100-to-1 odds to win the 1967 American League flag in a photo finish over the Detroit Tigers and Minnesota Twins, each one game out, and the Chicago White Sox, three games behind. The last-weekend victory by the Sox capped a rags-to-riches season in which the young Boston team, powered by Triple Crown winner Carl Yastrzemski, rose from ninth place in 1966 to first in 1967. Writers called the comeback "The Impossible Dream," taking the title from the featured song in the popular Broadway show *Man of La Mancha*.

Going into the last weekend of the 1967 season, Minnesota led Boston and Detroit by a game. Boston beat Minnesota twice at Fenway Park, then awaited the outcome of a season-ending doubleheader between Detroit and California. A sweep by Detroit would have forced a pennant playoff, but California won the second game to give Boston the pennant. The hero of the Red Sox drive was Yastrzemski, who had 10 hits in his last 13 at-bats to finish the year with league leadership in batting average, hits, runs scored, runs batted in, home runs, total bases, and slugging average. His 44 home runs and 121 runs batted in were career peaks.

Why were the New York Mets called "Miracle Mets" in 1969?

The New York Mets earned the "Miracle Mets" tag in 1969 because the team—never higher than ninth in seven previous seasons of existence—suddenly rose from the ashes to win a pennant and a World Championship with a brilliant stretch performance.

In early August, the team trailed the Chicago Cubs by nine-and-a-half games, but New York got hot just as the

Cubs wilted in the heat. The Chicago lead, two-and-a-half games on September 8, was gone three days later as the Mets roared to a 100-victory season, winning the National League East title by eight full games.

The Mets proceeded to sweep the Atlanta Braves, West winners, in the first National League Championship Series, and then won the World Series in five games against the Baltimore Orioles.

Stars of the team were pitchers Tom Seaver, Jerry Koosman, and Gary Gentry, relievers Tug McGraw and Ron Taylor, and big hitters Cleon Jones, Tommie Agee, Art Shamsky, and Donn Clendenon. Seaver had 25 wins and won the first of three Cy Young Awards for pitching excellence that summer.

Why did the Seattle Pilots have only one All-Star representative in their history?

First baseman Don Mincher, first pick of the Seattle Pilots in the 1968 American League expansion draft, represented the club in the 1969 All-Star Game because of league rules mandating at least one selection from each team. Since the club became the Milwaukee Brewers after that single season in Seattle, no other Pilot has ever appeared in an All-Star Game.

Why was the National League's Eastern Division dubbed "the National League Least" in 1973?

With only four days to go in the 1973 campaign, five of the six teams had a chance to finish first, with a remote chance that there could be a five-way deadlock—with all teams having an 80-82 record. But the New York Mets, rebounding from a 12-game deficit and last-place standing on July 8, managed to win without a playoff. The team's 82–79 record produced a .509 "winning" percentage, lowest ever recorded by a championship team, hence the nickname "National League Least." The Mets went on to topple favored Cincinnati, champions of the National League West, and take Oakland to a full seven games before losing the World Series. The Mets rode to the Series on the wings of Tug McGraw's magic motto: "You gotta believe."

Why were the Cincinnati Reds of the '70s known as "the Big Red Machine"?

In the 10-year span from 1970 through 1979, the Cincinnati Reds won four National League pennants and two divisional titles in the National League West—all but the '79 West title under Sparky Anderson.

The team was comprised largely of seasoned vets who made it run like a well-oiled machine. Since they wore uniforms highlighted in red, sportswriters covering the club called it "the Big Red Machine."

Key hitters were Pete Rose, Joe Morgan, Tony Perez, Johnny Bench, Dave Concepcion, and George Foster. The pitching stars seemed to change every year, but one thing was always constant: a competent bullpen led by people like Clay Carroll, Rawly Eastwick, or Pedro Borbon.

From 1970 to 1977, the Reds owned the National League's Most Valuable Player every year, with the lone exceptions of 1971 and 1974. Bench and Morgan won twice; Foster and Rose once each.

Seldom has one club dominated its league through an entire decade like "the Big Red Machine."

Why was Charlie Finley so controversial?

Charlie Finley bought the Kansas City Athletics in 1961 and remained owner of the team (which shifted to Oakland in 1968) through the 1980 season. Finley served as his own general manager and was the busiest trader in the game—even when his team was winning. Constant deals and managerial changes kept his club in the public spotlight—and promotions such as "Mustache Day" helped. Although he ran the team with a skeleton front-office crew and was often an absentee owner, Finley built the A's into a powerful club through an uncanny knack for recognizing young talent.

The A's were World Champions in 1972-73-74 and divisional winners in 1971 and 1975. But Finley was scorned for introducing colorful softball-style uniforms, white shoes, orange baseballs, and various other gimmicks, as well as for proposing night World Series games. Many of his suggestions were later adopted by baseball.

The major complaint against Finley came from his managers, who complained that he interfered with their operation of the club. Dick Williams resigned in 1973 after winning three straight divisional titles—two of them resulting in World Championships. Finley fought constantly with Baseball Commissioner Bowie Kuhn who voided Finley's attempts to sell his top stars before losing them to free agency. Crippled by free agency, the A's fell from second to last but regrouped to finish second, and then first, under Billy Martin in 1980-81.

Why did the Oakland Athletics once use four pitchers in a no-hitter?

On the last day of the 1975 American League season, Oakland manager Alvin Dark was getting his pitching staff ready for the Championship Series against the Boston Red Sox. Since the game against the California Angels would have no bearing on the final standings, Dark decided to use aces Vida Blue and Rollie Fingers at the beginning and end of the game, respectively, and second-liners Glenn Abbott and Paul Lindblad in between. The quartet, hyped for postseason play, was especially sharp against the Angels, then a hapless ballclub, and allowed no hits. Their no-hitter was a baseball first: the only time a no-hitter has been thrown by more than two pitchers.

Why do the Boston Red Sox dislike pennant playoffs?

Fenway Park, home of the Boston Red Sox, has been the site of two championship playoffs outside of the American League Championship Series. Unlike the National League, which used a best-of-three format to determine league champions when the predivisional schedule ended in a tie, the American League has always used a sudden-death arrangement. The Red Sox won coin flips to determine the playoff site but have never won the sudden-death game. In 1948, Cleveland won, 8–3, and in 1978, the New York Yankees staged a late comeback for a 5–4 win to take the American League East title.

Why was the midseason collapse of the Atlanta Braves in 1982 the fastest fall in major-league history?

On July 29, the Braves led the San Diego Padres by nine games and the Los Angeles Dodgers by 10½. But the Dodgers swept a doubleheader at Atlanta-Fulton County Stadium July 30 to start an Atlanta tailspin that produced 19 losses in 21 games. The Dodgers got hot simultaneously, vaulting into first place, with a half-game lead over the Braves, on August 10. The swing of 11 games in 12 days ranks as baseball's fastest fall, though the Braves were able to recover in time to finish first in the National League West, one game ahead of Los Angeles and two up on the revived San Francisco Giants.

Why are the New York Yankees so popular?

Because of unequaled success—33 pennants—and because of their location in the nation's media center, the New York Yankees have always drawn well, on the road as well as at home. If attendance can be gauged as a barometer of popularity, the Yankee record is indicative of their success; New York was the first team to exceed a million in attendance (1,289,422 in 1920) and the first to exceed two million (2,265,512 in 1946).

Why do teams feel they have an advantage playing at home?

In professional baseball, the home team bats last, giving it a distinct advantage if the game is tied when it takes its last turn at bat. The game ends immediately if the home team scores in the ninth inning or later in a tie game. It is for that reason that teams play to tie at home and win on the road; visiting managers invariably go for the big inning instead of the tie late in the game. Familiar surroundings, partisan fans, and the sudden-death situation of the home ninth (or beyond) are factors favoring the home team. So is the ability of grounds keepers to tilt foul lines to aid bunting clubs, keep infield grass short to assist slow-footed infielders, or alter the infield dirt to help or hinder running ball clubs. Since clubs play half their schedules at home, many teams are designed for particular parks. Case in point: the 1982 World Champion St. Louis Cardinals, a punchless team that thrived on pitching, speed, and the timely line drive in a spacious field carpeted by artificial turf (Busch Memorial Stadium).

Why is a deficit of three-games-to-one almost insurmountable in World Series competition?

Because the World Series is a best-of-seven affair, the

first team to win four times becomes the World Champion of baseball. Rebounding from a three-to-one deficit is difficult because it means that the team with the deficit must win three straight contests under extreme pressure against one of the toughest rivals in the game. The Pittsburgh Pirates have twice overcome the long odds—with victories in 1925 against the Washington Senators and in 1979 against the Baltimore Orioles—while the 1958 New York Yankees (against the Milwaukee Braves) and the 1968 Detroit Tigers (against the St. Louis Cardinals) have done it once each.

Why did free agency make trading difficult for major-league teams?

After the fall of the old reserve clause in 1976, unsigned players became free agents, able to sign with any club. To keep their best players, teams began signing athletes to long-term contracts, often with no-trade or limited-trade clauses included. Harry Dalton, general manager of the Milwaukee Brewers, explained the effect of free agency on trading: "Before, all you did was trade a service contract, usually an obligation for one year. There were few, if any, other restrictions. Now you have long-term guaranteed financial commitments, in some cases for four or five years, and in many cases for $1 million. First, it's tough for teams to take on that obligation and second, within the service contract itself, the player has the right to say no. Paul Owens of the Phillies might come up to me and offer a player. I'll say, 'What's his contract like?' He'll tell me and I'll say, 'I'm not interested.'"

Chapter 6

PLAYERS

Introduction

Almost every boy in America wants to be a major-league baseball player when he grows up. Never mind the minimum salary of $33,500 or the average big-league paycheck of more than $200,000 per year; most American kids want to play because they love the game.

That youthful enthusiasm remains with those good enough to reach the major leagues. Joe Torre, the National League's Most Valuable Player in 1971, explained the thinking of many when he said, "Baseball is never the same, never boring. Every aspect of the game is different. Playing every day is exciting. Roy Campanella once said that when you lose the little boy in you, it's time to quit. Somehow, the game manages to keep me young and that keeps me enthusiastic."

As a player, Torre was one of the best of his time—a batting champion, Most Valuable Player, and perennial All-Star who mastered several positions. But he was not able to advance into the elite echelon of athletes enshrined in the Baseball Hall of Fame.

Because admission to Cooperstown requires 75 percent of the vote, fewer than 200 baseball personalities have been enshrined. Although many excellent players don't come close in the balloting, they do make significant contributions to baseball history.

Consider Hoyt Wilhelm, the only man to pitch in more than 1,000 games. Or Harvey Haddix, who pitched 12 perfect innings before losing a 1–0 heart-breaker in the 13th. Or Roger Maris, who hit a record 61 home runs in 1961.

Don Larsen is remembered for his World Series perfect game of 1956—the only no-hitter in World Series history. Maury Wills earned a niche in history when he became the first man to exceed 100 stolen bases in a season. And Joe Adcock won't soon be forgotten by Brooklyn Dodger fans who watched him hit four home runs and a double in one game.

Even Adcock's performance pales when contrasted with the one-man show of Nate Colbert, an otherwise-forgotten slugger who exploded for five home runs and 13 runs batted in during a 1972 doubleheader in Atlanta. Only one other player has homered five times on the same day—and Colbert was seated in the St. Louis stands the day Stan Musial did it for the Cardinals.

Unlike Musial, who went on to a Hall of Fame career, Colbert was among thousands of men who have played major-league baseball with varying degrees of success over the last century. Some of those men have been related—Paul and Lloyd Waner were brothers who earned separate plaques in Cooperstown, but neither Dom nor Vince Di-Maggio could follow brother Joe into the Hall. None of the three Alous (Felipe, Jesús, and Matty) and only one of the five Delahantys (Big Ed) wound up in the Hall of Fame.

Jim Thorpe, famous for his Olympic exploits, was never a prospect for Cooperstown, but he's remembered as the ball player who got the game-winning RBI in the famous double no-hitter between Fred Toney and Hippo Vaughn (Vaughn gave up two hits in the 10th to lose the 1917 classic, 1–0).

Jimmy Qualls, who played just 63 games in his career, also proved a spoiler—delivering a one-out single for the Cubs in the ninth to spoil the attempted perfect game of the

Mets' Tom Seaver on July 8, 1969. Billy Sullivan was an even worse hitter (.212 lifetime) but lasted 16 seasons early in the century because he was such a capable catcher.

Bob (Hurricane) Hazle burned brightly for one summer. Called up to replace Bill Bruton in July, Hazle hit .403 down the stretch to help win the 1957 National League pennant for the Milwaukee Braves. Sold to Detroit after his bat cooled the following spring, Hazle was soon out of baseball.

Many fine books have been written about the men who play baseball and it would be impossible to include them all here. This chapter chooses instead to pinpoint some of the highlights.

Why were lefthanded pitchers scarce when baseball began?

Late into the 19th century, children with a natural inclination to be lefthanded were encouraged—often forced physically—to become righthanded instead. Being lefthanded was then thought to bring bad luck—hence the English word *gauche,* awkward, which means "left" in the original French.

Since children were discouraged from favoring their left hand (those who did sometimes had the hand tied behind their backs to force reliance on the right hand), baseball was virtually all righthanded in its early days. The first lefthanded pitcher, Robert Mitchell of the Cincinnati Red Stockings, didn't reach the National League until 1878—two years after the Senior Circuit was founded.

Today, no doubt because four baseball positions are closed to them (catcher, second base, shortstop, and third base), lefthanders comprise roughly 25 percent of the big-league pitching fraternity but only seven percent of the larger population of the Major Leagues (about the same percentage found in the United States).

Why did old-time players show off by catching balls thrown from the top of the Washington Monument?

Feats of agility and strength were once regarded as proof positive that a man was an exceptional athlete. Betting on such publicity stunts was common. On August 25, 1894, Chicago Cubs catcher William Schriver became the first man to catch a ball thrown off the top of the Washington Monument. But Gabby Street's 1908 catch from the same structure got more publicity, mainly because it was arranged by drama critic Pres Gibson, a friend of Street's, to prove a bet. Street stood at the base of the 508-foot monument while Gibson dropped 13 balls, one at a time. With the wind a factor, Street was able to catch only the last one dropped.

Eight years later, Brooklyn Dodger manager Wilbert Robinson decided to top Street's feat. Robinson, like Street, was a catcher during his playing days and was used to catching high pops. Robby hired an airplane and arranged to have aviatrix Ruth Law fly Dodger trainer Frank Kelly overhead. Kelly was to drop a ball over the side of the craft. The plane was up about 400 feet when Kelly made the drop—but he substituted a red grapefruit for the ball. Unable to distinguish the falling object, Robinson waited patiently. When the grapefruit hit, it splattered red juice in all directions. "Oh my God!" Robinson shrieked. "It broke me open! I'm covered with blood!"

Why did the same player appear in baseball's first game and in the modern era?

Jim O'Rourke, a catcher, played for Boston against Philadelphia on April 22, 1876, date of the National League's first game, and was a 52-year-old minor league manager in 1904 when he got another chance to play in the majors. John McGraw, manager of the New York Giants, agreed to

O'Rourke's request that he play in the big leagues one more time. On September 22, O'Rourke officially ended his career by playing the opener of a doubleheader against Cincinnati. He got a hit and the Giants won, 7–5, behind Joe (Iron Man) McGinnity to clinch the National League pennant.

Why was Roger Bresnahan's first game unusual?

Roger Bresnahan, known as the catcher who invented shin guards, chest protector, and an improved mask, was a star catcher for the New York Giants and other clubs from 1897 through 1915. But he made his debut as a pitcher— beating St. Louis for Washington of the National League, 3–0, on August 27, 1897. Bresnahan's strong arm proved a powerful weapon later in establishing his reputation as one of the all-time great catchers. He was elected to the Hall of Fame in 1945.

Why was Joe McGinnity known as an "iron man"?

Joe McGinnity of the New York Giants won the nickname "Iron Man" because of his amazing stamina on the mound. In August 1903, he pitched winning doubleheaders *three times.* McGinnity was blessed with a strong arm and an uncanny ability to throw strikes with an easy underhand delivery. The dead-ball era made it easier for pitchers to peform remarkable feats. Teams had small pitching staffs, relievers were seldom used, and star hurlers worked as often as possible. In addition to McGinnity, Ed Reulbach of the Chicago Cubs was an ironman pitcher of note. On September 26, 1908, he became the only pitcher to hurl two shutouts in one day—blanking the Brooklyn Dodgers by scores of 5–0 and 3–0. A Reulbach contemporary, Ed Walsh of the Chicago White Sox, also pitched both ends of doubleheaders on occasion. The last pitcher to win two complete games in a doubleheader was Emil Levsen of the Cleveland Indians in 1926.

Why was Mordecai Brown better known as "Three-Finger" Brown?

Mordecai Brown, the great Chicago Cubs pitcher of the early 20th Century, lost two fingers off his pitching (right) hand in a farm machine accident during his youth. Gripping the ball with two fingers missing sent the sphere spinning through the air with strange twists and paved the way for Brown to win 239 games and a niche in the Baseball Hall of Fame.

Why is Tinker-to-Evers-to-Chance baseball's best-known double-play combination?

Joe Tinker, at short, Johnny Evers, at second, and Frank Chance, the first baseman who doubled as manager, teamed up in the infield of the Chicago Cubs early in the century. Of the three, only Chance was an outstanding all-around player, but all were immortalized in legend when a disgruntled New York Giants' fan named Franklin P. Adams wrote a poem called *Baseball's Sad Lexicon:*

> These are the saddest of possible words:
> "Tinker to Evers to Chance."
> Trio of bear cubs and fleeter than birds,
> Tinker and Evers and Chance.
> Ruthlessly pricking our gonfalon bubble,
> Making a Giant hit into a double—
> Words that are heavy with nothing but trouble:
> "Tinker to Evers to Chance."

In actuality, the double-play combine produced only 31

twin-killings in four seasons—never more than 10 in any one season—hardly adequate by defensive standards of any era.

Why is Harry Steinfeldt remembered by trivia experts?

Harry Steinfeldt was the third baseman in the Chicago Cub infield that featured the Tinker-to-Evers-to-Chance double-play combination, popularized in the Franklin Adams verse. Steinfeldt hit .268 in a 14-year big-league career that included a five-year stint with the Cubs (1906–10).

Why was pitcher Wild Bill Donovan known as a great all-around player?

Wild Bill Donovan was a threat not only on the mound but also at bat and on the bases. The career leader in steals by a pitcher, Donovan stole successfully 36 times and is the only pitcher to steal a base in a World Series game (for the Detroit Tigers against the Chicago Cubs in 1908). Donovan's best day on the bases was May 7, 1906, when the Tigers faced the Cleveland Indians. Donovan singled in the fifth, then stole second easily when the Indians failed to pay attention to him on the base paths. The Indians again ignored Donovan—concentrating all their energies on hitter Ty Cobb instead—so the pitcher stole again, this time taking third base with relative ease. Cobb struck out but the No. 2 Tiger hitter reached first, setting up a double-steal with Donovan on the front end—giving him three stolen bases in an inning! Donovan won that game, 8–3, with the help of two hits and three stolen bases. Donovan won 187 games in his 18-year career, which ended in 1918. He had a .193 lifetime batting average—not bad for a pitcher—with six home runs and 93 runs batted in. In addition to his pitching assignments, Donovan played more than 50 major-league games at other positions.

Why were four Philadelphia Athletics known as "the $100,000 Infield"?

By the start of the 1911 season, Connie Mack had put together baseball's best infield: John (Stuffy) McInnis at first, Eddie Collins at second, Jack Barry at shortstop, and Frank (Home Run) Baker at third. Collins, who might have been the best second baseman in baseball history, compiled a .333 lifetime average, including 2,826 hits and 743 stolen bases. He also had a knack for survival that enabled him to play in the Major Leagues for 25 years—an amazing record of longevity. Baker was one of the feared sluggers of the dead-ball era, even though he never exceeded more than 12 homers in a season. He earned his nickname with crucial home runs against New York Giant stars Rube Marquard and Christy Mathewson in the 1911 World Series, which the A's won (Baker led both teams in hits, runs, runs batted in, and homers). Barry, a scrappy shortstop with a good glove, was a contact hitter who played on six pennant-winners during his 11-year career. The fancy-fielding McInnis, who had twelve .300 seasons and a career average of .308, holds the record of 1,652 chances in a season with only one error.

The Philadelphia quartet was known as "the $100,000 Infield" because Connie Mack could have acquired that sum in exchange for the contracts of his star infielders.

Why did Giant fans once resent Rube Marquard?

Late in the 1910 season, New York Giants manager John McGraw paid $11,000—a record for a player purchase at that time—to the Indianapolis minor-league team for the contract of Richard (Rube) Marquard. Cincinnati subsequently blasted the rookie, 7-1, in his debut and the Giants missed the chance to finish first as a result. Unhappy Giants fans began referring to Marquard as "the $11,000 Lemon"—a tag that stuck until 1911, when the young pitcher blossomed into a 24-game winner. In 1912, Marquard silenced his critics for good when he won a record 19 straight games en route to a 26-11 campaign.

Marquard was a contemporary of Rube Waddell, the great lefthander of the Philadelphia Athletics. After Marquard had won his first professional game, on Opening Day in Indianapolis in 1908, a local newspaper compared his style to Waddell's and teammates gave him a good-natured teasing about it, calling the young pitcher "Rube."

Why was Cy Young's farewell appearance a historic game?

At age 45, Cy Young pitched a masterful game in his last outing, on September 7, 1911. Young wound up a 1-0 loser to the Boston Braves when Philadelphia Phillies rookie Grover Cleveland Alexander outpitched him. Alexander was a rookie who went on to 373 lifetime wins, tying Christy Mathewson for the most in National League history. Young, with 511 lifetime victories, closed his career with more wins in the majors than any other pitcher (Walter Johnson ranks second with 414).

Why did Smokey Joe Wood become an outfielder?

The owner of a blazing fastball, Smokey Joe Wood was a 22-year-old righthander for the 1912 Boston Red Sox when he enjoyed one of the greatest seasons any pitcher ever had. He compiled a 34-5 record, with 35 complete games—10 of them shutouts—and a 1.91 earned run average, helping the Bosox win the pennant by a 14-game margin over Washington. Unfortunately the brilliant young hurler suffered a spring training accident in 1913 that brought his mound career to an end. He slipped on wet turf, fractured his thumb, and was never able to regain the old zip on his fastball. By 1918, he had become an outfielder, hitting as high as .366 in part-time duty with the Cleveland Indians three years later. Wood retired to be with his family after the 1922 campaign.

Why did his baseball ability cost Jim Thorpe two Olympic gold medals?

Jim Thorpe, an all-around athlete who later enjoyed a brief baseball career with the New York Giants, Cincinnati Reds, and Boston Braves (he hit .252 in a six-year career as an outfielder from 1913 to 1919), won two gold medals in the 1912 Olympics and became the only man to win both the pentathlon and the decathlon in the same Olympics. The United States Amateur Athletic Committee took his medals away six months later after it was learned that Thorpe had accepted payment of $2 per day to play baseball in a summer league in North Carolina prior to the Olympics. Thorpe claimed his entire life that he was a simple Indian schoolboy who did not know the rules regarding amateur status. Only in 1982 did the International Olympic Committee assent to requests from the Amateur Athletic Union and the United States Olympic Committee to restore Thorpe's medals posthumously (Thorpe died in 1953). Thorpe is remembered in baseball as the man whose 10th-inning single broke up the 1917 double no-hitter of Fred Toney (Reds) and Hippo Vaughn (Cubs).

Why was Casey Stengel a record-setter in his big-league debut?

In his first major-league game, on September 17, 1912,

Casey Stengel of the Brooklyn Dodgers was credited with four hits. Two other players—Willie McCovey of the 1959 San Francisco Giants and Mack Jones of the 1961 Milwaukee Braves—later tied this National League mark for most hits in a debut.

Why was Babe Ruth lifted for a pinch-hitter in his first game?

When Ruth reached the majors, he was a lefthanded pitcher with the Boston Red Sox. On July 11, 1914, he pitched Boston to a 4–3 win over the Cleveland Indians but was lifted for pinch-hitter Duffy Lewis in the seventh inning. Lewis singled to help set up the winning run but he wouldn't have pinch-hit for Ruth at all if not for the long-standing assumption that pitchers can't hit. Ruth turned out to be such a good-hitting pitcher that he was eventually converted to full-time duty in the outfield.

Why doesn't Walter Johnson hold the record for the best earned run average in a season?

Hall of Fame righthander Walter Johnson, long-time ace pitcher of the Washington Senators, had an exceptional season in 1913. But he missed a chance to record the best earned run average when a season-ending comedy game distorted his overall statistics for the year.

On October 4, 1913, the Senators faced the Boston Red Sox in a game that had no meaning in the American League pennant race. Washington used 18 players, including eight pitchers, and piled up a 10–3 lead by the ninth inning. Players on both sides were not taking the game seriously and even the umpires were laughing.

Walter Johnson had played the entire game in center field when he was asked to pitch in the ninth. He lobbed several pitches, yielded a single and double without retiring anyone, and returned to the outfield. Infielder Germany Schaefer took the mound and allowed both runners to score—inflating Johnson's earned run average because of the two earned runs he allowed that day. Johnson had taken a 1.09 earned run mark into the game, but emerged with a 1.14 average after the "comedy" runs were included.

The 1.14 earned run average stood until 1968, when Bob Gibson of the St. Louis Cardinals recorded a 1.12 mark. Had Walter Johnson eschewed the 1913 shenanigans, he would have maintained his grasp on the single-season ERA crown.

Why did Ernie Shore pitch a perfect game that was not a complete game?

When he was with the Boston Red Sox in 1917, Ernie Shore was chosen to relieve Babe Ruth, then a pitcher, in the first inning of a June 17 game against the Washington Senators. Ruth had been ejected for arguing a ball-four call on the first batter. The runner was erased trying to steal against Shore, who proceeded to retire the next 26 men in order and get credit for a perfect game—27 outs recorded without hit, walk, or error—but not a complete game.

Why did the Philadelphia Phillies once trade a pitcher who won 30 games?

After he went 30–13 for the Philadelphia Phillies in 1917, ace pitcher Grover Cleveland Alexander was drafted by the military for service in World War I. Owner William Baker, uncertain his star would return intact, swapped him to the Chicago Cubs. Alex pitched only three times for Chicago in 1918 but had 16 wins in 1919 and a league-leading 27 victories in 1920. He returned to the Phillies for his final major-league season 10 years later.

Why were fans able to set their watches by Grover Cleveland Alexander?

A great control pitcher, Grover Cleveland Alexander was very businesslike on the mound. He walked few and wasted little time in making mincement of National League hitters. In 1915, for example, Alexander walked only 64 men in 376 innings pitched and had a 1.22 earned run average en route to a 31-victory season for the Philadelphia Phillies. Because he was stingy in yielding home runs (even in compact Baker Bowl, where the Phils played half of their 154 games), twelve of Alexander's wins were shutouts. Average time of his games was one hour and thirty minutes, almost a full hour shorter than the average time of other games. Fans knew that ninety minutes would elapse from start-to-finish of games that Grover Cleveland Alexander pitched.

Why were Harry Gowdy and Hugh Mulcahy called "First in War" among ball players?

Harry M. Gowdy (Boston, National League) was the first major-league player to enter military service in World War I on June 27, 1917. Hugh N. Mulcahy (Philadelphia, National League) was the first to be drafted into World War II on March 8, 1941. (Although Pearl Harbor didn't occur until December 7, 1941, the draft was in effect before then.)

Why is Gavvy Cravath a forgotten home run king?

Clifford Carlton Cravath led the National League in home runs six times during his 11-year career and was the third-ranking home run hitter in baseball history when he retired in 1920. Although his 119 lifetime home runs seem insignificant by modern standards, they represent an amazing accomplishment because they were delivered between

1908 and 1920, the height of the dead-ball era. In 1915, when Cravath hit 24 homers and had 115 runs batted in for the Philadelphia Phillies, the next best "slugger" in the National League had only 13 home runs and the second-ranking home run-hitting team, the Boston Braves, hit only 17.

Cravath, a righthanded hitter, learned to hit to the opposite field with power—taking advantage of Baker Bowl's right field fence, which was only 280 feet from home. The dominant power-hitter of his era won his last two National League home run crowns while Babe Ruth was winning his first two in the American League (1918–19), but he was quickly forgotten when baseball entered the age of the lively ball, triggered by Ruth's gargantuan accomplishments.

Cravath got his nickname as a result of his hitting. When a long Cravath fly struck a seagull in flight during an amateur game in California, a Spanish-speaking spectator screamed, "Gaviota!" The Spanish term for seagull was later shortened to Gavvy.

Why was Joe Sewell regarded as baseball's toughest strikeout?

Sewell, a lefthanded batting shortstop who hit .312 in a career that stretched from 1920 to 1933, holds several records that reflect his excellent bat control. They include most consecutive games without striking out (115 in 1929), fewest strikeouts in a season (4 in both 1925 and 1929), and fewest strikeouts in a career (114 in 1,903 games over 14 seasons). Sewell, a member of the Baseball Hall of Fame, spent most of his playing time with the Cleveland Indians. He finally played out his career with the New York Yankees.

Why do many experts insist Rogers Hornsby was the greatest righthanded hitter of all time?

Rogers Hornsby, the only National Leaguer to win two

Triple Crowns, was a rare combination of high batting average and home run power. Like Ted Williams, the only American Leaguer to win the Triple Crown twice, Hornsby made good contact, keeping his strikeouts to a minimum, and was a tremendous student of hitting. Hornsby refused to go to the movies for fear that the darkness would weaken his keen eyesight. When Hornsby won his first Triple Crown, for the 1922 St. Louis Cardinals, he became the only player ever to exceed .400 and 40 home runs in the same season. His figures were .401, 42 homers, and 152 runs batted in. The powerful second baseman had a lifetime average of .358, second only to Ty Cobb.

Why did Lefty Grove cost the Philadelphia Athletics the unusual sum of $100,600?

After Lefty Grove posted a 26-6 mark for the old Baltimore Orioles of the International League in 1924, Connie Mack purchased his contract for the Philadelphia Athletics. Baltimore had had many offers for the star southpaw, but agreed to sell him to Mack "for more than the price of Babe Ruth." Mack, knowing that the New York Yankees had shelled out $100,000 to acquire Ruth from the Boston Red Sox in January 1920, agreed to throw in $600 extra—explaining the unusual price-tag.

Why did the Yankees fine Babe Ruth $5,000 for breaking training rules?

During spring training of 1925, Babe Ruth, then 30 years old, guzzled so many hot dogs, sodas, and beers that his stomach revolted just before the season opened—knocking him out of action for several months. Later, with neither Ruth nor the club faring well, the fun-loving slugger was found galavanting in the wee hours by a detective hired by manager Miller Huggins. The pilot delivered the report to Colonel Jacob Ruppert, the team's owner, and slapped Ruth with a $5,000 fine (a record for the time) for insubordination and breaking training rules.

Why was Mel Ott's professional baseball record unusual?

Mel Ott, a slugging outfielder known for lifting up his front foot as he began his swing, spent 22 years in the majors without ever playing in the minors—a record he shares with Al Kaline, a fellow Hall of Famer. Ott joined the New York Giants at age 16 in 1926 and retired after the 1947 season with a .304 batting average, 511 home runs, and 1860 runs batted in. Ott, who later managed the club, also had the unusual distinction of spending his whole career with one team, just as Kaline did with the Tigers (1953-74). No other major-leaguers have played so long in the majors without ever making a minor-league appearance. Among the top stars who bypassed the minors en route to the majors were Sandy Koufax, Catfish Hunter, Bob Feller, Frankie Frisch, and Eddie Plank.

Why was Hall of Famer Paul Waner such a great curveball hitter?

Paul Waner, an outfielder with the Pittsburgh Pirates (1926-40) and with three other clubs in a career that extended into 1945, had a lifetime batting average of .333—17 points higher than the average recorded by brother Lloyd, who also spent most of his career (1927-45) in the Pirate outfield. The Waners were able to record Hall of Fame credentials in the Major Leagues by handling the curveball with relative facility—a technique they developed as youths in rural Oklahoma. Unable to afford baseballs, the Waners followed the lead of their contemporaries and used corncobs as substitutes. Paul Waner explained how he sharpened his batting eye: "There were more curves in those corncob games than I ever saw in a real baseball game. You had to keep your eye on the cob because it would blind you if it hit you in the eye or hurt you if it hit you in the head. The constant practice of hitting the strange curves of the corncob did more than anything else to build up my batting."

Why did the Waner brothers launch a vaudeville tour?

In 1927, Lloyd Waner produced 227 hits—a rookie record—en route to a .355 season, while older brother Paul hit .380 to lead the National League. As a result, the Pittsburgh Pirates won the pennant and advanced into the World Series against the New York Yankees. Babe Ruth and Lou Gehrig led a Yankee sweep but the Waners performed just as well, resulting in instant popularity across the country. That convinced them to make some postseason money in vaudeville. With Paul playing the saxophone and Lloyd the violin, the Waners, outfitted in Pittsburgh uniforms, made $2100 per week (more than their baseball salaries) and shared the stage with Jack Benny, who served as their emcee.

Why was Walter Johnson's last game unusual?

Walter Johnson, second to Cy Young with 414 lifetime pitching victories, made his last major-league appearance not as a hurler but as a hitter. He came up to pinch-hit for pitcher Tom Zachary in the ninth inning on September 30, 1927, and flied out to right field. The ball was caught by Yankee rightfielder Babe Ruth, who hit his 60th home run in the same game.

Why was Ed Rommel's last win so difficult?

Although Ed Rommel won 171 games during his 13-year career—all with the Philadelphia Athletics—his last victory was certainly hard to come by. On Sunday, July 10, 1932, the A's went to Cleveland on a one-day trip (Sunday ball was banned in Philadelphia until 1934) and brought along only two pitchers, Lew Krausse and Rommel. Manager Connie Mack was hoping to rest the remainder of his weary staff, which had just weathered three straight doubleheaders and had another the following day. Mack thought he was safe because Rommel, who had pitched three innings the day before, was a knuckleballer whose arm could tolerate the strain of repeated outings.

When Krausse yielded four hits and three runs in the first inning of the game, the veteran righthander was waved in from the bullpen. Mack told Rommel that he would pitch the rest of the game no matter what happened. The pitcher almost made the manager eat those words; he gave up 14 runs and 29 hits but emerged as the winning pitcher when Philadelphia outlasted the Indians, 18–17, in 18 innings! (In the same game, Cleveland shortstop Johnny Burnett banged out nine hits, a record for one game.)

Why was Dizzy Dean upset with his brother for pitching a no-hitter?

Late in the 1934 season, the Deans were scheduled to pitch a doubleheader for the St. Louis Cardinals against the Brooklyn Dodgers. Dizzy, the older brother, pitched a three-hit shutout in the opener. Then Paul uncorked a no-hitter in the nightcap. After the second game ended, Dizzy chided his sibling: "Why didn't you tell me you wuz gonna pitch a no-hitter?" he drawled. "I woulda pitched one too!"

Why was Joe Medwick removed from a World Series game because of rowdy fans?

Joe Medwick, slugging leftfielder of the St. Louis Cardinals, became the only player to be taken out of a World Series game in order to prevent a riot during the 1934 Fall Classic against the Detroit Tigers. St. Louis held an 11–0 lead in the final game of the Series at Detroit when angry Tiger fans showered Medwick with fruit—symbolic of their irritation with an earlier play in which Medwick slid hard into Tiger third baseman Marv Owen. Commissioner Kenesaw Mountain Landis ordered Medwick removed so that order could be restored and the Series completed.

Why was weak-hitting Moe Berg added to the 1934 All-Star squad which toured Japan?

Although Moe Berg caught in only 38 games for the Boston Red Sox in 1934, he was added to the 1934 "All-Stars" by the United States government in order to photograph Tokyo for the military. Berg, a Princeton graduate and master of languages, learned Japanese in a two-month cram course and was able to pose as an "All-Star" by giving numerous lectures on the game to the Japanese. He became popular during the 1934 tour and was able to accomplish his mission with relative ease. Berg's clandestine movies of the Japanese capital were the principal reference for General Jimmie Doolittle's air raids over the city, which began on April 18, 1942.

Why did the Cubs trade for Dizzy Dean when they knew he was hurt?

On April 16, 1938, Chicago sent three players and $185,000 to the St. Louis Cardinals for Dizzy Dean. The 27-year-old righthander, victim of a broken toe when hit by an

Earl Averill liner in the 1937 All-Star Game, had sub-consciously altered his motion, damaging his arm. But the Cubs gambled he could help them win the pennant. The gamble paid off when Dean went 7-1 with a 1.80 ERA—the difference between first and fourth place. "We knew his arm was questionable," owner Phil Wrigley said after the season. "But I thought it was a pretty good deal. We won the pennant and set an attendance record. Dean had a psycho-logical effect on the team and that's what we wanted him for. We'd announce Dizzy Dean was going to pitch and we'd put on extra ticket sellers. People wanted to see whether his arm was good or bad."

Why did Hank Greenberg become an outfield-er?

Hank Greenberg, powerful righthanded slugger who played for the Detroit Tigers (1933–46) and Pittsburgh Pir-ates (1947), hit 58 home runs in 1938 but fell to a 33-homer campaign (with a .312 average and 112 runs batted in) in 1939. Detroit general manager Jack Zeller told Greenberg his salary would be cut $10,000—unless he moved from first base to left field to make way for rookie prospect Rudy York. Greenberg, who had worked hard to become a capable defensive first baseman, agreed to make the move on one condition: that he receive a $10,000 raise instead of a $10,000 cut. Zeller agreed and, in 1940, Greenberg became the first player to win the Most Valuable Player Award at a second position (he had won as a first baseman in 1935). With York's bat added to the lineup, the Tigers won the 1940 pennant.

Why did Lou Gehrig's playing streak end?

On June 1, 1925, Lou Gehrig of the New York Yankees replaced incumbent first baseman Wally Pipp, who had asked out of the lineup because of a headache. Gehrig performed so well that he remained in the lineup for a record 2,130 games—every Yankee contest until he benched himself on May 2, 1939. By that date, Gehrig was visibly suffering from amyotropic lateral sclerosis, the neuromuscular disease that ultimately claimed his life on June 2, 1941. The powerful slugger had begun losing his power in 1938 at age 35 (his 29 homers and 115 runs batted in were far off his usual output). By the spring of 1939, Gehrig was so clumsy and weak that his presence in the lineup was starting to hurt the team. After playing the first eight games of the season, Gehrig asked manager Joe McCarthy to take him out. Babe Dahlgren, his replacement, homered twice in a 22-2 Yankee romp. Although he remained in uniform, Gehrig never played again. On July 4, 1939, he received an emotional "day" from Yankee fans and players. It was on that day that he made his famous speech in which he called himself "the luckiest man on the face of the earth." Only Gehrig knew doctors had given him two years to live.

Why was Ted Lyons known as a Sunday pitcher?

Long-time Chicago White Sox starter Ted Lyons was approaching his 39th birthday when he got off to a fast start during the 1939 campaign. With his knuckleball dancing, the veteran pitcher started an extended winning streak after dropping the season's first decision. By chance, most of his starts seemed to fall on Sunday—a combination of scheduling, rainouts, and the coincidence of the team's rotation. White Sox officials noted larger crowds whenever Lyons pitched.

Manager Jimmie Dykes took note of the pitcher's uncanny knack for winning Sunday games and decided he would follow that routine with regularity. Only rain on Sunday would change the plan, which gave Lyons more days off between starts than normal—a factor which enabled the veteran to conserve his strength. In 1939, the

Chicago star went 14–6 (all six losses on the road) with a 2.76 ERA, second in the American League. He was equally effective in three more seasons of the Sunday regimen. Even in his last full year, 1942, Lyons was brilliant, with a 14–6 mark and league-leading 2.10 ERA. Moreover, he completed all 20 of his starts—a record last achieved in 1918 by Hall of Famer Walter Johnson. Military service intervened, but Lyons managed to win a game at age 45 in 1946 before hanging up his spikes to become White Sox manager.

Why hasn't there been a .400 hitter in the majors since 1941?

Although George Brett of the Kansas City Royals came the closest, with a .390 average in 1980, no hitter has been able to approach the .406 mark of Ted Williams (1941 Boston Red Sox) for several reasons: (1) coast-to-coast travel produces jet-lagged athletes who get to study each rival pitcher less frequently; (2) the development of relief pitching means that tired starters rarely stay in as long as they did 40 years ago; (3) the near-universal adoption of night baseball makes the ball harder to see and makes players more tired; and (4) constant publicity in the print and electronic media puts undue pressure on today's athletes. Some cynics would add that long-term, big-money contracts have taken away another key factor from would-be .400 hitters: incentive.

Why did Rip Sewell throw a blooper pitch?

For the first four seasons of his 11-year career with the Pittsburgh Pirates, pitcher Rip Sewell threw the conventional assortment of pitches: fastball, curve, and changeup. Then a freak hunting accident forced him to change his delivery. On the last day of the 1941 hunting season, a friend accidentally fired some buckshot into Sewell's right foot. Favoring the damaged foot, Sewell adopted the unorthodox delivery that produced the high, arcing blooper ball—dubbed the "eephus" pitch by outfielder Maurice Van Robays.

Probably the most famous moment for the eephus pitch occurred in the 1946 All-Star Game. Ted Williams capped a great individual hitting performance (four hits—including two home runs—plus a walk) by timing the eephus perfectly and depositing it in the right field bullpen at Fenway Park. Two men scored ahead of him.

Why did a 15-year-old once play in the majors?

The Cincinnati Reds sent lefthanded pitcher Joe Nuxhall into a game on June 10, 1944, when he was 15 years and 10 months old. Nuxhall, later a quality starting pitcher for the Reds, pitched only two thirds of an inning in an 18-0 loss to the Cardinals that day. If not for the depletion of big-league talent caused by World War II, Nuxhall's major league initiation almost certainly would have waited. The war years were marked by appearances of players too young, too old, or physically unqualified for military service.

Why did a one-legged man once play in the majors?

When clubs were strapped for players during World War II, the Washington Senators signed Bert Shepard, a pitcher with a wooden leg. As an Army Air Force flyer, Lieutenant Shepard had been downed over Germany on his 35th mission and captured by the enemy. Doctors amputated his leg, which had been crushed in the crash, and a fellow POW whittled a wooden leg for the 5-11, 185-pound lefthander. Shepard, who had no prior major-league experience, got into one game for Washington, yielding one run on three hits in 5 1/3 innings pitched. The record books credit

him with a lifetime earned run average of 1.69—compiled in
that one performance in 1945.

Why did the St. Louis Browns use a one-armed outfielder during the war?

Pete Gray, called up to the Browns in 1945 after hitting
.333 for Memphis as the Most Valuable Player in the Southern Association, was one of several handicapped athletes
who surfaced in the majors in the vacuum created by
departure of most major-leaguers for wartime military service. Gray hit .218 in 61 games for the Browns that year.

While in the outfield, Gray caught the ball with his glove
hand, tossed the ball in the air, placed the glove under the
stump of his missing left arm, caught the ball in his bare
hand, and threw back to the infield. He performed well
enough to keep his regular berth that season—but only
because the caliber of play was so poor that the players who
ranked second and third in the American League batting
race (Tony Cuccinello and Johnny Dickshot) were released
after the season.

Why did Johnny Mize have a reputation as a great streak hitter?

Between 1936 and 1953, first baseman Johnny Mize
starred as a slugger for the St. Louis Cardinals, New York
Giants, and New York Yankees. He had a .312 lifetime
average and 359 home runs and was known as a devastating
streak hitter who was almost impossible to retire when he
was hot. He hit three consecutive homers in a game four
different times and had a total of six three-homer games
during his career. Mize is the only man ever to hit three
consecutive homers in a game in both leagues.

Why did a major-league player wear No. 96?

Pitcher Bill Voiselle picked the unusual uniform number after his trade from the New York Giants to the Boston Braves in 1947. He chose it to remind observers that he hailed from Ninety Six, South Carolina.

Why did National League pitchers have a healthy respect for Ralph Kiner?

Although some experts dispute Kiner's qualifications for the Baseball Hall of Fame (he was elected in 1975), none can dispute his record as a slugger. He truly intimidated pitchers. Kiner, playing mostly for the Pittsburgh Pirates in a career that stretched from 1946 to 1955, had a lifetime average of .279 with 369 home runs. But from 1946 through 1952, he completely dominated the league's sluggers—earning a record seven consecutive home run crowns (Johnny Mize tied him twice). Babe Ruth won 12 league home run titles, another major-league mark, but never had as many as seven in a row.

Why do some experts call Joe DiMaggio the best pure hitter of all time?

In a career that stretched 13 years from 1936 to 1951, New York Yankees center fielder Joe DiMaggio hit .325 with 361 home runs. He had seven seasons of at least 30 home runs and nine seasons of at least 100 runs batted in. But DiMaggio, also an accomplished fielder, was not strictly a power hitter; he was such an excellent contact hitter that many observers say he was the best "pure hitter." He always seemed to get his bat on the ball. Of baseball's great sluggers, DiMaggio ranks first in home run-to-strikeout ratio with a .978 mark (361 home runs to 369 lifetime strikeouts). Yogi Berra ranks second and Ted Williams third. DiMaggio was particularly impressive as a contact hitter in 1941, the year of his 56-game hitting streak, when he fanned just 13 times while hitting 30 home runs. He had 541 at-bats that season.

Why did Boston Red Sox fans root for the Yankees' Joe DiMaggio?

Although the Boston Red Sox and New York Yankees have always been bitter rivals, fans of the Red Sox cheered the brother of their own Dom DiMaggio out of respect for his ability as well as his humility. Realizing he was playing hurt during a June 1949 series at Fenway Park, Boston fans cheered him wildly, prompting the visiting star to doff his cap and break into an uncharacteristic smile. DiMaggio had come into Boston in the wake of his father's death, coupled with the aftereffects of a painful heel injury that had failed to respond to treatment. Wearing a special orthopedic shoe, built up at the heel without spikes, DiMaggio singled and slammed a two-run homer to produce a 5-4 Yankee win in the opener. His three-run homer the next day reduced a 7-1 Red Sox lead to striking distance; a later two-run shot in the same game gave the Yankees a 9-7 win. Yet another DiMaggio homer—a three-run blast off Bosox ace Mel Parnell—led to a series sweep of the Yankees' chief pennant threat. DiMaggio called the series the greatest of his career and the most satisfying of his life. He was particularly cheered by thousands of letters and telegrams hailing his comeback.

Why wasn't Jackie Robinson the first black player?

Although Jackie Robinson is credited with breaking the color line by making the Brooklyn Dodger roster in 1947, he was not the first black player to reach the Major Leagues.

From 1882 to 1884, Providence of the National League had a catcher named Vincent (Sandy) Nava, a black Cuban, and in 1884, Toledo of the American Association, then a major league, had catcher Moses Fleetwood Walker and outfielder Welday Wilberforce Walker, a pair of brothers. Moses played in 42 games, his brother in five. The blacks in the majors and the 20-odd blacks in the minors were shunned by players, fans, and even the press—making their major-league tenures unpleasant at best. Hall of Famer Cap Anson, manager of the Chicago White Stockings of the National League, not only refused to play teams with black players but also was the chief architect of the unwritten "color line" that made Organized Ball off limits to black players between 1890 and 1946, when Robinson began his career with the Dodger farm at Montreal. Given few other options, black players formed the first professional all-black team in Babylon, New York, in 1885 and the first all-black league in Kansas City in 1920.

Why is Walt Dropo remembered for a hitting streak?

Walt Dropo batted only .270 while dividing his time among five teams between 1949 and 1961, but the 6-5, 220-pound first baseman found his way into the record book for a two-day splurge of hitting on July 14–15, 1952. Dropo, then with the Detroit Tigers, slammed 12 straight hits over a three-game span (including a July 15 twin bill) without any unofficial at-bats (walk, sacrifice, hit-by-pitch, etc.) intervening. It was the second time in baseball history that a batter had recorded 12 straight safeties, but the first time the hits had not been intertwined with unofficial at-bats. In 1938, Pinky Higgins, an infielder who hit .292 between 1930 and 1946, smacked 12 straight hits in successive doubleheaders on June 19th and 21st. The third baseman of the Boston Red Sox had two walks during his streak.

Why did a pitcher face both Babe Ruth and Mickey Mantle in regular-season play?

Al Benton had a long career that overlapped the end of Babe Ruth's career and the beginning of Mickey Mantle's. Thus he was able to face both of them. Benton was with the Philadelphia Athletics when he faced Ruth, then with the Yankees, in 1934. Benton was a member of the Boston Red Sox when he worked against Mantle, also with the Yankees, in 1952. Benton was the only pitcher to face both Ruth and Mantle.

Why was Bobo Holloman's 1953 no-hitter so unusual?

Alva Lee (Bobo) Holloman no-hit the Philadelphia Athletics for the St. Louis Browns on May 6, 1953, but never again pitched a complete game in the Major Leagues. Even more unusual was the fact that the no-hitter came in Holloman's first major-league start.

Why did Joe Adcock leave a big imprint in the memories of Brooklyn Dodger fans?

Joe Adcock, the slugging first baseman of the Milwaukee Braves, served as a one-man wrecking crew on July 31, 1954, when his team faced the Brooklyn Dodgers at Ebbets Field. On that day, Adcock blasted four home runs and a double for a record 18 total bases as the Braves won, 15–7. Adcock's victims were Don Newcombe, Erv Palica, Pete Wojey, and Johnny Podres. Adcock said later that his double, off Palica, was the ball he hit the hardest that day. It missed home run territory by a foot.

Why was the Cy Young Award created?

After considerable criticism that pitchers weren't receiving ample consideration in Most Valuable Player Award voting, baseball created the Cy Young Award for pitching excellence in 1956 (separate awards for each league were given, starting in 1967). Four of the first eight winners— Warren Spahn, Whitey Ford, Sandy Koufax, and Early Wynn—eventually won admission to the Baseball Hall of Fame.

Why did Hank Aaron benefit when Bobby Thomson broke his leg?

Bobby Thomson had just been acquired by the Milwaukee Braves from the New York Giants when he broke his leg sliding during spring training of 1954. Milwaukee manager Charlie Grimm replaced Thomson with a 20-year-old unknown infielder named Henry Louis Aaron. Aaron took to the outfield like a fish takes to water; he didn't leave the Braves' lineup for 21 years.

Why was the tandem of Hank Aaron and Eddie Mathews the greatest 1-2 punch in baseball history?

As teammates for the Milwaukee and Atlanta Braves, Hank Aaron and Eddie Mathews combined for 863 homers—exceeding the totals of Babe Ruth-Lou Gehrig (Yankees), Willie Mays-Willie McCovey (Giants), and Duke Snider-Gil Hodges (Dodgers) during the time they were teammates. Mathews, the only man to play for the Braves in three cities (Boston, Milwaukee, and Atlanta), reached the National League in 1952, two years before Aaron became his teammate, and left the Braves when he was traded to the Houston Astros after the 1966 campaign. The 863 home run figure spans the years 1954 (Aaron's first season) through 1966 (Mathews' last year with the Braves).

Why was Hank Aaron regarded as baseball's ultimate combination of power and speed?

In 23 major-league seasons, Hank Aaron hit a record 755 home runs and stole 240 bases in 313 attempts for a success ratio of .767, one point better than the mark achieved by Willie Mays. His best season may have been 1963, when he became the only player in baseball history to exceed 40 homers (44) and 30 steals (31) in the same year.

Why is a dramatic debut seldom a barometer of likely future success?

Whether a young player is a hitter or a pitcher, adjustment to the Major Leagues takes time—both for the athlete involved and for the men he faces. Probably the most dramatic debut by a pitcher was the performance of Karl Spooner for the Brooklyn Dodgers late in the 1954 campaign. He blanked the New York Giants, 3-0, and the Pittsburgh Pirates, 1-0, with a combined total of 27 strikeouts in successive September appearances. But he was an ordinary 8-6 the following year and left the majors with arm trouble at age 24.

Why did Herb Score's career end prematurely?

In his first two major-league seasons (1955-56), Herb Score compiled a 36-19 mark for the Cleveland Indians, leading the league in strikeouts both years. But on May 7, 1957, the fireballing righthander was struck in the face by a line drive off the bat of Yankee infielder Gil McDougald. Score was on the disabled list the rest of the season. When he finally returned, Score could not regain his prior form. He won only 17 more games over the next four-and-a-half seasons before retiring in 1962 with a career record of 55–46.

Why did a United States Senator once scout a Washington Senator?

When Harmon Killebrew was growing up in Payette, Idaho, U.S. Senator Herman Welker happened to see him play. Welker, a baseball fan and close friend of Washington Senator owner Calvin Griffith, advised the baseball magnate of his talented find. Griffith—more or less as a favor to his friend—sent a scout to see for himself. The Washington scout was duly impressed and Killebrew soon signed with the Senators. In 1959, his first full season, he hit 42 home runs at age 23. By the time he retired, Killebrew had accumulated 573 home runs, fifth on the all-time career list, playing all but one season for Griffith's teams in Washington and Minnesota.

Why was Von McDaniel such a disappointment in St. Louis?

On June 21, 1957, Von McDaniel blanked the Brooklyn Dodgers, 2–0, in his first major-league start. Soon after, he hurled a 4–0 one-hit shutout against the Pittsburgh Pirates. McDaniel, then 18 and just out of high school, had a 7–5 mark and 3.21 earned run average for the year and seemed to have an unlimited future. Cardinal fans envisioned two pitching McDaniels—Von and older brother Lindy, a successful relief specialist. But a mysterious inability to maintain his pitching rhythm forced a premature end to Von's career. He worked in only two more games, both in 1958, and was out of the majors by age 19.

Why did Hurricane Hazle help the Braves win a pennant?

Hurricane Hazle was a devastating storm of the early '50s—but was also a journeyman player who managed to get hot at the right time. In 1957, Bob Hazle was hitting .279 in Triple-A ball when he got a call-up from the parent Milwaukee Braves. He proceeded to hit .403 in 41 games as the Braves advanced to the World Championship. Not surprisingly, Hazle faded fast, was sold to Detroit in 1958, and quickly left the majors.

Why did a pennant playoff enable Eddie Mathews to win a home run crown?

Before the advent of divisional play in 1969, end-of-season ties between teams were settled through pennant playoffs (divisional ties are settled through one-game divisional playoffs). Before leagues were split in half, the National League used a best-of-three format to settle ties, while the American League used a single sudden-death encounter. Individual statistics from those playoffs (as well as current intradivisional playoffs) counted in regular-season statistics—unlike Championship Series statistics, which are kept separately. In 1959, when the Milwaukee Braves lost a two-game playoff to the Los Angeles Dodgers, Eddie Mathews of the Braves homered to break a deadlock for the home run title with Ernie Banks, whose Cubs finished last. Mathews wound up with 46 homers, but Banks—the runner-up with 45—was named Most Valuable Player that year. Both stars won eventual entry into the Baseball Hall of Fame.

Why was the Rocky Colavito deal unpopular in Cleveland?

On April 17, 1960, the Cleveland Indians angered their fans by sending popular slugger Rocky Colavito, a handsome outfielder, to the Detroit Tigers for singles-hitter Harvey Kuenn. Colavito had tied Washington's Harmon Killebrew for the 1959 American League home run crown with 42 circuit clouts, while Kuenn had led the league with a .353 batting average (but only nine home runs). The Indians missed Colavito's power, dropping from second in 1959 to fourth in 1960, and Detroit also dropped two notches, from fourth to sixth. The Colavito-for-Kuenn deal upset fans who liked Colavito's good looks and home run heroics—factors which had made him a matinee idol and franchise cornerstone in their eyes

The Colavito-for-Kuenn deal wasn't the only headline-catching swap between Cleveland and Detroit that summer; Indian general manager Frank (Trader) Lane also sent manager Joe Gordon to the Tigers for his Detroit counterpart, Jimmie Dykes.

Why was Dick Stuart called "Dr. Strangeglove"?

Dick Stuart, the regular first baseman of the World Champion Pittsburgh Pirates in 1960, was a solid home run hitter who was ill at ease while playing defense. In 10 seasons (1958–69), he committed more than his share of errors. When Stuart got married, he told a writer, "Behind every successful man there stands a good woman." The newsman responded, " . . . with a first baseman's mitt?" Stuart's lackluster defense won him the nicknames "Dr. Strangeglove" (after the popular movie *Dr. Strangelove*) and "Stonefingers" (since his hands seemed to be made of concrete).

Why do many experts consider Ted Williams the best hitter of all time?

Ted Williams is the only man to win more than two titles

in each of the three major batting categories: average, home runs, and runs batted in. He led his league in batting six times, in home runs six times, and in runs batted in four times. In his long career with the Boston Red Sox, 1939–60, Williams hit .344 with 521 home runs and 1,839 runs batted in. The slugging leftfielder's ability to win so many major batting honors seems even more significant when other greats of the game are considered. Babe Ruth won 12 home run crowns and six runs batted in crowns but only one batting crown, while Ty Cobb's record was 12 batting titles, one home run crown, and four runs batted in crowns. Stan Musial and Honus Wagner never won a home run crown, while Willie Mays never led his league in runs batted in.

Why were Ted Williams and Roger Maris lifted for pinch-hitters?

Roger Maris, a lefthanded hitter then in his second big-league season, was lifted for a righthanded pinch-hitter by the Cleveland Indians in 1958 because the opposing pitcher was lefthanded. Carroll Hardy proceeded to belt a game-winning home run—his only homer of the season—off White Sox ace Billy Pierce in that 11th-inning pinch-hit role. Hardy again substituted for a slugger of note on September 20, 1960—after Ted Williams of the Boston Red Sox fouled a first-inning pitch off his ankle. Hardy replaced him and lined into a double play.

Why was Clay Dalrymple an unlikely spoiler in Juan Marichal's debut?

Clay Dalrymple, light-hitting catcher for the Philadelphia Phillies, came up as a pinch-hitter with two outs in the eighth inning of Juan Marichal's debut on July 19, 1960. The Dominican righthander had not yielded a hit up to that point, but Dalrymple spoiled the potential no-hitter with a clean single.

It was the only hit yielded by the future Hall of Fame pitcher that day. The Giants won, 2-0.

Why was Charley Maxwell known as a "Sunday hitter?"

Charley Maxwell, an outfielder who played for three teams between 1950 and 1964, hit 40 of his 148 career home runs on Sunday—including four in a 1959 twin bill against the Yankees and three in a 1962 doubleheader against the same club. Maxwell became known as a "Sunday hitter" because he hit an inordinate number of his circuit clouts on that day. His second best day was Saturday; he hit 26 home runs on that day of the week.

Why was Willie Mays regarded as a great clutch hitter?

Although Hall of Fame center fielder Willie Mays never led the National League in runs batted in during a career that went from 1951 through 1973, he always seemed to come up with the big hit when his team needed it most. For example, Mays holds the record for most home runs hit in extra innings—22. He had a lifetime batting average of .302 and 660 home runs, third behind Hank Aaron and Babe Ruth on the career list.

Why did Mickey Mantle become an outfielder?

Mickey Mantle, the switch-hitting slugger who went on to a Hall of Fame career with the New York Yankees, began as an infielder, playing shortstop for Joplin, Missouri, of the Western League. The Yankees knew Mantle would hit but didn't want to trade incumbent shortstop Phil Rizzuto, who had been American League Most Valuable Player in 1950. So Mantle was moved to the outfield and opened the 1951 season in right field for New York, with Joe DiMaggio remaining in center. When DiMaggio retired after the '51 campaign, Mantle moved to center, where he remained until his own retirement in the spring of 1969.

Why did Mickey Mantle become a switch-hitter?

A natural righthander, Mickey Mantle learned to switch-hit at the suggestion of his father, Elven (Mutt) Mantle. During his career, the great Yankee center fielder hit more line drives righthanded but learned to loft the ball better lefthanded, allowing him to accumulate 536 major-league home runs, plus a record 18 more in World Series play. Ten times, Mantle hit home runs batting lefthanded and righthanded in the same game. Mantle's power stroke carried a consequence: too many strikeouts. Until Willie Stargell, Lou Brock, Bobby Bonds, Reggie Jackson, and Tony Perez passed him, Mantle owned the career record for most strikeouts as a batter.

Long before Mantle reached the majors with the 1951 Yankees, the art of switch-hitting was known in baseball. The first switch-hitter, second baseman-manager Robert Ferguson of the New York Mutuals (later Giants), played in 1871. Some of the better switch-hitters who followed, in addition to Mantle, were Max Carey, Frankie Frisch, Red Schoendienst, Maury Wills, Pete Rose, Ted Simmons, Willie Wilson, and Eddie Murray.

Why did a trade set the stage for a single-season home run record?

Just as the sale of Babe Ruth from the Boston Red Sox to the New York Yankees enabled the lefthanded slugger to establish numerous hitting marks, the trade of Roger Maris from the Kansas City Athletics to the New York Yankees set the stage for a long-distance hitting record.

Maris, like Ruth, was a lefthanded-hitting rightfielder who set his sights on the short right field porch at Yankee Stadium. With pitching diluted by expansion from eight to ten teams in 1961—his second season with the Yankees—Maris managed to hit 61 home runs, including the record-breaker on the final day of the season. It was the only time Maris hit as many as 40 home runs in a season.

Maris hit 33 home runs the next year, then 23, 26, 8, and 13 before the Yankees traded him to the St. Louis Cardinals for little-known third baseman Charlie Smith. Maris helped St. Louis win National League pennants in both 1967 and 1968, when he contributed both timely hits and a strong defensive performance in right field. After hitting just five home runs at age 33 for the Cards in 1968, however, Maris retired from baseball.

Why did Sandy Koufax credit a third-string catcher for his success?

Sandy Koufax, the Los Angeles Dodgers' Hall of Fame southpaw, had walked 295 batters in 512 innings during his first five years in the majors. In the spring of 1960, regular receiver John Roseboro was given a breather when the Dodgers went to Orlando, Florida, for an exhibition game against the Washington Senators (now Minnesota Twins). With Norm Sherry (later a manager and pitching coach) catching, Koufax walked the first three batters, using a curveball and changeup. Then he started throwing his fastball at full speed. Sherry immediately went to the mound, told Koufax to ease off on the fastball and let his fielders do the work. Koufax gave it a try and proceeded to strike out the side. He pitched four more scoreless innings, walking only one, and began to realize what he could accomplish by not overthrowing. In the next six seasons, Koufax won three Cy Young awards for pitching excellence, paving the way for eventual enshrinement in Cooperstown.

Why was Jack Reed's only home run especially timely?

On June 24, 1962, the New York Yankees and Detroit Tigers were locked in a 7–7 tie at Detroit. In the top of the 22nd inning, a light-hitting outfielder named Jack Reed, inserted earlier as a defensive replacement, came to the plate. With no pinch-hitter available, Yankee manager Ralph Houk had to let Reed hit. The result turned out to be a pleasant surprise: Reed's only major-league home run. The two-run shot off Phil Regan gave the pennant-bound Yankees a 9–7 victory. Not before or since has a home run been hit in such a late inning.

Why did Sandy Koufax quit baseball at age 30?

The great lefthander of the Los Angeles Dodgers retired in November 1966 after a 27–9 season that included a sparkling 1.73 earned run average. Doctors had warned the 30-year-old superstar, author of four no-hitters, that continued pitching might cause permanent disability to his arthritic left elbow. Sandy Koufax had endured constant pain and was forced to pack his elbow in ice after every game. He also had suffered a mysterious circulatory ailment in 1962.

Why was Jimmy Piersall's 100th home run significant?

Jimmy Piersall, known for his unorthodox behavior both on and off the field, hit his 100th major-league home run in

1963 while playing for the New York Mets. In celebration of this milestone, Piersall chose to run the bases *facing backwards*. The umpire ignored the gesture and permitted the run to count.

Why is the Lou Brock trade considered one of the most lopsided in baseball history?

On June 15, 1964, the St. Louis Cardinals sent 28-year-old righthander Ernie Broglio, veteran reliever Bobby Shantz, and reserve outfielder Doug Clemens to the Chicago Cubs for Lou Brock. At the time, it looked like the Cubs had made a steal, sending an erratic outfielder who struck out too much to a contending team for veteran pitching help. But it was Brock who literally made a steal of the deal—setting single-season and career marks for stolen bases, becoming an accomplished All-Star, and accumulating more than 3,000 hits. Broglio and Shantz left the majors quickly. Shantz retired after 1964, while Broglio lasted until 1966.

Why did Bert Campaneris play nine positions in one game?

Charlie Finley, owner of the Oakland Athletics, had Bert Campaneris play all nine positions in a 1965 game as a publicity stunt. Unfortunately, the versatile shortstop-by-trade was unable to complete the contest when he suffered a minor injury while catching the last inning. Three years later, the Minnesota Twins decided to prove that Cesar Tovar was equally utilitarian. He also played all nine positions in a game—striking out slugger Reggie Jackson while on the mound. Ironically, the first batter Tovar faced in the game was Bert Campaneris—the same man who had played all nine positions three years before.

Why did Willie McCovey receive so many intentional walks?

In 1969, when Willie McCovey was enjoying a Most Valuable Player season for the San Francisco Giants, the huge first baseman batted fourth in the lineup. By the time pitchers reached him, they had already gotten by Bobby Bonds, the leadoff man, and Willie Mays, who hit third. With no other power threats to worry about, hurlers often "pitched around" McCovey, preferring to give him one base on balls instead of having him hit the ball for four bases. That year McCovey led the National League with 45 homers, 126 runs batted in, and a robust .656 slugging percentage— helping the Giants finish a close second to Atlanta in the National League West. In the process, McCovey received a record 45 intentional walks.

Why were three Cy Young Awards presented in one year?

In 1969, Tom Seaver of the New York Mets won the first of his three National League Cy Young Awards for pitching excellence. The American League had two winners: repeat winner Denny McLain of the Detroit Tigers and Mike Cuellar of the Baltimore Orioles tied in the voting. McLain was 24-9 with nine shutouts, while Cuellar went 23-11 with a 2.38 earned run average, considerably better than McLain's 2.80. Their deadlock was the only tie in Cy Young Award history.

Why did the Perry brothers create baseball history?

Gaylord Perry and Jim Perry were the first brothers to each win 20 games in the same season. In 1970, Gaylord won 23 games for the San Francisco Giants and Jim won 24 for the Minnesota Twins. A year earlier, the Perrys combined for another mark when, on June 20, 1969, they won three games in one day. Another set of brothers, Phil Niekro of the Atlanta Braves and Joe Niekro of the Houston Astros, became the first brothers to reach 20 wins in the same *league* in 1979, when they each won 21 games to share National League leadership in victories.

Why did lefthanded pitcher Tommy John once throw righthanded at the All-Star Game?

On July 17, 1974, John was the leading Los Angeles Dodger pitcher with a 13-3 record when he ruptured a ligament in his left elbow. The injury required the complete reconstruction of his arm, a medical first. Dr. Frank Jobe placed a tendon from John's right forearm in his left elbow, putting the pitcher on the sidelines through the 1975 season. He split 20 decisions in 1976 before rebounding to a 20–7 mark in '77. He did appear in an All-Star Game while hurt— throwing out the first ball with his functioning right arm.

Why do Rookies of the Year rarely win other awards in their first year?

The baseball writers who do the voting for Rookie-of-the-Year generally feel that the rookie award is a significant enough honor for a first-year player. On two occasions, however, Rookies-of-the-Year were so outstanding that they won other major citations. Fred Lynn of the Boston Red Sox was MVP as a rookie in 1975, while Fernando Valenzuela of the Los Angeles Dodgers was the National League's Cy Young Award winner in 1981.

Why did a non-pitcher play in more than 100 games without batting?

Although American League pitchers rarely batted after 1972 because of the designated hitter rule (providing a substitute batter for the pitcher but not a defensive replacement), a non-pitcher managed to get into 105 games, spread over two seasons, without batting. He was Herb Washington, a Michigan State track star signed by maverick owner Charles O. Finley for the Oakland Athletics. Washington got into 92 games as a pinch runner for the World Champion Athletics in 1974 and 13 in 1975, scoring 33 runs and stealing 31 bases (in 48 tries). He appeared in three games of the 1974 World Series against the Los Angeles Dodgers.

Why was Lou Brock denied the Most Valuable Player Award the year he established a base-stealing record?

Lou Brock stole 118 bases for the 1974 St. Louis Cardinals to surpass the single-season record of 104 by Maury Wills of the 1962 Los Angeles Dodgers. Although Wills won the Most Valuable Player citation in his record-setting year, Brock was denied the honor because the Cardinals finished second, a game-and-a-half behind the Dodgers. The voters decided to give the Most Valuable Player award to durable Dodger first baseman Steve Garvey. Brock was justifiably miffed because, in 1962, Wills had won the award even though the Dodgers also wound up second—after suffering a playoff defeat at the hands of the San Francisco Giants. Voters in 1974 evidently decided Garvey was more valuable to the Dodgers than Brock was to the Cardinals.

Why was Brooks Robinson able to spend a record 23 seasons with one club?

Brooks Robinson spent his entire 23-year career with the Baltimore Orioles because he played third base—a position not easily filled—with extraordinary skill and was a fine clutch hitter. Robinson also played before the advent of the free agency era, when veteran stars routinely sell their services to the highest bidders.

Why did Ron Guidry develop a dislike for the name Mike?

In the 1978 season, Ron Guidry of the New York Yankees posted a 25-3 record. His only three losses were to lefthanders named Mike: Caldwell of the Brewers, Willis of the Blue Jays, and Flanagan of the Orioles. Guidry got his revenge by beating a righthanded Mike—Torrez of the Red Sox—in a one-game divisional playoff.

Why was Jim Bouton's comeback so remarkable?

As a righthanded fastball pitcher with the New York Yankees, starting in 1962, Jim Bouton enjoyed considerable success—once winning 21 games in a season. In 1969, however, he was sent to the fledgling Seattle Pilots (now Milwaukee Brewers) when it became evident his fastball had deserted him. Bouton tried to hang on with a newfound knuckleball but finally retired from the Houston Astros in 1970, yielding baseball for a budding television career.

Shortly thereafter, Bouton's "inside baseball" book *Ball Four* became a best-seller and short-lived television series while Bouton thrived as a New York sportscaster. Then the baseball bug bit him again in 1978.

Bouton finally arranged a spring training tryout—at his own expense—with the Atlanta Braves, a team then starved for pitching help. With 12 scoreless innings of pitching at the club's West Palm Beach, Florida camp, Bouton earned a Double-A contract at Savannah of the Southern League.

At age 39—long after most athletes have hung up their spikes—Bouton won 12 games for Savannah and was called up to Atlanta in September, capping a remarkable comeback after an eight-year absence from the Major Leagues. Bouton won one of four decisions for the Braves—proving the point he had made in the spring: he could still win at the major-league level.

Why did Dave Winfield's signing with the Yankees create such a controversy?

When slugging outfielder Dave Winfield played out his option with the San Diego Padres and signed a New York Yankee contract after the 1980 season, the terms stunned the baseball world. Winfield negotiated a 10-year pact worth anywhere from $15 million to $22,473,763 (depending on cost-of-living raises). He got a $1 million signing bonus, a first-year salary of $1.4 million, and a maximum cost-of-living raise of 10 percent each year, applied every other year. In addition, the rifle-armed Winfield won the opportunity to earn bonuses of $25,000 for playing 130 games, $25,000 for winning a Gold Glove (for fielding excellence), and $50,000 for winning the Most Valuable Player Award. The contract also includes a clause permitting the Yankees to buy out the pact's last two years at 50 percent of salary.

Winfield's signing was controversial because of the length of the contract and the enormous cost to the signing team. The two, taken together, were unprecedented in baseball history—and rival club owners feared Winfield's pact might establish a trend of longer contracts at higher prices for the game's top stars.

Why did an injury salvage Bruce Sutter's career?

The great righthanded reliever of the St. Louis Cardinals, Bruce Sutter, saved 36 games for the 1982 World Champions. He had come to the Cardinals only one year earlier—after establishing his credentials as a bullpen star with the Chicago Cubs. It was during his minor-league apprenticeship that Sutter suffered an injury that proved to be a blessing in disguise.

Shortly after signing with Chicago in 1972, Sutter hurt his elbow in a minor-league game and had to have surgery. When he was physically able to pitch, Sutter found that his fastball had deserted him. But Fred Martin, minor-league pitching instructor for the Cubs, showed Sutter a pitch that proved to be his ticket to the majors: a split-fingered fastball, close relative of the forkball.

Held with fingers spread as far apart as possible, the ball is stuffed between the fore and middle fingers, then thrown like a fastball. Batters see it as a fastball until it takes a sharp dip at the last minute. The pitch is effective for Sutter because he has very long fingers, enabling him to grip the ball with little pain. Many of his strikeouts come on balls that are only ankle-high by the time the catcher plucks them out of the air.

Sutter, the second National League reliever to win the Cy Young Award for pitching excellence (for the 1979 Cubs), throws the split-fingered fastball 90 percent of the time. He has used the pitch with devastating success, recording 215 saves in eight seasons through 1983. Only Rollie Fingers (301), Sparky Lyle (238), and Hoyt Wilhelm (227) had more lifetime saves heading into the 1984 season.

Why did one player bat safely for two teams on the same day?

When the New York Mets traded Joel Youngblood on

August 4, 1982, during their day game against the Cubs in Chicago, Youngblood—who had already singled in the game—had enough time to get to Philadelphia, where the Montreal Expos (his new team) were playing the Phillies that night. When Younglood also hit safely in that game, he became the only man in major-league history to bat safely for two teams in one day, though not the first to *play* for two teams in a day. In 1922, the Cubs and St. Louis Cardinals exchanged outfielders Jeff Heathcote and Max Flack between games of a May 30 doubleheader, permitting both men to appear in opposite uniforms during the nightcap. (Chicago won both games.)

Why do some pitchers work with a "designated" catcher?

Certain pitchers are fussy when it comes to working with a catcher. Such all-time stars as Bob Feller and Steve Carlton stated their preferences, and their managers, not wishing to upset their aces, obliged. Frankie Pytlak was Feller's personal caddy early in his career, while Carlton teamed with Tim McCarver whenever possible. When Mark (the Bird) Fidrych was en route to a stunning 19–9 season as a 1976 rookie of the Detroit Tigers, his catcher was always Bruce Kimm, normally a third-stringer. Kimm caught Fidrych in his debut and did so well defensively that Detroit pilot Ralph Houk was reluctant to break up the winning combination. Kimm caught all 29 Fidrych starts—even after injured regular Milt May returned to action.

Why can a pitcher hurl a no-hitter and still lose?

Games are won or lost on runs, not hits. Runs can be manufactured by hits but also by walks, hit batters, and errors. Only a no-hitter that is also a perfect game (no batters reaching base) cannot be lost.

Baseball history is filled with examples of nine-inning no-hitters that were lost when hits were surrendered in extra innings, but there are also examples of regulation no-hit games that were lost because of sloppy play.

In 1964, Ken Johnson, knuckleballing righthander of the Houston Colt .45s (later Astros), became the first modern pitcher to lose a nine-inning no-hitter when his own ninth-inning error allowed the Cincinnati Reds to score the lone run of the game.

Three years later, Steve Barber and Stu Miller of the Baltimore Orioles combined for a losing no-hitter against the Detroit Tigers. Barber walked 10, hit a batter, threw a wild pitch, and made an error in his 8 2/3 innings—allowing Detroit to eke out a 2–1 victory.

Why is earned run average (ERA) the best gauge of a pitcher's worth?

Quality pitchers employed by inferior teams may lose more games than they win because they get shabby offensive and defensive support. Their earned run average reflects the numer of runs-per-nine-innings "earned" by opponents rather than yielded by inept defenders. To calculate ERA, multiply the number of earned runs by nine, then divide the result by the number of innings pitched. A starting pitcher with an ERA below 3.00 or a relief pitcher (who works less innings) with an ERA below 2.00 can be proud of his performance. The lower the ERA, the better the pitcher.

Why were qualifications for the ERA title changed for relief pitchers?

Before 1950, pitchers had to complete at least 10 games to be eligible for the ERA crown. This obviously prevented any relief pitcher from winning it. But Jim Konstanty's 1950 season, with 16 wins and 22 games saved in 74 appearances for the pennant-winning Philadelphia Phillies, earned him the National League's Most Valuable Player Award and convinced baseball officials a change was needed in eligibility for the ERA title. Qualifications were changed to make all pitchers eligible who had worked as many innings as their team played games (154 then, 162 now). Hoyt Wilhelm became the first reliever to win the ERA crown in 1952, when he worked 159 innings for the New York Giants under the old 154-game format. (Mike Marshall holds the record for relief innings in one season: 208 for the 1974 Los Angeles Dodgers.)

Why is "the sophomore jinx" often a fact of baseball life?

Many players—flushed with the success of their initial year—have difficult times adjusting to their second seasons. Among those who have struggled are Vida Blue (1972), Carlton Fisk (1973), Al Bumbry (1974), and Dave Righetti (1982). The pressure of repeating a good performance is always enormous; veterans seem able to handle it better than inexperienced sophomores.

Why do veteran players sometimes opt for free agency?

Under terms of a Basic Agreement between labor and management signed in 1976 and amended several times since, major-league players with six years of service can sell themselves to the highest bidder after submitting to a reentry draft for negotiation rights.

The reentry system superseded the old reserve clause, which bound a player to his team pending trade, release, or demotion, after pitchers Andy Messersmith (Dodgers) and Dave McNally (Expos) tested the feasibility of "playing out their option" by not signing 1975 contracts.

Prior to 1975, the system in effect let clubs renew player contracts. Players did not have to sign but they were barred from selling their services elsewhere.

When the Messersmith-McNally case came before arbitrator Peter Seitz, he ruled that players were not bound to their teams after their contracts expired. Club owners appealed, but two courts upheld the decision, effectively terminating the traditional reserve system.

Prolonged labor-management negotiations created the reentry system, allowing stars to sell themselves on the open market. The direct result was the awarding of huge long-term contracts by teams hoping to keep their best players. By 1984, more than a dozen players were earning in excess of $1.5 million per year. The average salary had surpassed the highest individual salary paid in 1976: $225,000.

Chapter 7

MANAGERS AND STRATEGY

Introduction

Probably the most abused cliche in baseball regards the uncertain fate of the major-league manager. "Managers are hired to be fired," the saying goes. Invariably, the axiom proves true.

Even if a team advances to postseason play, the manager's job is not necessarily safe. The New York Yankees won the 1964 American League pennant but fired manager Yogi Berra anyway, replacing him with Johnny Keane, the man whose St. Louis Cardinals had defeated Berra in the World Series.

Only four years earlier, the Yanks had dismissed the legendary Casey Stengel—winner of 10 flags in 12 years—after Pittsburgh won the 1960 World Series on Bill Mazeroski's ninth-inning homer in Game 7.

When management or fans (or both) are unhappy with a team's play, the manager is generally the one to feel their wrath. The reason is simple: it's easier to ax one manager than 25 ball players.

Teams sometimes seem to change managers at the drop of a hat—even if those teams have winning records. One year after they represented the American League in the

World Series, the New York Yankees of 1982 employed three managers (Bob Lemon, Gene Michael, and Clyde King); two of the three had run the team in previous stints. A year later, New York brought back Billy Martin, winner in several cities, for his third term as a pilot in pinstripes.

Clubs tend to seek experience in selecting managers— explaining why nearly 50 managers since the century's turn have managed at least three teams each. Jimmie Dykes, part of that group, not only ran six different teams but was also involved in a trade for another manager. In 1960, the Detroit Tigers sent him to the Cleveland Indians in a swap for Indians' boss Joe Gordon. The unusual trade didn't work out; both men were let go by their new teams.

The most common reasons for a manager's dismissal include inability to win, failure to communicate with or control players, availability of a better man, or conflict with ownership. Successful managers must establish cordial relations with the media, keep 25 players happy even though only nine of them play at the same time, and argue with such diplomacy that neither manager nor players are ejected from the game.

Wilbert Robinson, who managed the Brooklyn Dodgers between 1914 and 1931, performed his tasks particularly well. Hall of Famer Dazzy Vance said of him: "Robbie was not the smartest baseball man, but he was the best psychologist. His aim was to get his players in the right frame of mind and keep them that way. Before games, he held a relaxation period. He chatted and told stories and poked fun at himself and others until everyone felt at ease."

Managerial style varies from quiet confidence to fire-and-brimstone. Leo Durocher, who tended toward a bombastic approach (at least in his dealings with umpires), lasted 24 years because he was a fiery, resourceful manager who always managed to outthink his opposition. Only a half-dozen others managed as long as the Lip in the Major Leagues.

None of today's managers doubles as a player, but that has not always been the practice. Early in baseball history, most teams employed player-managers who could lead by example. Active managers Frank Robinson and Joe Torre began their careers as strategists by doubling as players.

In general, however, baseball has become such a specialized sport—demanding a manager's full-time attention—that the use of the player-manager has gone out of vogue. (Don Kessinger of the 1979 Chicago White Sox was the last player-manager.)

Nor do any of today's pilots double as owners—a violation of current baseball rules. Past pilots did sometimes own their teams, as evidenced by Connie Mack of the Philadelphia Athletics. Mack had job security (he wouldn't fire himself) over a 53-year tenure as field manager, but he also had to worry about economics as well as victories. Twice, he was forced to sell off his stars to make ends meet. Championship clubs deteriorated as a result.

Mack, who compiled a managerial record of 3,776 wins and 4,025 losses, knew managing better than anyone else. He evaluated that job by percentages: "Talent comprises 75 percent of managing. Strategy is 12½ percent and the other 12½ percent is whatever a manager can get out of his team."

Although Mack had the most managerial wins, Joe McCarthy—one of three pilots to win pennants in both leagues—had the best winning percentage (.614). Frank Selee (.598) ranks second among managers and Earl Weaver (.596) third. All three were successful primarily because they were adept handlers of pitchers. But they were also capable strategists.

Managers must know when to switch lefthanders and righthanders—both in the field and at bat—and when to make pitching changes and other in-game personnel moves. They must establish pitching rotations, direct base runners through a series of signals, and offer hitting, pitching, and fielding expertise to their charges. They must also know such key intricacies of the game as working with grounds keepers to "fix the field" to the home team's advantage.

Team fortunes rest in the hands of competent managers. The pages that follow provide an inside look at the men who direct the teams and the game strategy that helps them win.

Why are managers fired so frequently?

When a team's fortunes change, it is easier to fire one manager than 25 ball players. Managing in the majors is not a job that has security. Consider the fact that the New York Yankees employed three different managers in 1982 alone (Bob Lemon, Gene Michael, and Clyde King). More than 600 men have managed in the majors, but only 16 have managed the same team at least 10 years. They are: Connie Mack, Athletics (50 years); John McGraw, Giants (29); Walt Alston, Dodgers (23); Cap Anson, Cubs (19); Wilbert Robinson, Dodgers (18); Fred Clarke, Pirates (16); Joe McCarthy, Yankees (15); Earl Weaver, Orioles, and Hugh Jennings, Tigers (14 each); Joe Cronin, Red Sox (13); Casey Stengel and Miller Huggins, Yankees, Jimmie Dykes, White Sox, Red Schoendienst, Cardinals, and Frank Selee, Braves (12 each); and Harry Wright, Phillies (10).

Why don't managers double as baseline coaches?

Managers once handled baseline coaching assignments. In fact, long-time New York Giant pilot John McGraw was called a "quitter" by rivals when he became the first manager to station himself in the dugout and direct his club from there. Pitcher Christy Mathewson, one of the all-time greats, pointed out that McGraw was better able to see everything and concentrate on the game from the bench. One of the last managers to serve on the coaching lines was Leo Durocher, with the New York Giants in the early '50s.

Why are club owners prohibited from managing their own teams?

Baseball Rule 20 (e) states that a manager may not have a financial interest in his team without special permission from the Commissioner. When Ted Turner made himself manager of the Atlanta Braves after the team had lost 16 straight games in 1977, National League president Chub Feeney exercised the rule, ending Turner's managerial career at one game (he lost, 2-1).

Earlier in baseball history, some owners had longer tenures as managers. Chris Von Der Ahe managed the St. Louis Browns (later Cardinals) in 1892 and parts of other years, and Charles Ebbets was in the dugout for the Brooklyn Dodgers when the 1898 season ended. Horace Fogel piloted the 1902 New York Giants for 42 games and Judge Emil Fuchs spent most of the 1929 season running the Boston Braves from the dugout. Connie Mack, John McGraw, and Clark Griffith all were owner-managers for years before anyone raised a question about the dual role.

In 1926, however, Rogers Hornsby was both player-manager and part-owner of the St. Louis Cardinals when he found himself traded to the New York Giants by Sam Breadon, who had controlling interest in the team. The National League held up the deal until Hornsby divested himself of the $60,000 he held in Cardinal stock.

Why do major-league teams need so many coaches?

Each major-league club carries four or more coaches in addition to the manager. Two flash signs to hitters and direct base runners from coaching boxes behind first and third base when their team bats; another supervises the bullpen; others, including hitting and pitching coaches, share the dugout with the manager.

A capable third base coach is particularly important because his decisions help or hurt the team score runs. Billy Hunter, who coached third base for the Baltimore Orioles for 14 years, once said that the third base coach controls the offensive end of the game more than the manager.

According to Hunter, who later managed in the majors himself, the third base coach watches the opposition club take infield practice, checks the throwing arms of rival outfielders, and knows what players handle cutoff plays smoothly.

"My theory at third," said Hunter, "was that if you had a 50-50 chance of making it, I sent the runner. You can only do that with a contending club because of the risk involved. I felt that if we made the other team throw, they made more mistakes. When you're cautious you might not score any runs. When you gamble, you might get two or three."

Why are player-managers rare in the modern Major Leagues?

Modern baseball has become too specialized and complex for individuals to devote full concentration to both playing and managing. Although the Chicago White Sox had a player-manager as recently as 1979 (Don Kessinger), the last player-pilot at the top of his game was Lou Boudreau, who guided the Cleveland Indians to the 1948 World Championship. (Boudreau was 24 when he took the job in 1942.)

In the early years of baseball, many top players managed their teams simultaneously. Among them were Ty Cobb (who once hit .401 as a player-manager), Tris Speaker, Bill Terry, Frankie Frisch, Gabby Hartnett, Rogers Hornsby, Joe Cronin, and Mickey Cochrane. The prevailing opinion about player-managers was best expressed by Brooklyn owner Charles Ebbets in 1898. Ebbets, who gave the Dodgers' ball park its name, said he preferred a player-manager to a bench manager because the former could lead by example. After World War II, however, the practice of employing player-managers faded from the game, with only a handful of exceptions.

Why was Cap Anson considered a great showman?

Cap Anson, player-manager of the Chicago National League club from 1879 to 1897, came up with some ingenious ways to draw crowds. He devised unique uniforms, paraded players to the park in open barouches, and initiated the practice of spring training to get players into top condition.

Why did Connie Mack manage a record 53 years in the majors?

Connie Mack never had to worry about the owner of the Philadelphia Athletics firing him; he was both owner and manager and wasn't about to fire himself. Mack, who wore a business suit with a high starched collar and straw hat (instead of a uniform) on the field, managed 20 years longer than John McGraw.

Why did the Yankees hire Miller Huggins?

Miller Huggins became manager of the Yankees in 1918—after a five-year stint as pilot of the St. Louis Cardinals—because Ban Johnson, American League president, initiated a meeting between Huggins and Col. Jacob Ruppert, co-owner of the Yankees. Johnson was eager for the Yanks to provide more competition for the powerful National League Giants, managed by John McGraw, and thought Huggins could be the catalyst. He was proven right when Huggins teamed with general manager Ed Barrow to piece together the original Yankee dynasty of the Babe Ruth era. Huggins remained manager until his death in 1929.

Why was Bucky Harris called "the Boy Wonder"?

Bucky Harris was a 27-year-old second baseman in his fourth season when he became manager of the Washington Senators in 1924. When he proceeded to win the pennant and the World Series, the press began to call him "the Boy Wonder" and the name remained with him through 29 years as a major-league manager.

Why was Joe McCarthy known as a "push-button manager"?

Jimmie Dykes, later a long-term manager himself, referred to Yankee skipper Joe McCarthy as a "push-button manager" because he felt that anyone could win with the talent the Yankees had. McCarthy, one of three pilots to win pennants in both leagues (Alvin Dark and Yogi Berra are the others), recorded a career winning percentage of .614 in 24 seasons. No pilot has done better.

Why was a major-league manager traded three times?

Rogers Hornsby, whose .358 lifetime batting average ranks second only to that of Ty Cobb in baseball history, was player-manager of the World Champion St. Louis Cardinals when he was traded to the New York Giants on December 20, 1926. Strictly a player under incumbent pilot John McGraw, Hornsby became a manager again when he was traded to the Boston Braves on January 10, 1928. Traded to the Chicago Cubs on November 7, 1928, Hornsby played under Joe McCarthy in 1929 and 1930, then replaced McCarthy as Chicago manager on September 23, 1930. He was released on August 2, 1932, signed as a player with the St. Louis Cardinals, then was released to become player-manager of the St. Louis Browns on July 27, 1933. He lasted slightly less than four years with St. Louis, ending his major-league playing career when the Browns let him go as a manager. Hornsby later returned to manage the Browns for part of the 1952 season and ran the Cincinnati Reds for part of that same season, as well as in 1953.

Hornsby frequently wore out his welcome because of his difficult disposition. He was outspoken, often unfriendly, and seldom related well to owners, team executives, or even teammates.

Why did Bill McKechnie manage three World Series teams?

Good managers are hard to find and Bill McKechnie was one of the best. Known for his ability to handle pitchers, McKechnie was the only man to manage three different franchises in the World Series: the Pittsburgh Pirates in 1925, the St. Louis Cardinals in 1928, and the Cincinnati Reds in 1939–40. McKechnie was also a coach for the Cardinals and Indians.

Why was Howard Ehmke a surprise starter in the 1929 World Series opener?

Although he pitched just 55 innings in the regular season, Howard Ehmke was a wise choice to start the 1929 World Series for the Philadelphia Athletics because he had secretly scouted the rival Chicago Cubs while nursing a sore arm during the season. Bypassing 20-game winners Lefty Grove and George Earnshaw, manager Connie Mack proved the wisdom of his choice when Ehmke fanned 13 Cubs—a World Series strikeout record later surpassed by Sandy Koufax (14) and Bob Gibson (17)—en route to a 3–1 victory.

Why did Connie Mack have to trade Jimmie Dykes?

Although Jimmie Dykes was the third baseman of Connie Mack's Philadelphia Athletics from 1918 to 1932, the manager was reluctantly forced to deal him when Bull and Eddie Kessler, two vociferous fans, unnerved Dykes during games at Philadelphia's Shibe Park (renamed Connie Mack Stadium in 1953). Mack tried to bribe the hecklers with season passes and eventually tried to silence them through court proceedings, but nothing worked. Given little choice, Mack sent Dykes packing to the Chicago White Sox—though he later brought him back to Philadelphia as his hand-picked managerial successor.

Why was Bill Terry a surprise choice as manager of the New York Giants after John Mc-Graw's retirement?

Bill Terry did not get along well with John McGraw and hardly talked to his manager during the last few years of McGraw's tenure. So his selection as McGraw's hand-picked successor in 1932 was a major surprise especially to third baseman Freddie Lindstrom, who had been regarded as McGraw's logical heir. Lindstrom was one of the few players who could talk back to McGraw and get away with it

Why did the Boston Braves once operate with two managers?

In 1943, manager Casey Stengel was struck by a taxi on a rainy night in Boston's Kenmore Square. Idled with a broken leg, Stengel watched co-managers George Kelly and Robert Coleman run the team.

Why did Dodger fans seldom see Burt Shotton when he managed Brooklyn?

Like Connie Mack, Burt Shotton preferred civvies to a baseball uniform. Wearing a suit instead of baseball flannels, Shotton always sent a coach, usually Clyde Sukeforth, to the mound to confer with his pitcher. Unless they peered into the dugout, Ebbets Field fans seldom saw the man who ran their club in 1947 and again from mid-1948 through 1950.

Why did Leo Durocher leave Brooklyn to manage the arch-rival New York Giants?

In 1939, Leo Durocher became manager of the Brooklyn Dodgers, then a mediocre team, won a pennant two years later, and guided the team to a club-record 104 victories in 1942 while finishing second. Lean years followed as World War II beckoned able-bodied athletes, but the Dodgers played well when they returned in 1946, losing the pennant in a postseason playoff against the St. Louis Cardinals. Durocher sat out 1947 when he was suspended for "conduct detrimental to baseball" by Commissioner A. B. (Happy) Chandler, but returned in 1948. Things weren't the same, though.

Dodger players had enjoyed playing for the calmer Burt Shotton in 1947 and couldn't respond to the high-pressure tactics of Durocher. In addition, Durocher had difficulty coexisting with general manager Branch Rickey, who had arrived from St. Louis in 1943 and whose development of a Dodger farm system was just starting to show dividends.

In midseason, Durocher stunned the baseball world when he suddenly resigned and moved crosstown to take charge of the New York Giants. The Giants had been last in 1946 and fourth in 1947 but were 11 games under .500 and fading when Durocher arrived. They rebounded to finish two games above the break-even level that year, blossomed into contenders, and won a miracle pennant in a photo-finish with Brooklyn in 1951.

Always a shrewd trader, sharp strategist, and expert motivator, Durocher also transformed weak clubs into contenders when he piloted the Chicago Cubs and Houston Astros later in his career. Durocher teams finished above .500 in 21 of the 25 seasons he managed—a record of excellence exceeded only by John McGraw (29 times above .500), Connie Mack (28), and Joe McCarthy (24).

Why did the fans manage the St. Louis Browns?

Colorful St. Louis Browns owner Bill Veeck, trying to drum up fan support for his lackluster team, created "Grandstand Managers Day" on August 24, 1951. More than a thousand fans seated behind the St. Louis dugout were given signs reading YES or NO and told to display them in response to visual questions posed by coaches. The fans voted to insert Sherm Lollar and Hank Arft for regulars Matt Batts and Ben Taylor, respectively, and the fan choices combined for four runs batted in to help Ned Garver beat the Philadelphia Athletics, 5–3. The fans also voted to keep Garver in the game after he had yielded five hits in the first inning; the decision paid off when Garver settled down to give up only two more hits in the remainder of the game.

Why did Alvin Dark refuse to manage the St. Louis Cardinals?

Alvin Dark is a teetotaler who rejected the job of managing the St. Louis Cardinals because of the club's affiliation with Anheuser-Busch breweries. The Cards became connected with Anheuser-Busch in 1953, when August (Gussie) Bush purchased the team.

Why did Al Lopez win a record number of games in a single season?

Al Lopez, a former catcher known as an excellent handler of pitchers, was able to coax an American League record of 111 victories from the 1954 Cleveland Indians because of their immense pitching talent. Lopez had a veteran staff consisting of Mike Garcia (age 30), Bob Lemon (33), Early Wynn (34), and Bob Feller (35). This foursome—together seven years—might have been the best starting quartet in baseball history. Lopez also had big hitters in Larry Doby, Al Rosen, Vic Wertz, and Bobby Avila.

Lopez teams always featured excellent pitching—but often did not have the offense to finish ahead of the powerful New York Yankees (1954 was a notable exception). When Casey Stengel won 10 times in 12 years for the Yankees from 1949 through 1960, Lopez was the only manager to beat him—first with the '54 Indians and then with the '59 White Sox. Lopez finished second 10 times.

Why did Preston Gomez twice remove pitchers during no-hitters?

Preston Gomez is probably the only major-league manager to twice remove starting pitchers who had hurled eight hitless innings in a game. As manager of the San Diego Padres in 1971, Gomez lifted Clay Kirby and, as manager of the Houston Astros in 1974, he lifted Don Wilson—using pinch-hitters for both in close games. Succeeding relievers blew both no-hitters in the ninth inning. Explained Gomez: "The name of the game is to win. Whatever you do on the field should be your own decision. If you lose, you can still feel good if you did your best. You have to forget about personal records and feelings."

Why did Sparky Anderson acquire the nickname "Captain Hook"?

As manager of the Cincinnati Reds from 1970 to 1978, George "Sparky" Anderson relied heavily on relief pitchers to win games for him. Because he was the man responsible for making the decision to pull starters quickly, players dubbed him "Captain Hook," after the *Peter Pan* character who had a metal hook in place of a missing hand. (In the days of vaudeville, unsatisfactory acts were literally pulled off the stage by long wooden hooks, just as Anderson yanked "unsatisfactory" pitchers.) The truth is that Cincinnati was blessed with a long line of quality relievers who made Anderson's decisions quite understandable.

Why was Frank Robinson's managerial debut memorable?

Frank Robinson was the first black manager hired (and later fired). In his first at-bat as the player-manager of the Cleveland Indians on April 7, 1975, Robinson homered, sparking a 5-3 victory over the New York Yankees. Robinson, at 39, was far off his Triple Crown form of 1966. He hit only eight more homers that year and three the next before retiring as a player.

Why was Earl Weaver regarded as one of the best managers in baseball history?

In 14½ seasons as manager of the Baltimore Orioles, Weaver had a won-lost mark of 1,354-919, a winning percentage of .596. Only Joe McCarthy (.614) and Frank Selee (.598) did better among pilots. The 1982 club, Weaver's last, was one of 12 Weaver teams to win at least 90 games. He won six American League East titles, four pennants, and one

World Championship. Although he was hated by umpires for loud, frequent, and often abrasive arguments, Weaver was a strategic genius and master motivator who used all 25 players on his roster and got the most out of each man. He kept extensive charts and detailed records which figured prominently in his version of platoon baseball.

Why did Casey Stengel have a hard time organizing the pitching staff of the New York Mets in 1962?

In addition to coping with a staff full of no-names, has-beens, and never-will-bes, Casey Stengel had two pitchers with the same name on his staff. Fortunately for Stengel, one Bob Miller was righthanded, while the other threw left-handed. The righthanded Robert Lane Miller had a 1–12 record as a starter but was later a crack reliever for several clubs. The lefthanded Robert Gerald Miller had a 2–2 record in relief.

Why did an ejection aid Walt Alston's major-league career?

When St. Louis Cardinals first baseman Johnny Mize was ejected during the last game of the 1936 season, future Hall of Fame manager Walter Alston replaced him in the field. In the lone at-bat of his major-league playing career, Alston fanned against Lon Warneke. Had Mize not been ejected, Alston might have missed the opportunity to bat in the majors.

Why did a modern Yankee manager fail to pilot the team in Yankee Stadium?

Bill Virdon, who managed several major-league clubs

following a successful career as an outfielder, happened to become Yankee manager in 1974, when the team played its home games in Shea Stadium, home of the Mets. Virdon was fired before the team finished its two-year residency at Shea during the renovation of Yankee Stadium. The Yankees have been continuous occupants of Yankee Stadium since 1923, except for the two-year period that included Virdon's managerial term.

Why was Alvin Dark the only man to manage All-Star teams for each league?

Traditionally, managers whose teams finish first the preceding year manage the All-Star teams of their league in midseason. Since only three managers have won pennants in both leagues, not many men have had the opportunity to manage All-Star teams for both the American and the National League. Joe McCarthy, the first manager to win pennants in both leagues, won with the Chicago Cubs before the advent of All-Star play in 1933, so he never managed a National League All-Star squad. Yogi Berra, who also won in both leagues, was fired by the New York Yankees after winning the 1964 pennant, so second-place pilot Al Lopez was named to head the American League All-Stars in 1965. That left Dark, who won with the Oakland Athletics in 1974 (and managed the 1975 American League All-Stars), and with the San Francisco Giants in 1962 (managing the National League All-Stars in 1963).

Why did Gene Mauch have a personal reason to celebrate when his California Angels finished first in 1982?

Until winning the American League West title with the 1982 California Angels, Gene Mauch had never managed a first-place team—in 22 seasons of managing. No manager had gone longer without winning. Mauch previously managed the Minnesota Twins, Montreal Expos, and Philadelphia Phillies. It was with the '64 Phillies that Mauch watched one of the greatest collapses in baseball history. Leading the National League by six-and-a-half games with 12 to play, the Phils lost 10 straight and wound up second, one game behind the pennant-winning St. Louis Cardinals. The '64 Phils will always be remembered as a "choke" team because of their great collapse.

Why has Billy Martin, a highly-regarded manager, lost so many jobs?

Although he is a master motivator of players and a shrewd strategist, Billy Martin has always been dogged by an explosive temper and occasionally by an affection for alcohol. He is not known for diplomacy in dealing with general managers or owners and his tendency toward brutal honesty and outspokenness has helped wear out the welcome mat in several cities.

Martin began his managerial career in the minors, then won the American League's Manager of the Year Award as the rookie pilot of the Western Division champion Minnesota Twins in 1969. He later piloted the Detroit Tigers, Texas Rangers, Oakland Athletics, and New York Yankees (beginning his third stint with the Yankees in 1983).

When he was named manager of the Athletics by Charley Finley in 1980, Martin tied the record of Charley Dressen, Rogers Hornsby, Bucky Harris, and Dick Williams for most different clubs managed (5), but he lasted only three seasons—including two as general manager and field manager—before ownership decided to terminate his services.

Martin has won several Manager of the Year awards and finished first five times (winning divisional crowns with the Twins and Athletics, pennants with the Tigers and Yankees, and a World Championship with another Yankee club).

Why do teams use signals?

Signals are used because it is impossible for players and coaches to communicate verbally. The element of surprise is essential in winning baseball games. In addition to the "hit" sign or "take" sign, flashed by baseline coaches to batters, signals order such plays as the stolen base, hit-and-run, sacrifice, or suicide squeeze. Coaches use six basic signs: bunt, take, hit-and-run, squeeze, steal, and forget-previous-sign. Defensive signals are also used, but usually with less camouflage than offensive signals.

Why is sign-stealing important?

Teams can anticipate enemy maneuvers in advance if signals are read with accuracy. In baseball, larceny is legal not only on the basepaths but also in the coaching boxes. There are no rules against stealing an opponent's signs— provided no mechanical device is used. Although the art of sign-stealing has decreased in recent seasons, stories of baseball's best sign-stealers abound. When he managed the Brooklyn Dodgers in the '50s, Charley Dressen was so adept at sign-stealing that he had a pregame meeting on the subject when he managed the 1953 National League All-Stars. Asked what signals he would use, Dressen said, "Don't worry about it, men. I'll give each of you the signals used on your own team!"

Why do managers platoon?

Platooning—playing certain players in certain situations—is practiced most often by managers who believe lefthanded hitters have an advantage against righthanded pitchers and righthanded hitters have an advantage against lefthanded pitchers. Platooning has been a hallmark of many managers dating back to George Stallings of the "miracle" 1914 Boston Braves. Tris Speaker employed a platoon system at first base and two outfield spots, helping the Cleveland Indians become World Champions in 1920, and Casey Stengel perfected the art of platooning during a 12-year tenure with the New York Yankees (1949–60) that produced 10 pennants.

Perhaps the classic example of successful platooning involved Art Shamsky, a slugging outfielder-first baseman for the Cincinnati Reds in 1966. On August 12, when a righthanded relief pitcher entered the game, manager Dave Bristol called on Shamsky to pinch-hit in the eighth inning. Shamsky homered. He stayed in the game and homered again in the 10th and 11th innings. But, the next day, he was not in the starting lineup because a lefthanded pitcher was starting against the Reds. A day later, with a righty working, Shamsky started and homered in his first at-bat, tying a mark shared by several players (four consecutive home runs).

Why do lefthanded batters have an advantage over righthanded batters?

Lefthanded batters stand several feet closer to first base than righthanded batters—a factor which can make an enormous difference in the number of infield hits fleet lefthanded hitters like Rod Carew and George Brett collect during a season. When a lefthanded hitter completes his swing, he is directly facing the first base bag—another advantage. From 1967 to 1980, 13 of 14 American League batting champions batted lefthanded, including 10 in a row from 1971 to 1980.

The advantage enjoyed by lefthanders is enhanced by the steady diet of righthanded pitching they face. A lefthanded batter facing a righthanded pitcher sees the ball delivered in his direct line of sight, with the curve breaking toward him rather than away from him.

The advantage of the lefthanded hitter was calculated in 1947 by a *New York Sun* sportswriter who used 1946 statistics to determine that southpaw hitters enjoyed an 18-point advantage over righthanded hitters. The figure wavers slightly from year to year, but there is little dispute over the benefits of hitting from the left side.

Why do switch-hitters often go against the percentages and bat lefthanded against lefthanded screwball pitchers?

Although normal baseball percentage indicates an advantage for a righthanded batter against a lefthanded pitcher, and vice versa, a lefty's screwball behaves like a righty's curve and breaks away from the righthanded hitter. That is the reason why Frankie Frisch, an accomplished switch-hitter, always batted lefthanded against Hall of Famer Carl Hubbell, a lefthanded screwball specialist.

Why is a hitter's number of total bases such an accurate barometer of his performance?

The number of total bases recorded by a player indicates the number of bases he reaches safely—not only with hits but also with such unofficial at-bats as those producing walks or times hit-by-pitch. Players with high figures in total bases are valuable because they reach base often and help their teams manufacture runs. Babe Ruth amassed a record 457 total bases for the 1921 New York Yankees. The only other man to reach 450 total bases in a season was Rogers Hornsby of the 1922 St. Louis Cardinals.

Why is on-base percentage such an important statistic?

On-base percentage, also known as on-base average

(OBA), is computed by taking hits, sacrifices, walks, interference calls, and times hit-by-pitch and dividing by the total number of appearances—both official and unofficial—at the plate. Hitters with good on-base averages are valuable to their teams because they are getting on base even though they may be slumping as hitters. Ted Williams, who walked often during his 17-year career, leads in lifetime on-base average with a mark of .483. Babe Ruth is next at .474.

Why is the suicide squeeze such a risky play?

A suicide squeeze occurs when there are less than two out and a runner on third breaks for home as the pitch is delivered. The batter attempts to bunt the ball out of reach of the pitcher so that the runner can score. (A safety squeeze—used only to push across the tying or lead run late in a game—occurs when the runner breaks *after* the bunt.)

The suicide squeeze can make a manager look like a genius or a dunce. If the batter misses the ball, the runner coming down from third is certain to be tagged out by the catcher. The batter must push the ball far enough from the plate so that the catcher can't reach it, yet out of reach of the pitcher. A good runner can make the squeeze work by not breaking for home too soon, a move which would alert the pitcher in time for him to make a pitchout and nab the runner coming home.

Why is hitting considered the most difficult job in sports?

A baseball takes only half-a-second, on the average, to travel from pitcher to hitter—and the hitter has only a fifth-of-a-second to move his bat from his shoulder to the contact zone. That leaves three-tenths of a second for him to (1) sight the ball, (2) determine what type of pitch is coming, (3) decide if it will be a ball or a strike, and (4) decide whether to swing or take the pitch. Given all these factors, it is amazing that Nellie Fox, second baseman for the Chicago White Sox in the '50s, once went a record 98 games without striking out and that Luke Sewell, catcher for several clubs between 1921 and 1942, twice played full seasons in which he struck out only four times.

Why is pinch-hitting such a difficult art?

Pinch-hitting involves coming off the bench in a crucial situation—invariably with no previous warm-up except for batting practice hours earlier—and making or breaking a team's chances. Pitchers, usually weak hitters, often depart for pinch-hitters in the late innings of close games—except in the American League, where the designated hitter always takes the pitcher's turn at bat. Dode Criss of the 1908 St. Louis Browns was the first heavy-duty pinch-hitter (12 hits in 41 at-bats). Manny Mota, last active with the 1982 Los Angeles Dodgers, had the most career pinch-hits (150).

Why was Del Unser's streak of three pinch-homers so unexpected?

Before Del Unser did it in 1979, no one in baseball history had managed to hit home runs in three consecutive pinch-hitting appearances. Unser, who hit a fourth pinch-homer for the Philadelphia Phillies that year, was an unlikely candidate for any record involving the long ball. As a rookie with the 1968 Washington Senators, the outfielder-first baseman managed only one home run in 635 trips to the plate—a line drive shot off Oakland's Jim Nash. Unser's father, Al, also hit a pinch-homer in the majors. It was a grand-slam for Detroit against the Yankees on May 31, 1944.

Why do catchers crouch just behind home plate?

Early catchers stood 20 feet behind home plate, well out of range of swinging bats—but also too far back to catch foul tips or throw out would-be base-stealers. It wasn't until 1909 that Jimmy Archer—wearing a newly-improved chest protector, shin guards, and helmet—became the first receiver to crouch behind the plate. Archer got the opportunity to carve a niche in the baseball history book when Johnny Kling, the regular catcher for the Chicago Cubs, decided to devote that season to his Kansas City billiard enterprise. The 26-year-old Archer hit only .230 in 80 games but showed a strong arm in revolutionizing the art of catching.

Why do all catchers throw righthanded?

The reason for the absence of lefthanded catchers is probably more traditional than practical. For many years, the answer to this question has been that catchers throw righthanded because most batters hit righthanded and a righthanded catcher has an easier throw to second with a righthanded batter at the plate (since a righthanded batter stands on the left side of home plate). For this reason, few lefthanded catcher's mitts have been made and few left-handed-throwing youngsters are encouraged to take up catching. If southpaw throwers were encouraged to become catchers, however, it is quite likely that they would do as well as righthanded throwers.

The last regular catcher who threw lefthanded was John Clements, who played for the Philadelphia Phillies at the turn of the century. Dale Long caught several games for the Chicago Cubs in 1958 and Mike Squires was pressed into service behind the plate for the Chicago White Sox in 1980.

Why do major-league teams prefer first basemen who throw lefthanded?

The throw is not an essential ingredient for a successful first baseman (scatter-armed Steve Garvey is a notable example); the ability to catch—especially errant throws—is much more important. Teams like lefties at first base because they wear their gloves on their right hand—the hand that faces the rest of the infield. That makes it easier for them to stretch, as evidenced by Willie (Stretch) McCovey, a lefthanded slugger who got his nickname because of his maneuverability around the bag for the San Francisco Giants. Another factor in the disproportionate number of lefties at first base is the limited number of positions open to them. With the exception of the mound and the outfield, first base is the only position a lefthanded thrower can play.

Why are all infielders *but* the first baseman righthanded throwers?

Third basemen must be righthanded to avoid awkward throws on balls hit to their right. Righthanded shortstops and second basemen also have a throwing advantage over lefthanders. In addition, the tough double-play pivot would be difficult for a southpaw second baseman (though it would be somewhat easier for a southpaw shortstop).

Why do infielders "cheat" in prospective bunt situations?

Both first basemen and third basemen play close to the plate in prospective bunt situations because stationing themselves close to home enables them to reach balls more quickly. If a first baseman makes the play, he may elect to try for the force play at second—nabbing the lead runner—or he can throw to first, with the second baseman covering. The third baseman would have the option of throwing to either base or, with runners on first and second, throwing to his own base, with the shortstop taking the throw. Hal Chase of the New York Highlanders was the first baseman who initiated the idea of coming in for the bunt, circa 1905, about the same time that converted catcher Fred Tenney of the Boston Beaneaters (later Braves) originated the 3-6-3 double play (first to second to first).

Why is the hidden-ball trick rarely successful?

The hidden-ball trick involves a fielder tagging a runner who thinks that the ball is in the hands of the pitcher. For the runner and base-line coaches to be duped in this way, timing is the key. Acting and confusion are also important for the play to be successful. Because it is difficult, at best, to engineer the proper set of circumstances, defensive players are seldom able to make the trick work. Regarded as the ultimate embarrassment in baseball, the hidden-ball trick did have several expert practitioners through the years. One-time Yankee shortstop Frankie Crosetti was a master of the play, while New York pitchers Lefty Gomez and Red Ruffing were expert at feigning possession. The hidden-ball trick was banned for a brief period because players hoping to pull it off took too much time setting it up. It is legal today, though seldom seen. In recent years, the most proficient hidden-ball expert was Gene Michael, an infielder for the New York Yankees.

Why is pitching considered to be 75 to 90 percent of the game?

Light-hitting teams with good speed and good defense behind quality pitching staffs have won pennants many times, while heavy-hitting teams with weak pitching seldom win. An excellent example is the 1930 Philadelphia Phillies, which had eight regulars top .300 and a team average of .315. The club finished dead last because its pitchers allowed rivals to score an average of 6.71 earned runs per game, a record for runs yielded.

Why is good control essential for a successful pitcher?

Pitchers who keep runners off base invariably win more than they lose. Those who issue walks frequently regret their wildness when those runners come around to score. Cy Young and Walter Johnson, who rank 1-2 in career victories, were masters of control. In 1904, Young walked 28 batters in 380 innings. Johnson walked 38 in 346 innings in 1913, when he won 36 games, including 12 shutouts.

Why don't pitchers win 30 games in a season anymore?

In the first decades of this century, pitchers often won 30 or more games in a season. Jack Chesbro won 41 in 1904, and Ed Walsh won 40 and Christy Mathewson 37, both in 1908. (There were no 30-game losers, but Vic Willis lost 29 in 1905 and four others lost 27 each between 1901 and 1910.) Pitching staffs were smaller and starters usually finished what they started—accounting for the high numbers of decisions they recorded. Although the season is now eight games longer than it used to be, modern managers go to their bullpens with increasing frequency, depriving potential 30-game winners of numerous opportunities in close games. Although Denny McLain of the Detroit Tigers managed a 31-6 season for the 1968 World Champions, the last 30-game winner before him was Dizzy Dean of the 1934 St. Louis Cardinals, also a championship club.

Why are pitchers sometimes required to cover first base?

First basemen play off the bag when a runner is not on base (especially with a righthanded batter up) or when the pitcher decides not to keep the runner close. If a ground ball is hit to the first baseman in such a situation, he sometimes does not have time to return to the bag. It is then the pitcher's responsibility to cover first. Charlie Comiskey, the first owner of the American League's Chicago White Stockings (and the man for whom the Chicago ball park is named), began the then-revolutionary practice of playing off the first base bag. Comiskey belonged to the St. Louis Browns of the American Association, then a major league, when he devised this defensive strategy during the 1880s.

Why is it widely accepted that the game is never over until the last man is out?

One-time National League president Harry Pulliam had a desk placard that read, "Take nothing for granted in baseball." That statement was underlined by Yogi Berra, who said, "It's never over until it's over." Twice, teams have rebounded from 12-run deficits to win one-run games. In one of those games, the Philadelphia Athletics enjoyed a 13-run eighth inning to beat the Cleveland Indians, 16–15, on June 15, 1925. Three teams have scored nine runs with two outs in the ninth inning of a regular-season game (once in the bottom of the ninth) and two teams have scored four runs with two outs in the ninth inning of a World Series game. Perhaps the most stunning upset occurred on May 23, 1901, when Cleveland had two outs and nobody on base in the home ninth inning when it erupted for nine runs to beat Washington, 14–13. (The biggest inning of the modern era occurred on June 18, 1953, when the Boston Red Sox notched 17 runs in the seventh inning against Detroit.)

Chapter 8

FAMOUS FEATS

Introduction

Every baseball season is different. The excitement provided by the pennant races, Championship Series, World Series, and All-Star Game varies from year to year, with different team and individual heroes.

Famous feats performed in the spotlight of national publicity give teams and players national recognition, but most milestones are recorded in the relative anonymity of the regular season. That is especially true in the post-expansion era that began in 1961.

Roger Maris hit 61 home runs in 1961 and Hank Aaron 755 lifetime, erasing Babe Ruth's season and career records. Maury Wills and then Lou Brock broke Ty Cobb's single-season steal record before Rickey Henderson topped them all with 130 stolen bases in 1982. Henderson seems likely to challenge Brock's career record as well.

Pete Rose passed Aaron to move into second place, behind Cobb, in career hits, while Nolan Ryan, the only pitcher to throw five no-hit games, became the career strikeout leader, surpassing Walter Johnson, until Steve Carlton, in turn, surpassed Ryan.

In the World Series, Don Larsen's 1956 perfect game for the New York Yankees against the Brooklyn Dodgers ranks as the supreme pitching performance, but fellow Yankee Floyd Bevens came within an out of a previous Fall Classic no-hitter nine years earlier. Instead, Bevens yielded a ninth-inning, two-run double to Brooklyn's Cookie Lavagetto and lost the game, 3–2.

Probably the biggest hit in World Series annals was Bill Mazeroski's bottom-of-the-ninth leadoff homer that gave the Pittsburgh Pirates a 10–9 win in Game 7 of the 1960 Fall Classic against the New York Yankees. New York had outscored and outplayed the Pirates throughout the Series but lost the clincher by a single run when Mazeroski homered—the only home run to decide a World Championship.

In 1975, Bernie Carbo of the Boston Red Sox tied the 1959 mark of Dodger Chuck Essegian with two pinch-homers in one Series, but Boston bowed to the Cincinnati Reds in a seven-game match that is generally regarded as one of the most exciting on record. Boston's appearance as champion of the American League ended a string of three straight World Championships by the Oakland Athletics.

The long list of World Series standouts includes Babe Ruth, the only man to hit three homers in a Series game twice; Mickey Mantle, who hit a record 18 homers in World Series play; and Reggie Jackson, whose five homers in a six-game Series stands as a slugging mark.

Ruth, Mantle, and Jackson have also shined in All-Star competition, which began on July 6, 1933, with Arch Ward's Dream Game at Chicago's Comiskey Park. Ruth's two-run homer gave the American League a 4–2 win in that initial encounter, but the National League has dominated over the last generation (with an 11-year winning streak ending in 1983).

All-Star starters have been selected by various means over the years, with a nationwide fan vote the current method. Managers—the pilots of the previous year's World Series entrants—fill out the remainder of their 28-man squads by selecting at least one man from each major-league team.

For All-Star hitting heroics, few could match Ted Williams. In 1941, the lanky leftfielder of the Boston Red Sox came to bat with two on and two out in the bottom of the ninth inning and the National League leading, 5–3. On a 2–1 pitch from Claude Passeau, Williams smacked a long home run to win the game for the Americans, 6–5. Five years later, Williams had two homers, two singles, and a walk in a 12–0 American League All-Star triumph.

The home run has also been a big weapon in League Championship Series and playoff games. Gary Matthews of the Philadelphia Phillies homered three times—tying Hank Aaron's 1969 Championship Series performance—to help his team win a four-game match with the Los Angeles Dodgers for the 1983 National League pennant.

The biggest home runs of playoff history were delivered by Bobby Thomson, whose 1951 ninth-inning blast capped a miracle comeback by the New York Giants against the Brooklyn Dodgers, and Bucky Dent, whose unexpected blow gave the New York Yankees a sudden-death win in a divisional playoff against the Boston Red Sox in 1978.

A single year can make a world of difference for a team. In 1945, the Chicago Cubs won the pennant after finishing 30 games behind the year before. The New York Giants were 35 games behind Brooklyn in 1953 and World Champions in 1954. Both the 1967 Boston Red Sox and the 1969 New York Mets won pennants after finishing ninth in 10-team leagues the previous season.

Predicting pennant-winners in advance is difficult because many unknown factors make preseason prognostications unreliable—even for writers who have been following the game for years. Trades, injuries, rookie surprises, veterans in sudden decline, unpopular owners and managers, and countless other variables influence each team's chances.

Before divisional play began in 1969, there were two pennant races—one in the American League and one in the National—with winners advancing to the World Series. The split into East/West divisions brought with it a best-of-five

Championship Series to choose league entries for the best-of-seven World Series.

Pennant races have wound up deadlocked several times. Prior to divisional play, National League teams tied for first in 1946, 1951, 1959, and 1962, and American League teams once, in 1948. After the split into divisions, ties forced divisional playoffs in 1978, in the American League East, and in 1980, in the National League West. Predivisional ties were settled by best-of-three playoffs in the National League and single-game, sudden-death showdowns in the American. Both leagues now settle divisional deadlocks with a one-game playoff.

World Series competition dates back to the 19th century postseason series between champions of the old American Association and the National League. Various formats were tried before the first modern World Series was staged between National and American League champions in 1903. The current best-of-seven format was adopted in 1905 and has been used since except for 1919, 1920, and 1921, when the 1903–04 best-of-nine format was reintroduced in the hope of building public interest as well as turnstile revenue.

Baseball history proves, without doubt, that the best method of arousing public interest that will produce a box office payoff is for a team or an individual to perform well. An ancient axiom contends that everyone loves a winner. In baseball, more than any other sport, that is the bottom line.

The pages that follow outline some of the famous and noteworthy feats by teams and individuals through the years. Many were publicized in the "Most Memorable Moments" fan poll during the 1969 Baseball Centennial, while others remain etched in history—worthy of a second look by fans who will recognize their significance.

Why is the World Series the highlight of the baseball year?

Postseason competition between league champions is a long-standing baseball tradition which first began in 1882, when the American Association joined the six-year-old National League as a major circuit. Chicago (National League) and Cincinnati (American Association) split four games before disputes shelved the rest of the series. In 1884, Providence of the National League beat the New York Metropolitans of the American Association three straight in a best-of-five match. An 1887 postseason tour between Detroit (National League) and St. Louis (American Association) included 15 games in 10 cities.

After the Players' League rebellion of 1890 killed the American Association, the National League took on four American Association clubs and held its own postseason competition: the Temple Cup. The league's two top teams competed in the first Temple Club series after the 1894 season and the competition lasted three more seasons, using the best-of-seven format now used in the World Series.

After the birth of the American League in 1901, American League and National League winners met in the World Series every year, beginning in 1903. A best-of-seven format was used with the exception of 1903 and 1919–21, when best-of-nine matches were played. There was no World Series in 1904 because John McGraw, manager of the National League champion New York Giants, refused to recognize the rival American League. The World Series was renewed in 1905 under the supervision of the three-man National Commission which then governed the game.

Why is it rare for starting pitchers to win three World Series games?

Only six pitchers have won three games as starters in

the same World Series under the best-of-seven format: Christy Mathewson (1905), Babe Adams (1909), Jack Coombs (1910), Lew Burdette (1957), Bob Gibson (1967), and Mickey Lolich (1968). (Stan Coveleski won three games under the best-of-nine format existing in 1920.) Three other three-game winners (Smokey Joe Wood in 1912, Red Faber in 1917, and Harry Brecheen in 1946) earned one of their victories in relief. Winning three World Series games is rare today because managers depend heavily on relievers; because increased emphasis on speed and power has made life harder for starters; and because the divisional playoff system before the World Series often ties up top starters who are unavailable for World Series Game 1.

Why were the losers paid more than the winners in the first World Series?

A portion of each team's World Series receipts go to the club and a portion to the players. But, in 1903, Pittsburgh Pirates owner Barney Dreyfuss was in a generous mood and tossed the club's losing World Series shares into the player pool. This allowed members of the losing Pirates to get $1,316 each, while players on the winning Boston Americans received only $1,182 each (Boston owner Henry Killilea kept his club's share of $6,699.56).

Why was the 1905 World Series known as the "Series of shutouts"?

All five games in the World Series between the New York Giants and the Philadelphia Athletics in 1905 were decided by shutouts. Christy Mathewson, ace righthander of the Giants, pitched three of them in a six-day span, winning 3–0, 9–0, and 2–0. Joe (Iron Man) McGinnity got the other Giant win, a 1–0 triumph in Game 4, while Chief Bender took Game 2 for the A's, 3–0. All three Philadelphia runs in Game 2 were unearned, giving the Giant staff a composite 0.00 earned run average for the World Series.

Why did a team once use only two pitchers in a World Series?

Early in the century, pitching staffs were smaller and relief pitchers were used only in the event of injury or illness to a starter. Pitchers were expected to finish what they started and the best pitchers were asked to work often (few teams had trainers and managers put more emphasis on durability than long-range conservation of a pitcher's arm). In the 1910 World Series, the Philadelphia Athletics of the American League used only Chief Bender and Jack Coombs to defeat the National League's Chicago Cubs, four games to one. No other team has ever used so few pitchers in the Fall Classic.

Why is 1912 remembered as "a pitchers' year"?

Three pitchers established record winning streaks during the 1912 campaign: Rube Marquard, who won 19 in a row for the New York Giants; Walter Johnson, with 16 straight for the Washington Senators; and Smokey Joe Wood, who won 16 in a row for the Boston Red Sox. (Marquard's National League mark was subsequently bettered by Carl Hubbell of the Giants, who won 24 straight in 1936–37, but Wood and Johnson continue to share the American League record, along with Lefty Grove of the 1931 Philadelphia Athletics and Schoolboy Rowe of the 1934 Detroit Tigers.)

Wood's 1–0 victory over Johnson on September 6 was his 14th straight triumph (Johnson's streak had ended with a relief loss on August 26). Wood won twice more before he finally was defeated on September 20, one of only five losses incurred in his 34-win campaign. Johnson, no slouch either, enjoyed a 32-victory season for the Senators in 1912.

Why was a key World Series error called "the $30,000 Muff"?

In the eighth game of the 1912 World Series (Game 2 was a tie), the New York Giants took a 2-1 lead in the tenth inning with Christy Mathewson on the mound against the Boston Red Sox. Clyde Engle led off for Boston with an easy fly to center field, but Fred Snodgrass dropped it, allowing Engle to reach second. Harry Hooper lined to Snodgrass, who caught the ball. Steve Yerkes walked. Tris Speaker then popped up near first, but Fred Merkle failed to go after it and catcher Chief Meyers couldn't reach it. Given a new life, Speaker singled to score Engle with the tying run. Yerkes went to third and scored on a sacrifice fly by Larry Gardner. Had Snodgrass not dropped the fly ball to set up the inning, the Giants might have held onto their lead and won the World Championship. His error was called "the $30,000 Muff" because he denied his 16 teammates the difference between the winners' share of $4,025 and the losers' share of $2,566.

Why did a rundown play result in a World Championship?

A botched rundown play in the fourth inning of 1917 World Series Game 6 helped the Chicago White Sox become World Champions over the New York Giants. The inning started when two runners reached base, thanks to errors by Heinie Zimmerman and Dave Robertson. Happy Felsch grounded to Giants' pitcher Rube Benton, who threw to Zimmerman at third when Eddie Collins broke from the base. Ball in hand, Zimmerman chased Collins home—running him past catcher Bill Rariden, who was up the line for the apparent rundown play. Neither Benton nor first baseman Walter Holke thought to cover the plate, allowing Collins to score easily. Chick Gandil followed with a two-run single, capping the inning, and the Sox went on to a 4-2 victory.

Why was a World Series game once played for charity?

On October 5, 1922, the New York Yankees and New York Giants were tied, 3–3, after 10 innings of play at the Polo Grounds when umpire George Hildebrand called the game because of "darkness." The decision caused a near-riot by fans who reasoned that at least 30 minutes of daylight remained. Commissioner Kenesaw Mountain Landis agreed with the fans, and decided to donate the entire day's gate receipts—some $12,000—to charity.

Why was an entire World Series played in the same park?

On several occasions, teams that shared home fields have won pennants in the same year. In 1921–22, the last two seasons before Yankee Stadium opened, the New York Yankees were tenants of the New York Giants at the Polo Grounds and both clubs won pennants. In both World Series, the two teams alternated as home team.

In 1944, both St. Louis teams finished first, making Sportsman's Park (later called Busch Stadium) the sole Series field. The Cardinals were designated as home team for Games 1–2 and 6–7, while the Browns were "home" for Games 3-4-5.

Why was Grover Cleveland Alexander an unlikely hero in the last game of the 1926 World Series?

At age 39, Grover Cleveland Alexander was 9–7 with two saves for the St. Louis Cardinals after his early acquisition from the Chicago Cubs. He continued to excel in the World Series, posting complete-game victories over the New York Yankees in Games 2 and 6. No one—Alexander included—expected him to appear in the seventh game, but manager Rogers Hornsby decided to go with experience when Game 7 starter Jesse (Pop) Haines ran into trouble in the seventh inning. Alexander, tired from his 10–2 triumph the day before, worked two-and-a-third innings of shutout ball to preserve a 3–2 victory and bring the World Championship to St. Louis. The only runner he allowed was Babe Ruth, who walked in the ninth and was then retired trying to steal second.

Why did Chicago Cub fans vilify home run star Hack Wilson for his World Series play?

Hack Wilson, the slugging center fielder of the Chicago Cubs, incurred the wrath of Chicago fans when he lost two fly balls in the sun during World Series Game 4 in 1929. The misplays helped the Philadelphia Athletics to erupt for 10 runs in the seventh inning and gain an incredible 10–8 win in a game in which the Cubs had led 8–0. Philadelphia proceeded to wrap up the World Championship with a 3–2 win the next day. Since Games 4 and 5 took place in Philadelphia, the Wrigley Field faithful had to wait until 1930 to vent their displeasure on Hack Wilson. At the start of the season, Wilson was pelted with lemons when he took his position in the outfield. Only a record-smashing season that included 56 home runs and 190 runs batted in quieted the irate spectators. (The 190 runs batted in represent a major-league mark; the 56 home runs a National League record.)

Why did the "Homer in the Gloamin'" help win a pennant?

On September 27, 1938, the Chicago Cubs were one-and-a-half games behind the Pittsburgh Pirates in the National League race as the two clubs began a crucial three-game series in Wrigley Field, home of the Cubs. Dizzy Dean won the opener for Chicago, 2–1, to narrow the gap to a half-game. With the score tied, 5–5, and two outs in the ninth inning of the second game, Gabby Hartnett came to bat as darkness and haze threatened to suspend play. The 37-year-old catcher slammed a home run—barely visible in the fading light—to win the game and catapult the Cubs into first place. The Cubs won again, 10–1, in game 3 and went on to the National League crown. All agreed that Hartnett's "Homer in the Gloamin'" was the turning point.

Why does Mickey Owen own an infamous entry in the World Series record book?

In Game 4 of the 1941 World Series, Mickey Owen, catching for the Brooklyn Dodgers, failed to hold Hugh Casey's game-ending third strike, allowing Tommy Henrich to reach first safely. Instead of gaining a 3–2 win, knotting the Series at two games each, the Dodgers saw the New York Yankees go on to steal the game by scoring four runs with two outs in the ninth and take a lead of three games to one. The Bronx Bombers wrapped up the World Championship the next day. Things might have been different had Mickey Owen held that elusive third strike. However, in all fairness to Mickey, it must be noted that Casey confessed years later that the pitch that got away was a spitter—a notoriously hard pitch to hit or to catch.

Why did slugger Enos Slaughter surprise the baseball world by winning a World Series with his base running?

Enos Slaughter led the National League with 130 runs batted in during the 1946 season, but the St. Louis Cardinals outfielder was not known for having much speed on the bases. Yet it was Slaughter's hustling on the base paths that helped the Cards topple the Boston Red Sox during the 1946

World Series. In the final game, with the score 3–3, Slaughter singled to lead off the eighth. Told to take any risk in an effort to score, Slaughter broke for second as Harry Walker dropped a Texas Leaguer between shortstop and center field. Slaughter reached second while the ball was still in the air and took third easily. Then, remembering that rifle-armed regular Dom DiMaggio had been replaced by Leon Culberson, Slaughter dashed for home. Shortstop Johnny Pesky had his back to the infield while awaiting the relay throw. When he got the ball and wheeled to throw, he was so surprised to see Slaughter streaking for home that he hesitated for just an instant. That gave Slaughter the split second he needed to beat the throw home. Slaughter's mad dash gave St. Louis a 4–3 victory and the World Championship.

Why were the three most memorable players of the 1947 World Series out of baseball by 1948?

The New York Yankees defeated the Brooklyn Dodgers in a seven-game World Series following the 1947 season, but the irony of that Fall Classic was that three World Series heroes found themselves out of the majors before the next season opened. In Game 4, Yankee pitcher Bill Bevens came within one out of the first World Series no-hitter when Dodger pinch-hitter Cookie Lavagetto delivered a two-run double—the only Brooklyn safety—to notch a 3–2 victory. In Game 6, Al Gionfriddo, a light-hitting outfielder, replaced Eddie Miksis in left field at the start of the sixth inning. With two on and two out in a game the Dodgers led, 8–5, Joe DiMaggio sent an apparent home run toward the bullpen in left-center field. Gionfriddo made a twisting, glove-handed catch near the 415-foot sign to preserve the Dodger lead. By 1948, however, none of the 16 teams in baseball wanted Bevens, Lavagetto, or Gionfriddo. Bevens, plagued by wildness even in his near-no-hitter, was 30 when released. Gionfriddo, whose inability to hit matched Bevens' inability to find home plate, was 25. Lavagetto, a light-hitting infielder used only sparingly by the Dodgers in 1947, was 34.

Why did Ralph Branca pitch to Bobby Thomson in the fateful ninth inning of the 1951 Dodger-Giant playoff?

Ralph Branca, normally a starting pitcher, was working in relief of Don Newcombe in the ninth inning of the decisive third pennant playoff game in 1951. Newcombe, the starter for the Brooklyn Dodgers, had taken a 4–1 lead into the bottom of the ninth inning at the Polo Grounds, home of the New York Giants. Alvin Dark and Don Mueller singled to start the inning. Monte Irvin popped up for the first out, but Whitey Lockman doubled home a run, cutting the score to 4–2. Mueller, hurt sliding into third, was removed on a stretcher, providing ample time for a pitching change. Dodger manager Charlie Dressen called for Branca, who had started and lost the first playoff game, to face Thomson, the Giants' leading home run hitter (31 during the regular schedule plus another—off Ralph Branca—in the playoff opener).

Branca could have walked Thomson intentionally to load the bases and set up a force at home, and perhaps a game-ending double-play, but the pitcher and catcher Rube Walker—subbing for injured regular Roy Campanella—decided that on-deck hitter Willie Mays, then in his rookie season, was too dangerous. They elected instead to try their luck with Thomson.

Branca threw a high, inside fastball, then decided Thomson would be looking for something low and away—anything other than the same pitch again. It was a sad miscalculation for Brooklyn. Branca threw another high, inside fastball and Thomson deposited it in the left field stands for a pennant-winning three-run homer, capping "the Miracle of Coogan's Bluff," a stunning comeback drive by the Giants. The blast is known to this day as "the Shot Heard Round the World."

Why is Gil Hodges remembered as a symbol of World Series futility?

The great first baseman of the Brooklyn Dodgers, Gil Hodges, is remembered as a symbol of World Series futility because of his failure to get a single hit during his team's seven-game setback in the 1952 Fall Classic against the New York Yankees. Counted on for his power (370 lifetime homers) and ability to produce in the clutch, Hodges was 0-for-21 in the Series, matching the record of ineptitude shared by Jimmy Sheckard of the Chicago Cubs and Billy Sullivan of the Chicago White Sox, both in 1906, and John Murray of the New York Giants, in 1911. Although Dal Maxvill later broke the record with an 0-for-22 showing as the St. Louis Cardinals shortstop against the Detroit Tigers in 1968, Maxvill—unlike Hodges—was a weak hitter who had not been counted on for offensive contributions.

In later World Series, Hodges regained his usual batting prowess and ended his career with an average of .267, 5 home runs, 21 runs batted in, and a .412 slugging percentage.

Why was the first game of the 1954 World Series so ironic?

The 1954 World Series between the Cleveland Indians and the New York Giants opened in the horseshoe-shaped Polo Grounds, a ballpark with dimensions so unusual that a pop fly could become a home run and a long drive could be turned into an ordinary out. That's exactly what happened in the opening game. Cleveland first baseman Vic Wertz sent a 460-foot drive to center, where Willie Mays made a back-to-the-plate catch that ranks as one of the great fielding plays of all time. But Dusty Rhodes, a 10th-inning pinch-hitter with two men on, won the game for New York with a 260-foot fly that fell into the right field stands for a game-winning home run. Bob Lemon was the victim. The Giants proceeded to sweep the favored Indians in four straight games.

Why did Sandy Amoros make a timely appearance as a World Series defensive replacement?

The Brooklyn Dodgers, seeking their first World Championship, took a 2-0 lead into the sixth inning of the seventh game of the 1955 World Series against the New York Yankees. In the top of the sixth, Dodger manager Walter Alston used George Shuba as a pinch-hitter for second baseman Don Zimmer. In the bottom of the same frame, left fielder Junior Gilliam moved from left field to second base, replacing Zimmer, and Sandy Amoros became the new left fielder. The timing couldn't have been better for Brooklyn. With runners on first and second and no one out for the Yankees, Yogi Berra sent a hard liner to the left field corner. Amoros, running full tilt, not only reached the ball but whirled in time to make a double play at first base. The Dodgers maintained the 2-0 lead behind Johnny Podres and became World Champions.

Why did shoe polish help decide a World Series game?

In the fourth game of the 1957 World Series, the New York Yankees took a 5-4 lead into the bottom of the 10th inning at Milwaukee. The first batter was Nippy Jones, pinch-hitting for Braves' pitcher Warren Spahn. Home plate umpire Augie Donatelli ruled the first pitch from Tommy Byrne a ball but Jones retrieved the ball and showed the arbiter a smudge of shoe polish. Donatelli reversed his call, ruled that the pitch had struck Jones in the foot, and awarded him first base. Milwaukee proceeded to score three runs for a 7-5 victory that tied the Series at two games each.

The Braves went on to become World Champions after winning a decisive seventh game.

Why did broadcaster Bob Prince fail to ask Bill Mazeroski about his game-winning homer following the seventh game of the 1960 World Series?

Bob Prince, then the No. 1 broadcaster for the Pittsburgh Pirates, was en route to the clubhouse when Bill Mazeroski led off the bottom of the ninth inning with the home run that gave the Pirates a 10–9 win and the World Championship. When Prince arrived in the Pittsburgh clubhouse, he encountered a wild victory celebration but had no idea how the game had ended. Among those he interviewed, per chance, was Mazeroski. Since the announcer did not know Mazeroski had hit the game-winning homer, he never questioned him about it.

Why did the Tigers play an outfielder at shortstop in the 1968 World Series?

When the Detroit Tigers won the 1968 American League flag, their regular shortstop was light-hitting Ray Oyler, who hit .135 in 111 games. Dick Tracewski, the backup, wasn't much improvement (.156 in 90 games). Manager Mayo Smith needed to get more punch at short, and also needed to return superstar Al Kaline to his normal position in right field. In Kaline's absence, Mickey Stanley, Willie Horton, and Jim Northrup had done a fine job in the outfield, but Smith knew Stanley was versatile enough to play elsewhere. So, he made a bold move: Stanley went from center to shortstop, Northrup from right to center, and Kaline returned to right. Those moves paid off as the Tigers rebounded from a 3–1 deficit to defeat the St. Louis Cardinals in seven games.

Why did a player get more hits in the World Series than in the regular season?

Prior to the 1983 season, six players—all of them pitchers—managed to get more hits in a World Series than in the regular season. Joe Hoerner, a St. Louis Cardinals relief pitcher who rarely batted, was the first to do it (1968). Like Hoerner, who had no regular-season hits but one in the World Series, the other pitchers who turned hitters are of relatively recent vintage: Bill Lee (Red Sox) and Will McEnaney (Reds) in 1975 and Tim Stoddard (Orioles) in 1979 managed one hit each in the World Series, while Ken Holtzman (Athletics) and Luis Tiant (Red Sox) had two hits each in 1974 and 1975, respectively. Stoddard's situation was the most unusual because he got his hit in the first plate appearance of his major-league career.

Why is the All-Star Game played in the middle of the season?

Midseason scheduling of the All-Star Game is a baseball tradition that began in 1933, when *Chicago Tribune* sports editor Arch Ward created the "Dream Game" concept as an adjunct to Chicago's Century of Progress exposition, a World's Fair. Most club owners originally opposed the idea of a three-day suspension of play for an exhibition game between "all-stars" of both leagues, but Commissioner Kenesaw Mountain Landis and the league presidents supported Ward's suggestion. The original intent was to stage a one-time-only All-Star Game, but fan reaction was so overwhelming that the game became an annual event. Fourteen of the 36 All-Stars of 1933 eventually made the Hall of Fame. Among them was Babe Ruth, whose two-run homer in the third inning gave the American League a 4–2 victory in the game, played at Comiskey Park on July 6, 1933.

Why do fans pick the All-Star starters?

The process of selecting All-Star starting lineups has changed several times through the years. In the first game, in 1933, an informal *Chicago Tribune* poll of readers gave managers John McGraw of the National League and Connie Mack of the American League suggestions for player selection, but the pilots—named by the league presidents—were free to pick their own 18-man squads. A newspaper fan poll was used again in 1934, but baseball executives considered the fan vote a farce because managers were not in agreement and chose other players. The fan poll was scrapped in 1935. That left selection in the hands of the managers, but favoritism prevailed, causing constant criticism in the media.

The fans got the vote back from 1947 through 1957, but ballot-stuffing by Cincinnati partisans in 1957 persuaded Commissioner Ford Frick to give the vote to the players, coaches, and managers—who were barred from voting for teammates in the hope of making the vote more objective.

Player voting was successful, and respected by fans, but Commissioner Bowie Kuhn restored the fan vote in 1970 through a computerized ballot distributed at ballparks. With all controls lifted, the new system gave an enormous advantage to teams with good attendance figures. It also limited selection to players lucky enough to find their names listed on the ballot; only two write-ins (Rico Carty in 1970 and Steve Garvey in 1974) were elected in the first 13 years of the restored fan voting. A 1974 poll of readers (mostly fans) in *The Sporting News* showed 74.2 percent of respondents dissatisfied with the voting system; many preferred to see voting returned to the players.

Why is Carl Hubbell's All-Star pitching remembered as an exceptional feat?

On July 10, 1934, Carl Hubbell, lefthanded screwball

specialist of the New York Giants, became the star of the second All-Star Game when he fanned, in succession, five future Hall of Famers: Babe Ruth, Lou Gehrig, Jimmie Foxx, Al Simmons, and Joe Cronin. Bill Dickey ended Hubbell's mastery with a single in the second inning. Hubbell's feat was so exceptional because it was difficult to strike out any of the sluggers in the American League lineup—let alone the five most dangerous long-ball hitters. The National League, leading early 4-0, eventually lost the '34 game, 9-7. Van Lingle Mungo of the Brooklyn Dodgers was the losing pitcher and Mel Harder of the Cleveland Indians the winner. But Hubbell was the star.

Why was Mickey Owen's All-Star Game homer so unexpected?

Mickey Owen, catcher for the Brooklyn Dodgers, did not hit a home run during the entire 1942 season—but he did connect as a pinch-hitter in that year's All-Star Game (the first pinch-homer in All-Star history). Needless to say, neither teammates nor rivals expected Owen's circuit clout. (Owen played in 133 games during the season.)

Why did a pitcher win an All-Star Game without throwing a pitch?

Dean Stone of the Washington Senators was the winning pitcher in the 11-9 victory of the American League in the 1954 All-Star Game. But he didn't throw a pitch. Stone entered with two outs in the top of the eighth and the Nationals leading, 9-8. With Duke Snider at bat, Red Schoendienst broke from third in an attempt to steal home. But Stone's throw to catcher Yogi Berra was in time to retire Schoendienst for the third out. Larry Doby, pinch-hitting for Stone, homered in the home eighth, helping the American

League take an 11–9 lead into the ninth, and the Americans won by that score when Virgil Trucks protected the lead for Stone, the pitcher of record.

Why was Red Schoendienst an unlikely hero in the 1950 All-Star Game?

Red Schoendienst, the spray-hitting second baseman of the St. Louis Cardinals, won the 1950 All-Star Game with a 14th-inning home run at Chicago's Comiskey Park. His blast, which gave the National League a 4–3 triumph, was totally unexpected because Schoendienst seldom hit with power during his career. He hit only seven home runs during the 1950 regular season and just 84 in a long career that included 8,479 official at-bats.

Why did the leagues play two All-Star Games for several years?

From 1959 through 1962, two All-Star Games were held each summer to provide double doses of assistance for the almost-insolvent players' pension fund. But, lagging fan interest, coupled with the reduced prestige of the All-Star Game, prompted a return to a single game in 1963.

Why was Willie Mays regarded as the king of the All-Stars?

The long-time center fielder of the Giants (in New York and San Francisco) starred in All-Star play. In 24 games, he had 23 hits, 20 runs, 40 total bases, and six stolen bases.

Why did the 1964 All-Star Game have a dramatic ending?

The American League took a 4–3 lead into the bottom of the ninth inning of the 1964 All-Star Game at New York's Shea Stadium. The Nationals pushed across the tying run before Johnny Callison, the slugging outfielder of the Philadelphia Phillies, slammed a Dick Radatz delivery over the fence for a game-winning homer.

Why did Fred Lynn create All-Star history with a home run?

Playing in the 50th anniversary All-Star Game at Chicago's Comiskey Park on July 6, 1983, Fred Lynn became the first player to hit a grand-slam home run in an All-Star Game. Lynn, center fielder of the California Angels, connected off Atlee Hammaker of the San Francisco Giants in the second inning of the game, won by the American League, 13–3. The win—which snapped an 11-game winning streak by the Nationals—also gave the American League a record for most runs scored in an All-Star Game.

Why did the media name three Most Valuable Players in the 1981 World Series?

Although writers and broadcasters have selected Most Valuable Players in the World Series since 1955, there has never been more than one winner per year until 1981, when Dodger teammates Ron Cey, Steve Yeager, and Pedro Guerrero finished in a three-way tie. Yeager and Guerrero homered twice, Guerrero led Los Angeles batters with seven runs batted in, and Cey survived a Rich Gossage beaning to hit .350 for the Series, with two hits in the decisive sixth game.

Why was a 1917 contest regarded as the ultimate pitching duel?

On May 2, 1917, opposing pitchers for the Chicago Cubs and Cincinnati Reds pitched no-hitters against each other in the same game! Fred Toney of Cincinnati completed his no-hitter through the 10th inning, when the Reds finally got to Chicago's Jim (Hippo) Vaughn for two hits and an unearned run. The Reds won, 1-0.

Why did Harry Heilmann like odd-numbered years?

The Hall of Fame outfielder, who played from 1914 through 1932, had a lifetime batting average of .342—matching Babe Ruth—but did especially well in odd-numbered years. From 1921 through 1927, Heilmann won American League batting crowns in 1921, 1923, 1925, and 1927. His averages in those years were .394, .403, .393, and .398, respectively.

Why was Wilbert Robinson more than an interested spectator when Jim Bottomley collected 12 RBIs in a single game?

Jim Bottomley of the St. Louis Cardinals knocked in a record 12 runs during a 17-3 victory over the Brooklyn Dodgers on September 16, 1924. Dodger manager Wilbert Robinson not only suffered a humiliating defeat but also watched his own record disappear in the process. On June 10, 1892, Robinson had collected 11 runs batted in while his Baltimore Orioles, then in the National League, smashed the St. Louis Cardinals, 25-4. Robinson had gone 7-for-7 in that contest with six singles and a double.

Why did Ted Williams risk his .400 season by playing on the last day?

When Ted Williams hit .406 in 1941—the last time any-one reached the .400 level—he insisted on playing both ends of a season-ending doubleheader against the Philadelphia Athletics. He took an average of .39955 into the twin bill, which would have been entered in the record books as .400, but he wanted to achieve a true .400 average. He finished at .406 after going 4-for-5 in the opener and 2-for-3 in the nightcap.

Why was Roger Maris rarely walked during his 61-homer season?

When Roger Maris of the New York Yankees was en route to a 61-home run season in 1961, the man hitting behind him in the batting order was Mickey Mantle, a better all-around hitter who also had enormous power. Pitchers hated to walk Maris, who finished the year with a .269 average, because Mantle would then have the opportunity to plate two runs with a single swing. So Maris seldom received a walk—and received the grand total of zero intentional walks. Mantle and Maris staged a two-man chase of the single-season home run mark in 1961 and ended the season as the most prolific 1-2 power punch for a single season. Mantle's season total, his career high, was 54 home runs.

Why was the numerology of Denny McLain's 30-win season unusual?

When Denny McLain posted a 31-6 record for the American League champion Detroit Tigers of 1968, it was the first time a pitcher had won at least 30 games in 34 years.

In 1934, Dizzy Dean of the St. Louis Cardinals had gone 30–7 for another championship club. What made the numerology unusual, in addition to the 1934-plus-34 sequence, is that both McLain and Dean were righthanders who wore No. 17 and pitched for pennant-winning clubs. In 1934, Dean's Cardinals beat the Tigers in a seven-game World Series; in 1968, the Tigers, with McLain, beat the Cardinals in a seven-game World Series.

Why was Hoyt Wilhelm able to pitch in more than 1,000 games?

Hoyt Wilhelm enjoyed a 21-year career that ended just shy of his 49th birthday in 1972. He was able to pitch in a record 1,070 games because he was primarily a relief specialist whose pet pitch, the knuckleball, placed little strain on his pitching arm. Lindy McDaniel ranks second to Wilhelm with 987 appearances, while Cy Young holds third place with 906.

Why was 1968 known as "the Year of the Pitcher"?

Falling batting averages, a rise in the number of low-scoring games, a total of 335 shutouts, and spectacular performances by Bob Gibson, Denny McLain, and Sandy Koufax made 1968 a pitcher's year. In no other season have pitchers from both leagues made a clean sweep of Most Valuable Player honors.

But McLain, with a 31–6 record for the Detroit Tigers, and Gibson, whose record 1.12 earned run average, 13 shutouts, and 268 strikeouts led the National League, deserved the awards. Gibson, who had a 22–9 record for the St. Louis Cardinals, proceeded to fan a record 17 Tigers (exceeding the Koufax record of 14) in the World Series opener, but lefty Mickey Lolich was a bigger surprise when he won three games, including the decisive seventh, for Detroit.

The futility of the batters in 1968 was best illustrated by American League batting king Carl Yastrzemski, who skidded from a Triple Crown performance in '67 to a rather anemic .301, lowest ever for a batting champ. One factor to be considered is that six American League starters, including McLain and two members of the Cleveland Indians (Luis Tiant and Sam McDowell), allowed an average of less than two earned runs per game.

Don Drysdale was close—thanks to a record 58 2/3 consecutive scoreless innings—but only Gibson kept his ERA under 2.00 in the National League. Neither Gaylord Perry (Giants) nor Ray Washburn (Cardinals) could do it, though they did exchange no-hitters in the same series—a baseball first—on September 17-18.

It seems "the Year of the Pitcher" was a fitting epitaph for the 1968 campaign.

Why did Steve Carlton lose his 19-strikeout game?

Although Steve Carlton, then with the St. Louis Cardinals, became the first pitcher to strike out 19 men in a game (against the New York Mets on September 15, 1969), he wound up on the short end of a 4-3 score. Between strikeouts, New York outfielder Ron Swoboda socked two Carlton deliveries over the fence—each time with a runner on base. Swoboda connected in the fourth and eighth innings. Since the initial 19-strikeout game, Carlton's record has been tied by Tom Seaver of the New York Mets and Nolan Ryan, then with the California Angels.

Chapter 9

LANGUAGE AND NICKNAMES

Introduction

Baseball's rich heritage is best expressed in its colorful language, most of which has found its way into everyday usage. Among the baseball terms now in popular use are *fan, ace, southpaw, rookie, doubleheader, rhubarb,* and *charley horse.*

If a businessman fails at a particular task, he has *struck out.* If a girl rejects a boy's advances, he can't get to *first base.* If a luncheon speaker can't keep his date, he asks for a *rain check* or, if that proves impractical, sends a *pinch-hitter.* A competitor who loses out on a bid is *shut out.*

An entirely different language is used in the dugouts, where players refer to *pull* or *spray* hitters, enjoy *taking a cut* at the plate but not at the salary table, and resent managers who use a *platoon* system or *go by the book.*

Many prominent quotations have stemmed from baseball personalities, both on the field and off. The best known is Leo Durocher's "Nice guys finish last," a rephrasing of the manager's actual quote about the New York Giants. Durocher, then running the rival Brooklyn Dodgers, was talking to a reporter when he noticed several Giants wandering around in the New York dugout, not far from manager Mel Ott.

"Look at them," said Durocher. "All nice guys but they'll finish eighth for him."

Since the National League then had eight teams, writers interpreted Durocher's remark to mean, "Nice guys finish last."

Certain other baseball lines have been quoted with more accuracy. Lefty Grove, the Hall of Fame pitcher of the '30s, made headlines when he said after a close game, "I'd rather be lucky than good." And Pirate slugger Ralph Kiner, whose home runs in the '40s and '50s paved his path to Cooperstown, coined the oft-quoted line: "Home run hitters drive Cadillacs, single hitters Fords."

The young Yogi Berra once said, "Bill Dickey is learning me all his experiences," while the seasoned Branch Rickey confided, "The trades you don't make are your best ones."

There is little denying the contributions baseball has made to American language, but considerable controversy remains about the origin of many colorful terms and expressions. There is also disagreement about the derivation of many of baseball's popular nicknames—both for teams and for individual players.

Nicknames, an important aspect of baseball language, began in baseball after more than one team surfaced in the same city. In pre-Civil War days, newspaper baseball reports referred to the New Yorks, the Bostons, or the Chicagos. But the first nickname had already been created—though it later surfaced in basketball—with the formation of Alexander Cartwright's Knickerbocker Base Ball Club of New York.

The Knicks began play in 1845, but it wasn't until 1864 that a lasting baseball nickname came into being. That was the year that the Athletic Base Ball Club of Philadelphia was born. The name Athletics remained with the team after it joined the American League in 1901 and lasted through franchise shifts to Kansas City and Oakland. Headline writers created a nickname for a nickname when they shortened Athletics to A's for the sake of brevity.

Years after the Cincinnati Red Stockings became the

first professional club in 1869, press box occupants shortened that title to Redlegs and later Reds. Baltimore teams have always been known as Orioles—for the bird of the same name—but the St. Louis Cardinals and Toronto Blue Jays acquired their nicknames for different reasons (explained in this chapter).

Like team nicknames, player nicknames sometimes come from the animal kingdom. Jim (Hippo) Vaughn weighed 230 pounds, while Walter (Rabbit) Maranville was a diminutive shortstop. Broad-shouldered Jimmie Foxx was called "the Beast" because of his strength—the same factor that inspired the nicknames King Kong for Charlie Keller and Kong Kingman for Dave Kingman. Mike (the Bear) Garcia and Fred (Big Bear) Hutchinson were burly pitchers of note, while 6-foot-6-inch Dick (the Monster) Radatz was an intimidating fireballer who frightened batters with hard-to-hit late-inning relief. Lou Gehrig's durability made him "Iron Horse" to colleagues, while Charles Radbourn, a 60-game winner in 1884, was called "Old Hoss" because of his willingness to work often and perform well.

Babe Ruth was among a handful of players who also had a nickname used only in the dugouts; teammates called him "Jidge," a deliberate mispronunciation of his given first name, George.

Ted Williams and Joe DiMaggio carried longer, more poetic nicknames, used primarily by the press. Williams was "the Splendid Splinter" and DiMaggio "the Yankee Clipper," at least in the eyes of the people who wrote about them. Such monickers are as unusual today as they were during the '40s—mainly because brevity has always dominated the world of nicknames. Whatever fits best in newspaper headlines seems to stick best in the minds of the fans as well.

The origin of baseball nicknames—as well as other baseball terminology—is outlined in the pages that follow. This chapter includes information both known and unknown, with an eye toward clearing up some long-standing discrepancies.

Why is a baseball field called a diamond?

Although Alexander Cartwright's 1845 design for a "regulation" field, with bases 90 feet apart, is actually a square, the field appears to be diamond-shaped from the catcher's perspective. (A true diamond has two acute and two obtuse angles.) Another theory on the application of the term to baseball stems from American urban planning of the 19th century. Towns were generally built around squares featuring public buildings. In the east, those squares were known as "diamonds."

Why does baseball call two games in one day a "doubleheader"?

The term "doubleheader" stems from railroading, which has provided many terms for baseball. Trains with two engines were called doubleheaders. Baseball picked up the usage for two games between the same opponents on a given day. The first baseball doubleheader was played on October 9, 1886, with Philadelphia at Detroit.

Why is a first-year player called a "rookie"?

In chess, the rook—buried in the corner of the board—is often the last piece to be used in a game. In the early part of the century, older players shunned newcomers and first-year players were often the last to capture the attention of their teammates. The term was first mentioned in print in *The Chicago Record-Herald* in 1913.

Why is a baseball sometimes called an "apple"?

The baseball has always been compared with other round objects, especially of the food variety. From time to time, players have referred to it as an apple, orange, tomato, onion, or potato—with home runs frequently referred to as "taters," slang for potatoes.

Why is the 5-4-3 double play called "around the horn"?

A 5-4-3 twin-killing goes from third base (5) to second (4) to first (3), or "around the horn" of the infield—touching all bases. (The numbers 1-9 are used in scoring to refer to each of the nine field positions.) The phrase "around the horn" stems from nautical jargon, with reference to the difficult journey around Cape Horn at the tip of South America (before the construction of the Panama Canal).

Why is a compact ballpark called a "bandbox"?

At the turn of the century, small towns often had tiny wooden stands where bands performed. Small ballparks with easy-to-reach fences, such as Ebbets Field in Brooklyn and Fenway Park in Boston, were sometimes called bandboxes because they reminded observers of the tiny band shells in small-town America.

Why is the pitcher-catcher combination called "the battery"?

In the military, one man provides ammunition for an artillery battery and another man fires it. In the analogy, the catcher is the "commander" providing ammunition (balls) for the pitcher to fire. The term "battery" was originally used to describe only the pitcher in an 1867 issue of *The Ball Players' Chronicle,* writing about a hitter in an amateur game.

Why do hitters await their turns to bat in the "on-deck circle"?

In an effort to keep games moving, and to remind both offensive and defensive teams of the batting order, hitters due to bat next kneel in a designated circle somewhere between their dugout and home plate. The term "on-deck" was first used in 1872, when a sailor was the official scorekeeper of a game between Boston and the little seaport town of Belfast, Maine.

Why are "pushed" (versus struck) infield grounders called bunts?

The word "bunt" is a derivation of "butt"—to push with the head. When batters push the bat at the ball, hoping to deaden it so that infielders can't handle it quickly, their efforts are called "bunts." Dick Pearce of the Brooklyn Atlantics dropped the first successful bunt on record in 1866.

Why is a spray hitter sometimes called a "banjo" hitter?

The term "banjo hits" originally was used to refer to "lucky" grounders that found their way through the infield (now known as "seeing-eye" singles). Ray (Snooks) Dowd of the 1924 Jersey City club was believed to be the first one to apply the banjo reference when he suggested that balls hit by "banjo" hitters make "plunk" sounds as they strike the bat. The implication was that balls hit by "banjo hitters" may turn into hits but are not necessarily hit very well. One of the famous "banjo hitters" of recent vintage was Maury Wills, who anchored shortstop for the Los Angeles Dodgers through the '60s. He turned out to be enough of a banjo hitter to finish with a .281 average after 14 seasons.

Why is a short home run also called a "Chinese" home run?

Two New York sportswriters of the '20s used the word Chinese in describing "unworthy" home runs. *New York Tribune* sports editor Bill McGeehan noted that the right field wall of the Polo Grounds, home of the New York Giants, stood just 258 feet from home plate and looked thick, low, and not very formidable—like the Great Wall of China. *The Journal's* T. A. Dorgan, who enjoyed deprecating Giant victories, had another motivation. He came from San Francisco, which had America's largest Chinese population, but did little to make it feel welcome (even denying it the right to vote). The Chinese provided a vast labor force which was willing to work for small wages. To the baseball writer, Chinese (cheap) labor and Chinese (cheap) home run seemed a simple analogy.

Why is a reserve player called a "bench-warmer"?

Because a substitute sits on a bench, which he keeps warm, he is known as a bench-warmer. The term first appeared in *The Saturday Evening Post* in 1912, when a story included this line: "A certain rich man offered a manager $10,000 if the manager would carry his son as a combination of mascot and bench-warmer."

Why is the term "bush" or "bush-leaguer" considered an insult by ball players?

Anything that is "bush" or "bush-league" is below major-league standards, according to baseball insiders. The term "bush-league" first appeared in *American Magazine* in 1910: "The scouts returned from the deepest parts of the bushes proclaiming that the crop was poor." Two years later, the same journal referred to players from such leagues as "bushers." Major-leaguers often refer to any action they dislike as "bush"—particularly a contrary decision by an umpire.

Why is a brushback pitch sometimes confused with a beanball?

A brushback is meant to warn the batter against digging in too comfortably at the plate, while a beanball is actually aimed at the batter's head (or bean). Since the intention of the pitcher is not always accurately gauged, a hitter may think a brushback is actually a beanball—an interpretation that can spark an on-the-field altercation. Early in the century, Chief Bender was accused of relying too much on the beanball by sportswriter Charley Dryden. Baseball history is dotted with references to "beanball wars," involving retaliation by one team against another that relies too heavily on inside pitches.

Why is a team's best pitcher called its "ace"?

Although some historians suggest a team's No. 1 pitcher is called its ace because the ace is the best card in the typical deck, there is another explanation. When the Cincinnati Red Stockings, the first professional team, went unbeaten in 1869, Asa Brainard pitched every game. Thus, in future years, whenever a pitcher of the period did especially well, he was called an "asa." Later, that term was shortened to "ace."

Why are baseball spectators called fans?

During the late 1880s, German-born Chris Von der Ahe, owner of the St. Louis Browns of the American Association (then a major league), was discussing a devoted St. Louis patron with sportswriter Sam Crane. "Dot feller is a regular FAN-a-tic," said the executive, emphasizing the first syllable of the last word in his thick German accent. Crane proceeded to put the abbreviated word into everyday usage.

Why are cheap outfield seats called bleachers?

Although Webster says the term bleachers was used as early as 1550, most baseball historians believe the century-long baseball use of the term began because long wooden benches used for less affluent fans changed color with exposure to the sun. They took on a "bleached" look and thus were called bleachers.

Why are scouts called "bird dogs"?

Bird dogs are trained to track birds, just as baseball scouts are trained to track potential major-league talent. Like hunting dogs, baseball's "bird dogs" are paid commissions to relay information about amateur talent to staff scouts who do the actual signing.

Why is a spectacular catch sometimes called a "circus" catch?

A spectacular catch is a crowd-pleaser—much like a circus—and has been referred to as a "circus catch" since 1885, when a Chicago sportswriter first drew the parallel. A circus catch should not be confused with a "hot dog catch," which is a routine play deliberately made to look spectacular by the fielder. Players who show off in the field are known to colleagues as "hot dogs" or "showboats." Willie Montanez, a first baseman for several National League teams in the '70s, was a leading "hot dog" fielder of recent vintage.

Why is the relief pitchers' enclosure called the "bullpen"?

At the century's turn, most American ballparks featured a large outfield billboard for Bull Durham tobacco. The company popularized its name by offering $50 to any player who hit the bull with a batted ball. Pitchers warmed up under the sign, which was often located in fair territory deep in the outfield.

Some baseball historians suggest that the bullpen got its name from the log enclosure pioneers used to fend off Indian attacks—or from the makeshift jail of Wild West days. Both enclosures were called bullpens.

There are other theories, too. In bullfighting, the bulls are kept in separate pens, then let out one at a time to do battle with the matador. In baseball, pitchers are let out one at a time to do battle with the batter.

It is also possible that the term "bullpen" might have come to baseball from railroading. Bill Friel, a former railroader who spent the summer of 1901 as a utility infielder for the Milwaukee Brewers of the American League, noted that railroads had shanties with benches at intervals along the roadbed so that workers could sit and talk during breaks. When Friel played, pitchers not working sat on a similar bench in foul territory near the right field line. He referred to it as the bullpen since the railroad bench had the same name.

Why are bloop hits called "Texas Leaguers"?

Art Sunday joined Toledo of the International League from Houston of the Texas League in 1889 and immediately proceeded to collect a series of bloop hits—too far out for the infielders and too far in for the outfielders. Because of the league he had just left, his bloops were dubbed "Texas Leaguers."

Why do unrelated players sometimes refer to each other as "cousins"?

When a pitcher is able to retire a hitter regularly without difficulty, he might refer to him privately as his cousin. The term was first used during the Babe Ruth era, when Waite Hoyt was pitching for the Yankees. Since Hoyt's day, the term "cousin" has also picked up the opposite meaning. When a hitter handles a pitcher with no trouble, that batter might refer to the pitcher as his cousin. In baseball, it's obvious that almost everything is relative.

Why is a good hitter called a "country" hitter?

Early in the game's history, most batters settled for singles, in-between shots, and Texas Leaguers instead of swinging for the fences. The rare exceptions were muscular youths from farm country, who often played ball at country fairs where they could show off their strength. Batters with power picked up the name "country fair hitters," later changed to "country hitters" or "fair country hitters."

Why is a relief pitcher called a "fireman"?

Because a relief pitcher is expected to extinguish the "fire" left smoldering by the starter (or by another reliever), he is often called a "fireman." The fireman label was first applied to Johnny (Grandma) Murphy, star reliever for the New York Yankees in the '30s. Some have taken the firefighting analogy a bit further; when the California Angels had a weak bullpen in the late '70s and early '80s, writers dubbed the corps "the Arson Squad" because it usually made a bad situation worse.

Why is a home run pitch called a "gopher ball"?

Lefty Gomez, Hall of Fame pitcher for the Yankees in the '30s, called home run pitches "gopher balls" because they "go for" homers. That term survives in current baseball lingo.

Why is a baseball referee known as an "umpire"?

In its original Middle English form, "noumpere" means an arbitrator, or extra man, called in when two parties disagreed. This third party is supposed to be neutral and therefore able to impartially settle the dispute. The "n" was eventually dropped and the word Anglicized, leaving "umpire" a part of baseball's lexicon when Alexander Cartwright wrote the original rules of 1845.

Why is third base known as "the hot corner"?

After watching Reds' third baseman Hick Carpenter catch seven scorching liners in an 1889 game, a Cincinnati sportswriter wrote, "The Brooklyns had Old Hick on the hot corner all afternoon and it's a miracle he wasn't murdered."

Why is a leg injury often called a "charley horse"?

The term "charley horse" has its roots in a lame horse named Charley; but there are several conflicting explanations. One involves the 1886 Chicago White Stockings of the National League. When morning rains postponed their scheduled afternoon game, players looked for something else to do. One found a dry race track seven miles away and the team departed *en masse*. Getting a "hot tip" from a teammate about a horse named Charley, the White Stockings placed their bets on him. As luck would have it, the "favored" horse broke last, stayed last, and finished last. The next day, when a Chicago player pulled up lame, a quick-witted colleague called him "Charley horse."

A few years later, another horse named Charley—overworked from pulling a cab in the days before the automobile—was used to drag the infield for Sioux City of the Western League. The aged, tired animal moved each leg with difficulty and seemed to suffer from arthritis. It wasn't long before players started referring to any limp or leg injury as a "charley horse."

Why is a high-bounding ball called a "Baltimore chop"?

In 1896, the hard-driving Baltimore Orioles, scourge of the National League, found they could get infield hits by banging the ball down on their rock-hard infield. The *Baltimore News* described it this way: "A middle-height ball is picked out and is attacked with a terrific swing on the upper side. The ball is made to strike the ground from five to ten feet away from the batsman and, striking the ground with force, bounds high over the head of the first or third baseman."

Why is a short major-league trial called a "cup of coffee"?

It usually doesn't take long to drink a cup of coffee, so a brief stay in the big leagues is frequently referred to as a "cup of coffee." Nearly 600 players have appeared in only one major-league game—the shortest cup-of-coffee imaginable. John Paciorek, brother of later major-league standout Tom Paciorek, hit 1.000 in the only three at-bats of his career for Houston in 1963. But the one-game career of Arliss Taylor, lefthanded pitcher with the Philadelphia Athletics, was more colorful. He worked just two innings in a late-summer start against Cleveland in 1921. Arliss, hit hard, yielded seven hits and struck out only one—but the man he fanned was Joe Sewell, the toughest man to strike out in major-league history.

Why is a home run with the bases loaded called a "grand-slam"?

Baseball takes the term "grand-slam" from the card game of bridge. The ultimate hitting achievement is clearing the bases and scoring oneself—a "slam" that is indeed "grand" because it's impossible to do any better.

Why is an unsigned player called a "holdout"?

When a player refuses to accept salary terms—particularly if he also refuses to report to spring training by March 1—he is usually referred to as a holdout. The term was first used in 1888 by the *New York Press,* but caught on five years later, when Brooklyn pitcher Tommy Lovett held himself out of the game for a full season while engaged in a bitter salary dispute.

Why is a player with great nerve said to have a lot of "moxie"?

Moxie was a Southern soft drink, similar to root beer or cola, that was said to provide a refreshing lift. Beginning around 1930, Southern players used the term to describe a player who performs well under pressure—specifically a man who can "reach back for something extra."

Why is a team's top pitcher called a "bellwether"?

A wether, or male sheep, often leads the rest of the flock and usually wears a bell. A top pitcher, capable of pitching 300 innings or winning the big game, is the team leader, or bellwether.

Why is a curveball with a wide arc called a roundhouse curve?

Like "doubleheader" and "bullpen," the baseball term "roundhouse curve" traces its origin to railroading. A "roundhouse" is a locomotive storage building marked by a revolving center floor that turns to provide tracks for each engine to enter or leave. Roundhouse curves are easier to time than sharp-breaking curves; batters, given a choice, would choose roundhouse curves over any other variety.

Why is a lefthanded pitcher called a southpaw?

Before the turn of the century, when baseball was played only during the daytime, ballparks were laid out with the pitcher's mound set east of home plate—the idea being that the sun, setting in the west, would not interfere with a batter's vision. Therefore, a lefthanded pitcher, as he prepared to face the batter, held the ball in the hand (or paw) that faced south.

Why is the letter K used to signify a strikeout in baseball scorebooks?

New York Herald baseball writer M. J. Kelly, devising a system of single-initial scoring in 1868, used "K" for strikeout because it was the last letter of the word "struck." He could not have used "S" because it might have been confused with "sacrifice" or "shortstop."

Why were line drives once known as "Titanics"?

In the wake of the Titanic disaster of April 1912, ball players referred to line drives as "Titanics" because they were sinking liners. The term fell out of dugout usage as the Titanic fell from memory.

Why are minor-league clubs known as "farm teams" for the majors?

The term "farm team" came into usage at a time when some minor-league clubs operated as independents while others affiliated with major-league clubs. The independents subsisted by selling or trading players to the majors, while the subsidized "farm teams" provided a place where big-league clubs could "grow their own" athletes and "harvest the crop."

Why is a baseball fight a "rhubarb"?

The term "rhubarb" was first used to describe a baseball brawl in 1938, when Garry Schumacher of the *New York Journal-American*, writing about a battle between the New York Giants and Brooklyn Dodgers, explained that winners of fights in Brooklyn usually forced the losers to swallow terrible-tasting rhubarb tonic.

Why is Boston's team known as the Red Sox?

Harry Wright, a former cricket player, organized the

Cincinnati Red Stockings—the first professional team—in 1869 and, together with brother George, contributed greatly as a star player to the club's wildly successful seasons in 1869–70. But the Wrights, unhappy with new ownership of the club after the 1870 campaign, accepted an enticing offer from the directors of a new team in Boston. The Wrights took the established "Red Stockings" nickname with them and it was later shortened to Red Sox. The Cincinnati team retained the same name, later shortened to Reds.

Why is San Francisco's team called the Giants?

The New York National League team, which moved to San Francisco in 1958, was originally known as the Green Stockings and later as the Mutuals. It acquired its present nickname in 1885, when manager Jim Mutrie jumped for joy after a big play and cried, "My Giants!" A sportswriter heard him and the name stuck.

Why did Giant fans give the Dodgers their nickname?

Brooklyn, always an arch-rival for the affection of New York fans, was crisscrossed by numerous trolley-car lines at the turn of the century. Brooklynites therefore were known in not-so-polite circles as "trolley dodgers." In a derogatory reference to Brooklyn baseball, Giant fans called the Brooklyn team "Trolley Dodgers" and the name was abbreviated. The team had earlier been known as the Bridgegrooms, Superbas, Atlantics, Kings, and Robins.

Why did the White Sox take their nickname from the National League?

"White Stockings" had been a popular name in Chicago

long before the Chicago White Sox became a charter member of the American League in 1901. The National League franchise now known as the Cubs first used the "White Stockings" label because their uniforms came equipped with white stockings. The National League team changed its nickname to "Colts" in 1869 after manager Cap Anson appeared in a Syracuse, New York play called *A Runaway Colt.*

The discarded "White Stockings" title (later shortened to White Sox by sportswriters Carl Green and I. E. Sanborn) was picked up by the American League entry in an attempt to capture an early fan following.

Why is Pittsburgh's team called the Pirates?

Although the Pittsburgh club's players had a fearsome look around 1890, the team was known as the Pirates because it signed a player who rightfully belonged to another club. Writers also referred to the club as Buccaneers (another term for Pirates), or Bucs for short.

Why is the New York American League franchise known as the Yankees?

The New York Yankees were not a charter member of the American League. There was no New York franchise when the league began play in 1901. The team that became the New York Highlanders in 1903 began life as the Baltimore Orioles. New York's original nickname stemmed from the elevated position of its park at the entrance of Manhattan Island. New York carried the name "Highlanders" for nearly a dozen years—"Hilltoppers" was also used at times—before *New York Press* sports editor Jim Price and *New York Globe* newsman Mark Roth (later a Yankee official) decided either name was too long to fit into a headline. They created the name "Yankees," which went on to become one of the best-known nicknames in the history of sports.

Why is the St. Louis team known as the Cardinals?

Contrary to popular belief, the St. Louis Cardinals did not get their nickname from the bird. The team was initially known as the Maroons, and then as the Browns, because of their uniform color. When the club switched to new red-tinged suits at the century's change, a female fan, expressing delight with the new outfits, shouted, "My, what a lovely shade of cardinal!" Writers overheard, and the nickname stuck. But the St. Louis Browns were not dead; when the Milwaukee club transferred to St. Louis in 1903, it resurrected the old nickname and cavorted about in flannels fringed in brown. The Browns became the Baltimore Orioles in 1954 and took on the nickname of the well-known bird that has always symbolized baseball in that city. The only other team bearing a bird-related nickname is Toronto, which began life as the Blue Jays in 1977 after a fan suggested the blue jay is known for its tenacity and aggressiveness.

Why is Oakland's club known as "Athletics"?

In 1864, the Athletic club of Philadelphia was formed. The name Athletics remained in use when that club evolved into a team and was used through franchise shifts to Kansas City and Oakland. The club often wore a script "A" on its hats and uniform shirts, so writers began using the word "A's" interchangeably with "Athletics."

Why was Cincinnati's team once called "Redlegs"?

Two years before it began paying players in 1869, Cincinnati's team was known as the Red Stockings. That was often shortened to Reds by press box occupants who wanted to save time and space in their papers. The name "Redlegs" was substituted at times when it was politically dangerous to be identified as Reds.

Why are many player nicknames taken from the animal kingdom?

Physical size and strength—or lack of it—is most apparent among athletes. In baseball, a game where nicknames prevail, it is only logical to expect nicknames to derive from comparisons between man and beast. Rabbit Maranville, a diminutive shortstop with large ears, had a nickname that fit so well that even his wife didn't call him by his given name of Walter. Dick (the Monster) Radatz, Mike (Bear) Garcia, and Jim (Hippo) Vaughn were hulking giants. Ron Cey earned "the Penguin" nickname because of his walk, while Charles (Old Hoss) Radbourn, a 60-game winner in 1884, got his because of his willingness to work often. Joe (Ducky) Medwick got his nickname from an adoring female fan, who screamed, "Isn't he a ducky wucky of a ball player?"

Why did a ball player give his nickname to the Speaker of the House?

Tip O'Neill, Speaker of the U.S. House of Representatives in 1984, got his nickname from a ball player named James O'Neill, baseball's batting champion in 1887. O'Neill hit .492 (walks counted as hits that year) and specialized in fouling off pitched balls to make pitchers work harder. The harder they worked, the more likely O'Neill would walk, inflating his batting average. Because of the volume of foul tips he produced on purpose, teammates on the St. Louis club starting calling him "Tip." The name caught on among fans—especially in the Irish-American community where he was a hero. Among the Irish-Americans who named their sons after him was Thomas P. O'Neill of Massachusetts, father of the boy who later became Speaker of the House. Like his father, the long-term Congressman developed a strong affection for baseball.

Why was Ty Cobb called "the Georgia Peach"?

Ty Cobb hailed from Georgia, the Peach State. In Cobb's case, the "Georgia Peach" monicker applied well; no one has topped his .367 lifetime batting average.

Why was Denton True Young better known as Cy Young?

Cy Young, whose 511 lifetime victories may never be equalled, was an innocent farm boy when he first tried out for the Canton, Ohio, team late in the last century. Hoping to impress the manager, he fired a blazing fastball past the Canton batters. Twice, the catcher missed the pitch and it smashed into the wooden grandstand behind home plate, sending wood splinters in all directions. The batter told his manager, "Sign that kid, boss. He did more damage to your grandstand than a cyclone." Young was called "Cyclone" Young for a while before the nickname was shortened to "Cy."

Why was George Herman Ruth called "Babe"?

Babe Ruth's nickname derives from his youth. Signed to

a contract by Jack Dunn's Baltimore Orioles of the International League in 1914, the 19-year-old Ruth had a round, cherubic face which accentuated his youth. The first time he appeared in uniform, a veteran teammate said, "Look at Dunnie's new babe!" The nickname was reinforced later that spring after Ruth nearly decapitated himself while joyriding in the elevator of Baltimore's training camp hotel in Fayetteville, North Carolina. After a stern lecture on safety from Dunn and several teammates, Ruth looked downcast. An older player, taking pity on him, shook his head and said, "You know, you're just a babe in the woods."

Why didn't Connie Mack use his real name in baseball?

Connie Mack, as a player and later as long-time manager and owner of the Philadelphia Athletics, felt his given name of Cornelius McGillicuddy was too long for players, fans or press to remember. He was one of numerous athletes who shortened their names to aid their careers. Mack also had several nicknames: "Slats," because of his lean frame; "Mr. Baseball," because of his immense knowledge of the game; and "The Tall Tactician," because he was a master strategist who projected a lanky image, accented by his constant appearance in high starched-collar street clothes.

Why was Charles Dillon Stengel better known as Casey?

Long-time major-league manager, Casey Stengel, who was also a better-than-average outfielder for several clubs, used to sign his name "Charles Stengel, K.C.," with the initials representing his hometown of Kansas City. Spotting that designation on his luggage, players picked up the "K.C." and dropped the "Charles." Some historians suggest

Stengel got his well-known nickname from the poem "Casey at the Bat," since the central character struck out in the end. Stengel fanned frequently early in his career, but overcame that reputation by homering twice for the New York Giants against the Yankees in the 1923 World Series.

Why were Al Schacht and Max Patkin each known as "the Clown Prince of Baseball"?

Al Schacht was more successful at clowning than at pitching. After three so-so seasons with the Washington Senators (1919–21), he became a coach and performed assorted madcap antics from the coaching box. He and Nick Altrock, a teammate with Washington, decided to pool their resources and take their act on the road. They toured ball parks, mostly in the minors, as a pregame promotion. Schacht referred to himself as "the Clown Prince of Baseball," a title later adopted by Max Patkin, a one-man show who began his clowning career in 1951. Patkin, known for his uncanny ability to twist his body into all kinds of odd positions, traveled more than three million miles on tour. In a career that stretched more than 30 years, Patkin performed in more than 4,000 ball parks.

Why was Harold Traynor better known as "Pie"?

Pie Traynor got his nickname as a kid when he ran grocery errands for his mother. The shopping list invariably ended in "pie."

Why did their fastballs produce nicknames for Hall of Fame pitchers Walter Johnson and Christy Mathewson?

Mathewson, long-time star for the New York Giants,

was called "Big Six" after a speedy fire engine of his era. Johnson was known as "The Big Train" because locomotives were known for their speed and power—just as Johnson was known for his smoking fastball.

Why was Carl Hubbell called "the Meal Ticket"?

Carl Hubbell, long-time star lefty of the New York Giants, was the stopper of the Giant pitching staff, the man who could "keep groceries on his manager's table." Thus, he was called "the Meal Ticket."

Why did Pepper Martin have two nicknames?

Always an aggressive, gung-ho player—the Pete Rose of the '30s—John Martin picked up his "Pepper" nickname at Fort Smith, Arkansas, where he played in 1925. Team president Blake Harper hung the nickname "Pepper" on Martin because he added spice to the play of the Fort Smith team. Later, Martin's heroics in the 1931 World Series victory by the St. Louis Cardinals over the Philadelphia Athletics led a St. Louis newsman to call him "the Wild Horse of the Osage," in reference to Martin's swift play in center field, his daring base running, and his Oklahoma heritage (Oklahoma is home of the Osage Indian tribe). Martin hit .500 in the '31 World Series to deprive Connie Mack of a third straight World Championship.

Why was Lou Gehrig called "The Iron Horse"?

The nickname "Iron Horse" was a tribute to Lou Gehrig's remarkable durability. Until sidelined in 1939 by the effects of amyotrophic lateral sclerosis—the neuromuscular disease that took his life in 1941—the powerful first baseman played in a record 2,130 consecutive games for the New York Yankees. Seemingly made of iron, Gehrig left behind a .340 lifetime batting average and 493 home runs. He won one batting, two slugging, three home run, and five runs batted in titles—and holds the American League record for most runs batted in for a season, 184.

Why was Charlie Gehringer known as "the Mechanical Man"?

Charlie Gehringer, Hall of Fame second baseman for the Tigers for almost 20 years (1924-42), went about his business so smoothly and quietly that few fans noticed. But he compiled a .320 lifetime average, played a near-perfect second base, and hit with some power (184 lifetime homers). It was teammate Doc Cramer who first called him "the Mechanical Man" because the game seemed so easy for him.

Why was Johnny Murphy called "Grandma"?

There are two theories about the derivation of the Yankee relief ace Johnny Murphy's unusual nickname. The most common attributes it to the "rocking-chair motion" Murphy used when he pitched. A second notes that Murphy's New York teammates in the '30s called him "Grandma" because he frequently complained about meals and accommodations on the road. Teammates insisted he acted like a grandmother.

Why was Joe DiMaggio called "the Yankee Clipper"?

Because he was such a swift, smooth center fielder,

Yankee broadcaster Arch McDonald pinned the "Yankee Clipper" tag on Joe DiMaggio, a player whose grace reminded him of the famed New York-to-Boston train. DiMaggio was also known as "Joltin' Joe" because of his hitting heroics. A 1941 song introduced by Les Brown made that reference after DiMaggio's famous 56-game hitting streak.

Why was Joe DiMaggio's brother called "the Little Professor"?

Joe DiMaggio's younger brother Dominic just didn't look like a ball player. Small and bespectacled, he seemed almost out of place in a baseball uniform. Dom DiMaggio looked like a college professor instead of an outfielder, but he played for the Boston Red Sox from 1940 to 1953, with three years out for military service during World War II. The 5-9, 168-pound righthanded hitter had a .298 lifetime batting average with 87 home runs.

Why were the Walker brothers known as "Dixie" and "the Hat"?

Fred (Dixie) Walker and Harry (the Hat) Walker, baseball brothers who won National League batting titles with different teams in the '40s, earned their nicknames in different ways. Fred, who played from 1931 to 1949 for the Yankees, White Sox, Tigers, Dodgers, and Pirates, was called "Dixie" because his father Ewart had worn the same tag as a minor-league pitcher in 1909 (presumably because of his Southern accent and mannerisms). Harry, who was with the Cards, Phils, Cubs, and Reds (1940–55), had a habit of tugging at his cap between pitches, thus wearing out nearly two-dozen caps per season (the average player uses three). Harry was sometimes called "Little Dixie," but that nickname never caught on. But Dixie's other nickname, "the

People's Choice" (pronounced "Cherce" in Brooklynese), was widely used by fans of the Brooklyn Dodgers.

Why was LeRoy Paige known as "Satchel"?

LeRoy Paige picked up his famous nickname "Satchel" as a youth when he carried luggage at the Mobile, Alabama train station. Despite his true age, Satchel Paige always seemed youthful. Late in his long career, he said, "Age is a matter of mind over matter; if you don't mind, it doesn't matter."

Satchel Paige was at least 42 years old when he first reached the Major Leagues with the 1948 Cleveland Indians. He had been restricted to the Negro Leagues during his prime because of the major-league "color line." Pitching since 1926, Paige was still active as recently as 1965, when he hurled three innings as a publicity stunt for the Kansas City Athletics against the Boston Red Sox. His age at that time was believed to be at least 59.

Sportswriters sometimes referred to Paige as "Old Man River," after the song from *Show Boat,* because he always kept on rolling—even though men half his age fell by the wayside.

Why was Harold Reese called "Pee Wee"?

Harold (Pee Wee) Reese was not so nicknamed because of his size; at 5-foot-10, he was taller than most other National League shortstops. Reese, who hit .269 with 126 homers for the Brooklyn Dodgers between 1940 and 1958, got his nickname at age 12, when he won a marble-shooting contest known as a "pee wee championship." According to Duke Snider (and many sportswriters), despite his nickname, it was Pee Wee who kept the great Dodger teams of the '40s and '50s on their toes. He was their leader.

Why is Phil Rizzuto known as "Scooter"?

Phil Rizzuto, the popular broadcaster of the New York Yankees, acquired his nickname of "Scooter" long before he became the team's regular shortstop in 1941. During his amateur days, rivals noted the way the 5-foot, 6-inch infielder "scooted" after hard-hit grounders. Such agility, coupled with his diminutive stature, produced the nickname, and it stuck like glue—even after Rizzuto traded his glove for the Yankee microphone in 1957.

Why is Lawrence Peter Berra better known as "Yogi"?

Hall of Fame catcher Yogi Berra, later a pennant-winning manager in both leagues, earned his nickname as a youth in St. Louis. Young Berra had a habit of crossing his legs while watching movies and was doing just that when he and some friends went to see an Indian travelogue that featured a Hindu fakir. Jack Maguire, later with the New York Giants, turned to Berra and said, "You know, you look just like that Yogi. That's what I'm going to call you—Yogi Berra!"

Why did Mickey Cochrane's nickname become Mickey Mantle's real name?

Gordon Stanley (Mickey) Cochrane, a Hall of Fame catcher and manager, got his nickname when he played for the Dover minor-league team in the Eastern Shore League. He looked Irish, so his manager started calling him Mickey. Mantle's father, a Cochrane fan, later gave the name to his son in tribute.

Why did Willie Mays get the nickname of "the Say Hey Kid"?

Sportswriter Barney Kremenko pinned the name "the Say Hey Kid" on Willie Mays when he first reached the majors with the New York Giants. The gifted center fielder, who appeared to be timid in his overwhelming surroundings, said little other than "Hey!" when he first came up from Minneapolis, then a Giant farm.

Why was Orlando Cepeda called "the Baby Bull"?

Orlando Cepeda, a slugging first baseman for the San Francisco Giants and several other clubs (1958–1974), was the son of "the Babe Ruth of Puerto Rico," a man fans knew as "the Bull." So Orlando became "the Baby Bull"—though he was hardly a baby anything to National League pitchers. In 1967, Cepeda's slugging led the St. Louis Cardinals to the World Championship as he became the first unanimous choice in the history of National League Most Valuable Player voting. Two years later, Cepeda helped his new team, the Atlanta Braves, become the first winner of the National League West as baseball inaugurated divisional play. Cepeda was best-known for his years of service with the San Francisco Giants, where he teamed with Willie Mays and Willie McCovey to form a formidable trio of sluggers in the heart of the lineup.

Why was Phil Regan called "the Vulture" by other pitchers?

In 1966, Phil Regan was a 29-year-old righthanded relief pitcher who provided airtight late-inning pitching for the pennant-winning Los Angeles Dodgers. Regan compiled a

14-1 record, 21 saves, and a 1.62 earned run average in 65 appearances, spanning 117 innings. It seemed he would get a win or a save every time he appeared, while other pitchers worked harder and more often with nothing to show for their efforts. Tired of seeing Regan pile up his incredible record—often working an inning or less per outing—starter Claude Osteen pinned "the Vulture" tag on him. Other hurlers in Dodger blue, and soon pitchers on other clubs, subsequently referred to a save as a "vulch."

Why did Sandy Koufax and Don Drysdale call Hank Aaron "Bad Henry"?

Reverse nicknames are common in baseball. Hank Aaron was called "Bad Henry" because he was so good—just as George Haas was called "Mule" because he was so fast. Aaron was also called "Bad Henry" because his arrival at the plate often meant bad news for rival pitchers.

Why did Reggie Jackson win the nickname of "Mr. October"?

Reggie Jackson has always played his best baseball in postseason games—helping the Oakland Athletics become World Champions in 1972-73-74 (Jackson missed the '72 World Series with an injury) and the New York Yankees do likewise in 1977-78. Several other Jackson-led teams won divisional titles without making it to the Series. In 1982, when Jackson was in his first year with the California Angels, he hit his 18th postseason home run, tying Mickey Mantle (who had 18 World Series homers before the advent of divisional play). Other than Babe Ruth, who did it twice, Jackson is the only man to hit three homers in a World Series game (1977). He had a record five home runs against the Dodgers in that six-game classic. Since Jackson seems to save his heroics for postseason play, which takes place in October, he is known as "Mr. October."

Why were three members of a World Championship club known as "the Three Stooges"?

Ken Singleton, slugging designated hitter for the Baltimore Orioles, gave the team's seventh, eighth, and ninth-place hitters the nickname "Three Stooges" (after the inept movie trio) because they were weak hitters on a strong-hitting 1983 team. Rich Dauer hit .235, Rick Dempsey .231, and Todd Cruz .208 during the regular season but maintained their spots in the batting order with strong defensive play. In the five-game World Series victory against the Philadelphia Phillies, Dempsey tried to prove he didn't belong in the group; he hit .385 (5-for-13) with four doubles, a home run, and two runs batted in—good enough to earn the car presented annually to the Most Valuable Player of the World Series.

Chapter 10

HONORS, TRADITIONS, AND SUPERSTITIONS

Introduction

Baseball is a game of tradition; it is slow to change. It is, in the words of long-time club owner Bill Veeck, a game to be savored and not gulped.

When change does occur in baseball, it is often implemented many years after it was originally suggested.

Consider the designated hitter rule, introduced by the American League in 1973. Although it was considered a radical innovation, the idea for the designated hitter had brewed for 45 years—since it was first proposed by National League president John Heydler in 1928.

The seventh-inning stretch, spring training, and the trading of players are baseball traditions that trace their roots to the 19th century. Uniform numbering, first tried before the century changed, became universal shortly after the Yankees became the first team to wear numerals regularly in 1929 (Babe Ruth wore no number when he hit his epic 60th home run in 1927). Retiring of uniform numbers as a tribute to great stars is a relatively new tradition; it began much more recently.

Perhaps the biggest tradition in baseball is the act of honoring outstanding performances. Each year, the American and National League select Most Valuable Players,

Rookies of the Year, Managers of the Year, and Comeback Players of the Year, as well as recognizing the best pitchers through annual Cy Young Awards and fielding wizardry through Gold Glove Awards.

The very best players, managers, umpires, and media representatives may receive baseball's biggest honor: enshrinement in the National Baseball Hall of Fame in Cooperstown, New York. Induction day for new members each summer is a festive affair featuring an exhibition game between two major-league teams. That game is played at Doubleday Field, believed to be the site where Abner Doubleday "invented" baseball in 1839 (most baseball historians say the Doubleday story is mere legend).

Despite the controversy over Abner Doubleday, the Hall of Fame opened in 1939, a year chosen to coincide with the centennial of Doubleday's alleged invention. Through the years, many baseball insiders have sought to move the Hall of Fame out of Cooperstown, a rural hamlet without easy access by automobile or mass transportation (especially during the harsh winters of Upstate New York). That movement has failed, however, because the Cooperstown location is *traditional* even if not entirely justifiable.

Baseball is steeped in tradition. As long ago as 1910, William Howard Taft became the first President to throw out the first ball on Opening Day; many others have followed suit—even after the game abandoned Washington in 1972. When a President is unavailable, other celebrities have been selected for first-ball ceremonies. That is especially true on Opening Day, when ceremony mixes with celebration as the new season opens in high spirits.

The seventh-inning stretch is another baseball tradition—and some historians suggest that President Taft was responsible for that one too. Others contend the practice of rising before the home seventh began in the 19th century, when college fans, seated on uncomfortable wood board benches, rose to stretch their weary frames.

Taking batting practice, shagging flies, and even chewing tobacco are among the many traditions players and fans take for granted. But loving good-byes to retiring stars are emotional affairs invariably etched in memory. Few witnesses will forget the tearful Yankee Stadium speeches made by Lou Gehrig and, years later, Babe Ruth—once-powerful sluggers wracked by illnesses that would claim their lives.

Some stars simply announce their retirement, then go out with a bang. Ted Williams, who homered in his last at-bat, was one of those. Carl Yastrzemski and Johnny Bench, who were not, still had the satisfaction of receiving 'round-the-league salutes, from rivals as well as home fans, before they bowed out in October 1983.

Unlike endings, beginnings are not necessarily historic occasions; if they are, only those who can foresee the future know about them. But spring training is as much a baseball tradition as the planned farewell.

The six-week training grind allows managers to decide who will make the opener and who will receive farewell notices. It also allows players to prep for the 162-game regular season of night games, doubleheaders, constant travel, and a fishbowl existence caused by the national media spotlight.

Eighteen teams train in Florida, seven in Arizona, and one in California. But it has not always been that way—especially when wartime travel restrictions were in force.

Even during the spring, players practice various superstitious rituals—mainly in the belief that they will try anything they think can help them. Many superstitions are also traditions: not mentioning a no-hitter in progress, not stepping on the foul lines when changing sides, not wearing uniform No. 13, and not talking to anyone before big games.

Superstitions have developed over time, but even those few relatively recent in origin have become entrenched in the minds of the major-leaguers. It is traditional to be superstitious in baseball but it is also traditional to deny that one believes in superstition, once called "the religion of feeble minds" by Edmund Burke.

This chapter examines the traditions of baseball, from

the honors players covet to the superstitions they deny—
with much more in between.

Why is the Baseball Hall of Fame located in Cooperstown?

The sleepy Upstate New York village of Cooperstown—
halfway between Schenectady and Utica—was chosen as
the site for the Baseball Hall of Fame and Museum because a
special commission reported in 1907 that Abner Doubleday
"invented" baseball in Cooperstown in 1839. Most historians
now believe that Doubleday, who was a West Point plebe at
the time, did not even get to Cooperstown in 1839. Nev-
ertheless, the Hall of Fame opened in 1939, 100 years after
the alleged Doubleday invention.

Why has there never been a unanimous selec-tion to the Hall of Fame?

Too many factors weigh against a unanimous selection.
Some voters feel no candidate deserves enshrinement in his
first year of eligibility no matter what his record. Hank
Aaron, the all-time home run champion, received 97.8 percent of the vote, second highest percentage to Ty Cobb in
voting for the Hall, but was left off nine ballots completely.
When Willie Mays was elected, 23 writers omitted his name.

Why is baseball's biggest loser in the Hall of Fame?

Baseball's biggest loser is also its biggest winner. Cy
Young, a righthander who pitched from 1890 to 1911, won 511
games and lost 313 (though there is some dispute over the
accuracy of old records). In Young's day, hurlers worked
more frequently and relievers were seldom used—factors

which account for the unusually large number of decisions he recorded.

Why is a pitcher with a losing record enshrined in Cooperstown?

Satchel Paige was only 28–31 in the majors, and he didn't make the grade until he was at least 42 years old—when the 1948 Cleveland Indians purchased his contract shortly after the "color line" was broken by Jackie Robinson's arrival in Brooklyn. Paige was immortalized because of his years of stardom in the Negro Leagues and on the barnstorming circuit. A wiry righthander with pinpoint control, Paige was rated by many who saw him as the greatest pitcher in baseball history

Why are there no relief pitchers in the Baseball Hall of Fame?

Because the science of relief pitching is relatively new—making the career reliever a recent occupational development—Hall of Fame electors may not be weighing relief pitching statistics heavily enough when they consider candidates for enshrinement. The leading Cooperstown candidate among relievers is Hoyt Wilhelm, the only man in major-league history to pitch in more than 1,000 games. Wilhelm posted 123 relief wins, 227 saves, and a 2.52 earned run average before ending his 21-year career at age 48 in 1972, but even those statistics have been overshadowed by the record of Rollie Fingers, the American League's Most Valuable Player and Cy Young Award winner in 1981. Fingers has saved more than 300 games (a major-league record) since coming to the big leagues with the Oakland Athletics in 1969. Fingers will not be eligible for the Hall of Fame until five years after his retirement from the active ranks.

Most managers paid scant attention to relievers until 1950, when Jim Konstanty of the Philadelphia Phillies worked in 74 games, all in relief, and pitched the "Whiz Kids" to a surprise National League pennant. Although Konstanty was named Most Valuable Player after the season, it was another 10 years before teams began to depend heavily on relief pitchers. By 1983, however, relief specialists dotted the rosters of all 26 big-league clubs.

Why were Hall of Fame requirements waived for Addie Joss?

When a player's career is curtailed by death or injury, eligibility requirements for the Hall of Fame, such as the mandatory five-year waiting period for enshrinement, are sometimes waived. Addie Joss was one game short of becoming a 10-year man in the majors when he was stricken by tubercular meningitis just before the 1911 season opened. A week later, he died at age 31. Joss won 160 games and recorded a career earned run average of 1.88, second only to the 1.82 mark of Ed Walsh. Although his record was remarkable, Hall of Fame eligibility is restricted to those who have pitched at least 10 years. Taking into account the sudden illness which claimed his life just short of his 10th season, however, electors lifted the restriction and enshrined Joss posthumously in 1978.

Why do uniforms have numbers?

Identification of players, coaches, and managers was difficult in the early years—mainly because megaphone men (the forerunners of public address announcers) were usually too ineffective to be heard all over the ball park. The Cincinnati Reds of the American Association, then a major league, experimented with numbers for a short time during the 1888 season but the idea failed to catch on. The Cleveland Indians of the American League took the field on June 2, 1916, with numerals pinned to their shirts by business manager Robert McRoy but, again, the concept proved to be short-lived. It took more than a dozen years before the New York Yankees became the first team to wear numbers on a regular basis (in 1929). Once teams started wearing numerals, identification of field personnel became easy for fans, who only had to match shirt numbers with names and positions listed in scorecards. The American League mandated numbering by all clubs in 1931 and the National League did likewise two years later. Modern teams often outfit their players in uniforms bearing player names as well as numbers.

Why do teams retire uniform numbers?

Teams honor retired or deceased stars by retiring their numbers. More than 40 major-leaguers have been honored in this fashion. Hank Aaron's 44 and Casey Stengel's 37 have both been retired by two clubs. The New York Yankees lead the majors with nine retired numbers, honoring Babe Ruth (3), Lou Gehrig (4), Joe DiMaggio (5), Mickey Mantle (7), Yogi Berra and Bill Dickey (8), Thurman Munson (15), Whitey Ford (16), and Stengel (37). The Yankees are the only team to retire the same number (8) twice—once for Berra and once for Dickey.

Why does one retired number belong to an owner?

After the California Angels finished first in the American League's Western Division in 1982, the team decided to give a special tribute to Gene Autry, the erstwhile "Singing Cowboy" who owned the team. They picked out Uniform No. 26—because Autry was so supportive he seemed like the team's "26th man" on the roster (rosters are limited to 25 players)—and retired it in his honor.

Why did the Detroit Tigers fail to retire Ty Cobb's number?

Ty Cobb won a record 12 batting titles during his career (1905–28) and retired with a .367 lifetime average, the best in baseball history. But the Tigers were unable to retire his number in tribute because the team did not wear numbers during Cobb's tenure in Tiger livery. Cobb left the club in 1926, three years before the New York Yankees became the first team to wear numbers on a regular basis (making player identification easier for spectators as well as scorers, umpires, and other players). The Cincinnati Reds of 1888, the Cleveland Indians of 1916, and the St. Louis Cardinals of 1924-25 had experimented with sleeve numerals, but those first attempts at baseball numerology were only fleeting previews of what was to come years later.

Why was Honus Wagner's number retired if he wore no number as a player?

Honus Wagner's playing days with the Pittsburgh Pirates ended in 1917, long before teams started wearing numbers, but he spent many years with the Bucs as a coach. It was the No. 33 he wore in that role that the Pirates eventually retired in tribute to the great Hall of Fame shortstop.

Why did Babe Ruth wear No. 3?

When the Yankees decided to put numerals on the backs of their players, the most obvious system was to assign them in the sequence the players batted. So Ruth got No. 3, Lou Gehrig No. 4, and so on.

Why was someone able to wear No. 3 after Ruth and No. 7 before Mickey Mantle?

Cliff Mapes, an outfielder who hit .242 in five seasons, happened to reach the majors in 1948, before the Yankees had retired Ruth's number. When the team decided to honor the dying slugger on Babe Ruth Day that summer, the number was retired and Mapes had to pick a new uniform. He chose No. 7, a number he relinquished when he left the team before Mantle arrived in 1951. Mantle's number was eventually retired as well.

Why do teams have spring training?

Spring training is one of the oldest traditions of baseball. Even before the Boston Nationals went to New Orleans before the 1884 season, teams limbered up for the season in warmer climes to the south. The first spring training regimen was undertaken by a newly-organized touring club from Chicago in February 1870. Tom Foley, molding top semipro talent in an effort to beat the undefeated Cincinnati Red Stockings, took his Chicago White Stockings to New Orleans to prepare for the challenge (it didn't help). Another Chicago White Stockings team—this one a charter member of the National League (founded in 1876)—is credited with staging the first "official" spring training in 1886. That spring manager Cap Anson, disgusted with the extra weight his athletes had put on during the winter, decided the proper therapy would be exercise and conditioning, coupled with dips in the soothing waters, at Hot Springs, Arkansas.

Why did Florida become such a hotbed of spring training activity?

Most teams worked out under the stands of their home parks, or traveled from one southern city to another, before the New York Giants established the first spring training headquarters, at Marlin Springs, Texas, in 1908. The Chicago Cubs followed suit, opening up on Catalina Island, off the coast of Los Angeles. Teams made occasional visits to Florida—notably the Philadelphia Athletics in Jacksonville—but it took a series of letters from former Pittsburgh resident Al Lang to spark serious interest in what is now "the Sunshine State." Lang, a baseball insider who had gone south for health reasons in 1911, initially contacted Pirate owner Barney Dreyfuss, a close friend, after he read that Pittsburgh had experienced snow and cold weather at Hot Springs, Arkansas.

When Dreyfuss couldn't be persuaded to come to St. Petersburg, Lang turned his attention to Branch Rickey, then running the St. Louis Browns. The Browns played in St. Petersburg in 1914 and the Philadelphia Phillies succeeded them the following spring. But, it wasn't until 1922 that the sleepy fishing village of 3,000 struck gold. The Boston Braves decided to train in St. Petersburg, bringing thousands of snow-weary New Englanders south to watch. They were joined five years later by the powerful New York Yankees. St. Petersburg has had baseball every spring since—and other Florida cities, realizing the benefits, have also attracted teams. By 1984, 18 of the 26 clubs trained in Florida, seven in Arizona and one in California.

Why are spring training exhibition games referred to as Grapefruit League or Cactus League games?

Since 18 teams train in Florida, the heart of the nation's citrus fruit industry, exhibition games in Florida are commonly called Grapefruit League contests, while games in Arizona are referred to as Cactus League encounters because of the preponderance of cactus plants in the desert southwest. Spring training results don't count and the listing of Grapefruit or Cactus League standings in newspapers is intended solely to satisfy baseball-starved fans hungering for news of their favorite teams.

Why is spring training an unlikely indicator of the season to come?

During spring training, optimism reigns supreme in every major-league camp. Players, coaches, and managers are relaxed because game results don't count. Stadiums are so intimate that players and umpires often converse with fans while games are in progress. All fields have natural grass, most games are played in daylight, and experimentation is the rule. Players try new positions, freshmen get a chance to impress, pitchers loosen their arms by working in stretches of three or four innings, and veterans are often excused from long bus rides. "Spring training is made for the owners, managers, and general managers," according to Hall of Famer Ralph Kiner.

Why did the New York Highlanders once train in Bermuda?

Arthur Irwin, business manager of the New York Highlanders (who became the Yankees during the 1913 season), had visited Bermuda—then developing its reputation as a semitropical winter paradise—and persuaded owner Frank Farrell that the 1913 Highlanders would become contenders if they trained there. Irwin noted that the Jersey City club had held training exercises in Bermuda in 1912 and would return to provide the New Yorkers with exhibition game competition. Farrell agreed and a diamond was laid out behind the team's hotel in Hamilton, the capital. The spring training period progressed well, but the regular season was another story. The team suffered 94 losses to finish next-to-last in the eight-team American League. Apparently the Highlanders/Yankees learned that it's not where you train your horses but what kind of horses you train that really matters in baseball.

Why did teams train in the north during World War II?

Because long train trips by major-league teams tied up transportation vital to the nation's war effort, Baseball Commissioner Kenesaw Mountain Landis instituted "the Landis Line" for the spring training periods of 1943-44-45. Under this ruling, no team could train south of the Ohio or Potomac rivers nor west of the Mississippi (with the exception of the two St. Louis clubs). As a result, "spring" training datelines in 1943 came from such places as French Lick, Indiana (Cubs); College Park, Maryland (Senators); Bear Mountain, New York (Dodgers); Washington, D.C. (Braves); Atlantic City, New Jersey (Yankees); and Wilmington, Delaware (Phillies).

The New York Giants returned to the Lakewood, New Jersey site they had last used in 1897, while the St. Louis Cardinals—ousted by flooding in Cairo, Illinois—finished their 1945 spring training at home.

On cold or snowy days, teams made use of whatever indoor facilities (such as armories or university gyms) were readily available. The Brooklyn Dodgers, for example, regularly worked out inside the West Point fieldhouse when conditions precluded outdoor play at Bear Mountain.

Why do the Cincinnati Reds always open the season at home?

Because Cincinnati had the first professional team, the National League salutes that heritage by allowing the Reds to open at home every year. The Reds have done so every year they have been in the league (they were out from 1881 to 1889) except for 1877, when rain forced cancellation of the opener for three days. Tired of waiting for the skies to clear, the Red Stockings boarded a boat for nearby Louisville, where they opened the season on a dry diamond.

Why did Washington always open the American League season at home?

When Washington had a team (until 1972), it always opened one day ahead of American League rivals as a salute to the nation's capital. Presidents were often in attendance. Benjamin Harrison was the first incumbent President to watch a game—on June 6, 1892, when Cincinnati topped Washington (then a National League team), 7-4. William Howard Taft was the first Chief Executive to throw out a first pitch, on April 14, 1910.

Why are doubleheaders so popular?

Because fans get two games for the price of one, doubleheaders are extremely popular. Modern baseball economics, however, has restricted the scheduling of doubleheaders because teams like to gain as many separate admissions as possible, thereby generating as much revenue as they can. Scheduled doubleheaders first began to proliferate during the dark days of the Depression, when teams were looking for gimmicks to bring fans through the turnstiles. Offering baseball "twofers" seemed like a good idea—and the innovation became a tradition. The record of consecutive doubleheaders figures to stand forever: the 1928 Boston Braves, bedeviled by a rash of rainouts, had to play nine straight twin bills, including four in a row against the New York Giants, September 10-14.

Why is the "magic number" so important in a pennant race?

The "magic number" reveals what combination of victories and defeats a team needs to win a championship. To calculate the "magic number" of a first-place team, compute the number of games to be played, add one, then subtract the number of games ahead of the closest opponent in the loss column of the standings. Any such combination of wins by the first-place team and losses by the second-place team will clinch the pennant for the team in the lead.

Why is trading an integral part of baseball?

There are various reasons for making deals. Sometimes a bad team deals in the hope new faces will bring new customers through the turnstiles. Salary disagreements, personality clashes, or a player's wish to be closer to home are other factors. When Bill Veeck owned the Cleveland Indians, he deliberately acquired the son-in-law of Washington owner Clark Griffith, who disapproved of Veeck's endless gimmicks. After Joe Haynes was secured from Chicago, Veeck was able to negotiate the deal with Washington which brought Early Wynn and Mickey Vernon to Cleveland in time to win the 1948 American League flag.

Why did baseball lift its early restrictions on night games?

Although night baseball—which began in the majors when the Cincinnati Reds installed lights in Crosley Field in 1935—was initially limited to seven games per season (ostensibly one against each rival in the eight-team league), baseball officials realized that baseball after dark was attracting crowds of fans who formerly couldn't come to weekday games. When President Franklin D. Roosevelt suggested during the war that more night games would hike the morale of war-plant workers, baseball teams were only too happy to oblige.

Why do teams take batting practice?

The tradition of batting practice traces its roots to Harry Wright, who managed the Philadelphia Phillies before the turn of the century. Wright required each player to hit 12 balls as part of a pregame exercise program. Wright ordered fungo hitters, standing down the foul lines, to hit fly balls to the outfielders. Before Wright launched the double-barreled routine, teams only loosened up by tossing balls around. Wright's routine attracted crowds who wanted to watch their favorites hit—even if only in practice. Modern "batting practice"—with players taking several swings in a batting cage before the game—evolved from Wright's innovation. It is interesting to note that baseball's pregame ritual—which can take one-and-a-half to two hours—is several times longer than that of any other major sport.

Why do teams use special pitchers for batting practice?

Before 1937, when the Yankees' Paul Schreiber became the first batting-practice pitcher, teams routinely used regular pitchers to throw batting practice. But the risk of injuring or simply tiring a regular hurler seemed too great, so clubs began to hire specialists who could reach the plate consistently. The function of a batting-practice pitcher is to help the batters get into a groove; unlike a regular pitcher, the batting-practice pitcher does not try to outfox or overpower the batters he faces.

Why did rookies once have a tough time getting batting practice?

Years ago, veteran players treated rookies in much the same way that fraternity brothers treat pledges—with disdain, indifference, and occasional vindictiveness. Veterans, fighting hard to hold onto their jobs in the face of challenges from talented rookies, often made it hard—if not impossible—for freshmen to take swings in the batting cage. Rookies sometimes came to the park to find their bats sawed in half, their clothes tied in knots, or their shoes nailed to the floor. By the time they got straightened out, batting practice was over.

Why do teams use scouts?

Advance information is very helpful in winning a game. Scouts sign players, scour major- and minor-league cities to check on potential trades or free agent acquisitions, and gather information about teams their clubs will face next. Scouts commonly rate each player's throwing ability, defense, running speed, hitting, and power, and include suggestions on how to pitch opposition hitters. They also monitor pitchers and provide suggestions for their own team's hitters. In scouting, the best information is current, since a hitter might be in a slump or a fielder might have a sore throwing arm.

The patron saint of scouts is Howard Ehmke, a Philadelphia Athletics pitcher who was sidelined briefly with a sore arm during the 1929 season. Connie Mack, manager of the Athletics, sent Ehmke to scout the Chicago Cubs, who went on to win the National League pennant. Since his arm had a chance to rest, Ehmke regained his strength in time to open the 1929 World Series as a surprise starter. Armed with the knowledge he acquired on his scouting mission, Ehmke went all the way to beat the Cubs, 3–1. Philadelphia took the World Series in five games.

Among the best scouts today are Jim Russo of the Baltimore Orioles and Eddie Lopat of the Montreal Expos.

Why is the infield "dragged" in the fifth inning?

Although "dragging the infield" smoothes the field and makes for better baseball, the fifth-inning routine is a relatively new concept. It began in the Pacific Coast League in 1949, when Hollywood Stars manager Fred Haney decided that fans would buy more concessions during a 10-minute break in the middle of the game. Haney came up with the brainstorm—now universal in professional baseball—while pondering a question from concessions chief Danny Goodman on how to hike business.

Why is the National Anthem played before games?

The pregame playing of "The Star-Spangled Banner" began as a morale-builder in 1942, the first full year of U.S. involvement in World War II. Fans objected to pre-game prayers, and the playing of the National Anthem, accompanied by a standing salute to the flag, seemed like a gesture of loyalty that would provoke little opposition.

Why are certain habits believed to bring good luck in baseball?

Although Edmund Burke once called superstition "the religion of feeble minds," ball players have always felt good-luck rituals *might* help and *couldn't* hurt. Among the things which are supposed to bring good-luck are: knocking on wood; carrying a rabbit's foot, four-leaf clover, or other charm; swinging two bats as well as the regular bat while loosening up; seeing empty barrels; putting on the left shoe first; having the pitcher receive the ball from the same man each inning; finding a lucky hairpin that will inspire a slew of hits; stepping on third base or another base before taking a fielding position; and wearing the same clothes, eating the same food, and doing the same things while in a hot streak.

Why do players avoid certain patterns of behavior?

Just as there are numerous good-luck charms and rituals, there are a number of habits believed to be associated with bad luck. Players say it is bad to chew gum instead of tobacco (many chew a mixture); walk between the catcher and umpire when coming to bat; step on the foul lines; put a hat on a hotel bed; open an umbrella in a room; see a black cat; or have anything to do with the No. 13. One of those who wore No. 13 was Ralph Branca, who threw the home run ball that won the 1951 pennant for the New York Giants in the bottom of the ninth inning of the playoff finale.

Why are ball players always chewing?

Players chew gum, licorice, tobacco, and a variety of other items because they need moisture (especially in the field, where there is no access to a drinking fountain). Constant exercise of the jaw muscles helps relax nerves and keeps concentration high.

Why was 56 a lucky number for Joe DiMaggio?

During Joe DiMaggio's record 56-game hitting streak between May 15 and July 16, 1941, the Yankee center fielder also collected 56 singles and scored 56 runs—making the number 56 appear particularly lucky for him.

Why did Ralph Branca change his uniform number after giving up the famous "shot heard 'round the world" by Bobby Thomson?

Ralph Branca of the Brooklyn Dodgers was wearing No. 13 when he yielded the three-run, bottom-of-the-ninth home run that Bobby Thomson hit for the New York Giants in the decisive third National League playoff game of 1951. Thomson's blast, generally considered to be the most dramatic home run in baseball history, capped a sensational comeback drive by the Giants, who had trailed the Dodgers by more than a dozen games in August. The home run also achieved fame of sorts for Branca, who was embarrassed by the notoriety and sought to change his luck. The pitcher wore No. 12 during the 1952 season, but then figured his uniform number had little to do with actual performance. He resumed wearing No. 13 in 1953.

Why didn't broadcaster Bob Wolff mention Don Larsen's World Series no-hitter in progress?

On October 8, 1956, righthander Don Larsen of the New York Yankees pitched the only no-hitter in World Series history. In fact, Larsen's 2–0 victory over the Brooklyn Dodgers was a perfect game. During the contest, Bob Wolff refrained from mentioning the no-hitter because he subscribed to the ancient baseball superstition that it is bad luck to mention a no-hitter in progress. But Wolff, a fine sportscaster, dropped many hints to the vast radio audience. He said things like "Larsen has set down 18 in a row" and "There's nothing but goose-eggs on the scoreboard for the Dodgers." He even said, "There are only four hits in this game and the Yankees have all of them." Wolff said he was influenced by the fact that Red Barber did mention a World Series no-hitter in progress by Floyd Bevens of the Yankees in 1947—and that Bevens lost both no-hitter and game with two outs in the ninth inning. Barber received much flak for violating baseball superstition, but Wolff, highly praised for his poise during Larsen's gem, used the situation as a springboard for his career.

Why did Rollie Fingers grow his famous mustache?

Rollie Fingers, the star relief pitcher, who increased his record total of saves to 301 during the 1982 campaign, originally grew his Snidely Whiplash mustache at the suggestion of Oakland Athletics owner Charlie Finley in 1972. Finley, constantly searching for gimmicks to generate publicity, paid members of the A's $300 apiece to grow mustaches for postseason games in 1972. Fingers, knowing he had a good thing g(r)owing, decided to keep it. "It just so happened we won the Series that year so I figured I'd keep mine for another year. In 1973, we won again, so I thought I might as well keep a good thing. We won again in 1974 and I've had it ever since. I'm going to keep it until I retire and then I'm going to shave it off and live like a normal person."

Why is the hot dog so closely associated with baseball?

Veteran ballpark vendor Harry M. Stevens, who created the first scorecard in Columbus, Ohio, before the turn of the century, began to handle concessions for the New York Giants in 1894. Seven years later, ice cream wasn't selling on a cold spring day, so Stevens sent out for sausages, boiled them, slipped them lengthwise into rolls, and sent his hawkers through the stands shouting "Get 'em while they're hot!" Cartoonist Tad Dorgan supplied the name "hot dog" to the Stevens sausages, which reminded him of dachshunds. It was also Harry M. Stevens who came up with a workable way to keep hot dogs hot; his vendors paraded around ballparks with frank-loaded hot water tanks strapped to their necks.

Why do fans stand for the "seventh-inning stretch"?

In most parks, fans stand to stretch before the home seventh inning—often to the tune of organ music and clapping hands. There are several theories about the origin of this tradition. Some historians insist that the fans of the Cincinnati Red Stockings, the first professional team in 1869, stood in the seventh to gain temporary relief from the hard wooden benches then in use. Others say that fans in Washington stood out of respect for President William Howard Taft, who attended the 1910 opener but appeared to be leaving in the seventh inning (he was merely stretching himself). Still other researchers claim that the seventh-inning stretch started in 1882, when Brother Jasper, coaching the Manhattan College team, instructed his student-spectators not to move about or leave their seats with a game in progress. He apparently relented in the seventh inning on an afternoon when the fans seemed particularly restless. The coach stopped the game and told the fans to stretch their legs.

Why did a .267 hitter once win the Most Valuable Player Award?

In 1944, Marty Marion was named Most Valuable Player in the National League because his expert glove work at shortstop made champions of the St. Louis Cardinals. Marion hit only .267 for the season, but voting writers thought he merited the honor because of his defense and leadership. Years later, Roger Maris won the American League honor with an average only two points higher. But Maris, an outfielder for the New York Yankees, blasted a record 61 home runs when he won the prize (for the second straight year) in 1961.

Why are Gold Glove awards given?

Baseball's Gold Glove awards were created in 1957 as a joint venture of the Rawlings Sporting Goods Company and *The Sporting News,* a weekly sports publication. The award was initially to be given to one player for each position; separate teams in each league were named thereafter. The Gold Glove award is a gilded baseball glove presented before a game at each winner's home park. Repeat winners have an additional gold crest attached to their trophies.

Chapter 11

OUT OF THE MAJORS

Introduction

Professional baseball includes not only the Major Leagues, but also a complex network of minor-league teams, baseball in other countries, and—in the past—organized leagues that challenged the majors or gave those excluded from the big-leagues a chance to play for pay.

Minor-league baseball, the traditional training ground for the majors, gives talented players the chance to polish their skills and garner valuable experience that will eventually enable them to compete against the best ball players in the world.

Almost all major-league players spend time in the minors, though Sandy Koufax, Al Kaline, Catfish Hunter, and Bob Horner were notable exceptions. Ty Cobb, Rogers Hornsby, Babe Ruth, and Hank Aaron were among the game's immortals who began their pro baseball careers in the minors.

Cobb nearly jeopardized his career by considering an offer to jump to the upstart Federal League in 1914, but the veteran Detroit outfielder rejected a lucrative five-year pact—a wise decision in the wake of the Federal League's dissolution after only two years of operation.

The Federal League was the only serious threat to the stability of the majors in this century (though the Continen-

266

tal League, proposed by Branch Rickey, forced major-league expansion in 1960). A significant number of major- and minor-league players hopped into Federal League uniforms and several Federal League owners, as well as ballparks, were absorbed into the existing majors after the agreement that produced the Federal League fold of late 1915.

Except during the war years and the Great Depression, professional baseball has thrived throughout the century. But it probably would have done even better if it had taken in the top stars of the Negro Leagues, two six-club circuits comprised of baseball's best black talent. With blacks barred from Organized Ball by an unwritten agreement among owners, Negro League clubs provided outlets for many top players. A few—such as Satchel Paige, Monte Irvin, and Roy Campanella—eventually reached the majors, but most of those who did had spent their primes playing in obscurity.

Conditions in the Negro Leagues were far different from what they were in the majors—or even in the all-white minors. Although they had to cope with segregation and discrimination of every sort, black teams played so well that they invariably won when matched in exhibition play against white opposition from the majors and minors. Such black-white contests invariably occurred after the conclusion of the major-league schedule.

Modern Japanese teams would have much more difficulty beating major-league opponents than the old Negro League teams would have had. Baseball is also the national pastime of Japan, but Japanese players, as a rule, are not as big or strong as their American counterparts. Japanese ballparks are smaller, enabling the more wiry sluggers to reach the fences. Pitchers work often and don't go to the showers when knocked out of a game; instead, they head for the bullpen and throw until meeting the fans' approval. Lineups are selected during pregame practice, when managers and coaches determine which regulars look rusty and need a rest. All players have one-year contracts that include a tough reserve clause restricting free movement of players between teams.

Baseball out of the majors is noteworthy because many of the participants, today as well as yesterday, are professionals striving to meet certain levels of excellence. For some, achievement of those goals will mean a ticket to the Major Leagues.

This chapter looks at life outside the majors—not only as that life exists today but also as that life shaped baseball history. The record-breakers of professional baseball outside the majors are revealed and the deserving stars who never had a big-league chance are saluted. No one will know whether the Pittsburgh Crawfords, perhaps the greatest team of the Negro Leagues, could have played in the majors, but the thought will spark provocative discussion wherever baseball historians gather.

What we do know is that baseball outside the majors is too much a part of the game's heritage to be overlooked. The pages that follow attempt to fill some of those gaps in history.

Why was a National Association of Professional Baseball Clubs created for the minor leagues?

In September 1901, wanton raids by major-league teams threatened to ruin minor-league baseball. The National Association was created to provide strength through unity for independent minor-league team operators. The Association survives today as the umbrella organization of the minor leagues.

Why did the Federal League threaten the minors?

The Federal League began life as the financially unstable

United States League in 1912 and changed its name the following year. Late in 1913, Chicago coal magnate James Gilmore reorganized the league and started recruiting major-league talent by offering fat contracts and building new ballparks. Although several "name" players jumped the majors for the Federals, the league was unsuccessful in its bid to become a third major league because it was forced to rely chiefly on second-line major-leaguers and top-flight minor-league talent. That was enough to threaten several minor leagues, however, including the heretofore stable International League, first established in 1887 (as the International Association). Several International League clubs moved out of cities invaded by the Federals, giving the International League the uncomplimentary nickname "the Belgium of Baseball" (since it surrendered easily to invaders). When the Federal League folded after the 1915 season, minor-league baseball again began to grow and prosper.

Why did the Federal League fold?

The untimely death of Robert Ward, owner of the powerful Brooklyn Federal League team, coupled with several court actions and failing finances, forced the Federal League to suspend operations after the 1915 season. The National League struck a secret deal to buy out the loop (in the hope of luring deserting stars back) but American League president Ban Johnson, angered at the Federal's attempts to rival the majors, refused to give the Federal League owners a penny of settlement fees. A negotiated peace was finally struck on December 22 over the objections of the Baltimore Federal League team, which sued baseball for $1 million and ultimately lost in the historic United States Supreme Court decision of 1922 that exempted baseball from antitrust laws.

Why was Joe DiMaggio's minor-league hitting streak ironic?

When Joe DiMaggio was a minor-league outfielder for the San Francisco Seals of the Pacific Coast League in 1933, he mounted a strong challenge to professional baseball's record hitting streak of 69 games, by Joe Wilhoit of Wichita (Western League) in 1919. DiMaggio, then just 18 years old, hit in 61 straight games before his streak was stopped. The irony of his performance was that DiMaggio, unable to topple a minor-league record hitting streak, later established a major-league standard (56 straight games in 1941) that others couldn't exceed. DiMaggio batted .405 during his minor-league hitting streak—100 points below the mark Wilhoit recorded in his.

Why were the Baltimore Orioles once the terror of the International League?

When Jack Dunn ran the Baltimore Orioles of the International League, his players were outstanding—especially between 1919 and 1925. The 1920 edition of the Orioles had a season's batting average of .318 and won their last 25 games of the year to eke out a one-and-a-half game margin over second-place Toronto. The Maple Leafs went 20–2 down the stretch but it wasn't enough to overcome the Orioles, who erased Toronto's one-game lead of August 29. Baltimore's sizzling finish remains the greatest stretch-drive showing in the history of the minor leagues.

Why did major-league teams conceive the idea of grooming new talent in the minors?

In 1926, Branch Rickey's St. Louis Cardinals sought to purchase a player from the Joplin, Missouri club. When their interest became known, a bidding war ensued, forcing the economy-conscious Cardinals out of the running. Rickey approached Cardinal owner Sam Breadon and said, "If we can't buy the contracts of players we like, we'll have to grow our own." Cardinal scouts were hired to sign players and other teams followed suit—putting an end to the baseball tradition of independent minor-league operators selling their stars to the majors. By 1940, the Cards owned 32 teams and had working agreements with eight others. They controlled all the players in two separate leagues, prompting Commissioner of Baseball Kenesaw Mountain Landis to limit such working arrangements to one team per league.

Why is minor-league stardom no guarantee of major-league success?

Stardom in the minors is no guarantee of success in the majors because the overall caliber of play, the quality of facilities, and even the atmospheric conditions are often quite different at the minor-league level. Joe Bauman, for example, once hit 72 home runs—a professional record for a single season—but he did it for a Class C team in a league with short fences, weak pitching, and thin mountain air (conducive to long-ball production). Bauman never reached the majors, but Gene Rye did; he hit .179 with no homers in a brief Red Sox trial after once hitting three home runs in an inning as a minor-leaguer (1930). Joe Hauser was the only man to exceed 60 home runs in a season *twice* in pro ball, but he was nothing special in the majors. Steve Bilko, with two 50-homer seasons in the minors, also fizzled once he reached the big leagues. Among the players who made successful careers out of minor-league ability were Ox Eckhardt, Nick Cullop, Tom Winston, Smead Jolley, and Lou (the Mad Russian) Novikoff.

Why is Ron Necciai remembered for his minor-league pitching?

Although pitching success in minor-league baseball cannot be fairly compared with pitching in the major-leagues, Ron Necciai did achieve a professional baseball mark worthy of note. Pitching for Bristol of the Appalachian League on May 13, 1952, Necciai fanned 27 batters during a no-hitter against Welch, West Virginia. One out was recorded on a groundout, but Necciai was able to whiff 27 because his catcher missed a third strike, allowing a runner to reach first safely. Necciai failed to amount to much in a brief major-league fling. (The major-league mark for strikeouts in a game is 21, by Tom Cheney of Washington in a 16-inning game against Baltimore in 1962. Several pitchers share the nine-inning mark of 19 strikeouts.)

Why has barnstorming disappeared from baseball?

Barnstorming—tours of small (often farm) communities by teams of major-league players—went the way of the buffalo nickel with the advent of televised games. Prior to TV, baseball enthusiasts who lived far from major-league cities got their only chance to see the stars live through the postseason ritual of barnstorming. Both major-leaguers and Negro League stars regarded barnstorming as an economic necessity, even though they had to play under dim lights in county fair ballparks and live out of suitcases on buses or trains.

Some barnstorming has taken baseball players overseas. The first barnstorming tour, in fact, occurred in 1888, when A. G. Spalding's Chicago White Stockings and an all-star team headed by the New York Nationals' John Montgomery Ward launched an around-the-world tour. Stops included Colorado Springs, the Kingdom of Hawaii, Sydney, Cairo, Naples, Rome, Paris, and London. In 1913 and 1924, Giants' manager John McGraw headed similar junkets, helping to bring the game to Japan and China for the first time. The final game of the 1913 trip was played before 35,000 Britishers, including the King of England.

Why did minor-league baseball decline after a postwar peak?

In 1949, there were 448 minor-league teams in 59 leagues, the largest roll-call in National Association history. Attendance was 26 million—some two-and-a-half times what the 16 major-league teams drew that year. By 1963, however, the minors had slumped to 130 teams in 18 leagues. The biggest factors were (1) the end of the independent operator in the minors; (2) the advent of television and air-conditioning, which kept fans home; and (3) expansion of the majors and major-league TV into minor-league territory.

Why did the Hollywood Stars wear shorts?

The long-time Pacific Coast League Hollywood Stars, known for numerous innovations, unveiled a uniform combination of T-shirts and shorts in 1950. The suits weighed much less than traditional flannels and naturally retained less perspiration, so the players were pleased. The fans, however, were another story. With fan reaction negative, the Stars wore the short uniforms only sporadically after 1950 and never again after 1953. Some two-dozen years later, however, shorts were worn for the first time in the majors when Bill Veeck outfitted his Chicago White Sox in collared shirts and short pants. Veeck's experiment was even more short-lived than the innovation in Hollywood— mainly because players proved reluctant to slide without adequate protection for their shins.

Why was the old Atlanta park tricky territory for outfielders?

Ponce de Leon Park, long-time home of the powerful Atlanta Crackers, had a magnolia tree in center field. When the park was torn down after its last season in 1964, the magnolia tree was left untouched. A shopping center now surrounds the famous tree.

Why did minor-league baseball delay Warren Spahn's candidacy for the Baseball Hall of Fame?

After he left the National League at age 44 in 1965, the great lefthanded pitcher made token appearances (as publicity stunts) for minor-league teams in Tulsa, Oklahoma, and Mexico City. Since baseball rules stipulate that eligible players must wait five years after retirement—from any form of professional baseball—before they can be considered, Spahn's candidacy was delayed. The winner of 363 major-league games—all after World War II—was eventually enshrined, befitting a pitcher who won more games than any other southpaw.

Why did minor-league teams in Pawtucket and Rochester make national headlines in 1981?

Pawtucket and Rochester, farm clubs of the Boston Red Sox and Baltimore Orioles, respectively, carved a niche in the baseball record book when they played a 33-inning game—the longest in the history of professional baseball—in 1981. The game began on April 18, was suspended, then resumed until completion on June 23. The contest consumed eight hours and twenty-five minutes, exceeding the previous mark for longevity by four innings. Pawtucket won, 3–2.

Why did a minor-league team in Denver draw more than 65,000 fans to a game?

On July 3, 1982, the Denver Bears of the Class AAA American Association drew 65,666 fans to their annual Fireworks Night promotion, an event timed to coincide with Independence Day. The pyrotechnical display in Denver has become so impressive each year that crowds for the event increase annually. While Denver holds the record for the largest single-game crowd in the minors, the season mark belongs to the Louisville Redbirds of the American Association. In 1983, that club became the first minor-league franchise to top the million mark.

Why is there a limit to the number of times a major-league player can be optioned to the minor leagues?

Every big-league player can be included on the 40-man "protected" list of a major-league team and be sent back to that team's minor-league system six times. Once those options are exhausted, the major-league team must keep him or risk losing him to another organization through the annual winter draft of minor-leaguers. Those eligible for the draft include players not on the parent team's protected list as well as players whose options have expired, leaving them "frozen" in the minors and ineligible for recall. If a frozen player passes untouched through the draft, he may rejoin his parent team only if it reacquires his contract through purchase. This cannot happen until all other clubs have waived their right to claim him. Draft sessions are conducted in reverse order of the standings so that the weakest teams can obtain the best possible players first.

Why are there three Triple-A leagues in the minors?

An agreement between the major- and minor-leagues requires each of the 26 big-league teams to own or operate at least one team at each of the three minor-league levels (Class AAA, Class AA, and Class A). The 26 Class AAA teams in the United States and Canada are divided into three leagues for two reasons: geographic proximity and a size reasonable enough to permit proper scheduling and competitive pennant races. The three Triple-A, or Class AAA, leagues are the International League, based primarily in the East; the American Association, in the Midwest; and the Pacific Coast League, in the Far West. Triple-A teams operate in larger cities than those of Double-A or Class A and provide a direct pipeline of players to the majors.

Why are the Newark Bears remembered as a great minor-league team?

The New York Yankees' top farm, based in Newark, New Jersey, was a perennial minor-league power. In 1937, the Bears were so strong that 16 of their 17 players made the Major Leagues—nine of them in 1938. The Bears had a 109–43 record in 1937, but that was not the best in Triple-A history; the 1934 Los Angeles Angels of the Pacific Coast League were 137–50 for a remarkable .733 winning percentage.

Why was it difficult to keep league standings for Negro League clubs?

Before the Organized Ball color line was lifted in 1947, black ball players displayed their talents in the Negro Leagues, consisting of two six-club circuits. Games were played not only against league rivals but also against any opponent which promised a return at the gate. Thus, keeping track of wins and losses was not easy—especially because teams played an unequal number of games.

The average player salary in the Negro Leagues was $18-$20 per week—not much compensation for a circuit that depended for travel on small, cramped, steamy buses that broke down frequently (the Newark Eagles became the first team to buy a large, air-conditioned bus, but didn't do so until after World War II).

Life in the Negro Leagues was complicated by the fact that hotels in many towns refuse to board blacks, and restaurants often refused to serve them. Players were often housed in private homes, usually in poor sections of cities where they had scheduled games.

Why was Rube Foster called "the Father of Black Baseball"?

Rube Foster not only organized the first great black team, the Chicago American Giants, but organized the first black league (the Negro National League in 1920) and encouraged participants to maintain a high level of play so they would be ready when the doors to the all-white majors opened. A great fastball pitcher who later became a prominent manager in black baseball, Foster was elected to the Hall of Fame in 1981.

Why was Josh Gibson called "the black Babe Ruth"?

Josh Gibson was a power-hitting catcher who hit more than 70 homers in a season several times in the Negro Leagues. In 1930, his first season, the 19-year-old receiver slammed the only fair ball ever hit over the distant Yankee Stadium roof. From 1933 to 1945, he was chosen for the Negro Leagues' East-West (All-Star) Game every year but

1941, when he played in Mexico (Roy Campanella won the job in 1941). Gibson's batting average was .457 in 1936 and .440 in 1938—even though such freak pitches as the spitball, emery ball, mud ball, and shine ball (all banned in the majors) were legal in the Negro Leagues.

Why is Satchel Paige such a legendary figure in baseball?

Satchel Paige was called "the black Matty" after Hall of Famer Christy Mathewson. Paige, who began pitching for the Chattanooga Black Lookouts in 1926, enjoyed a long career as a Negro Leagues star, enterprising barnstormer, and standout major-leaguer—even though he reached the big leagues with Cleveland in his 40s, long after most men would have retired.

Thanks to a resilient right arm, Paige worked more than 2,000 games and threw more than 100 no-hitters. As a barnstormer, he sometimes made $35,000 per year—even during the Great Depression. Paige was advertised as "The World's Greatest Pitcher—Guaranteed to Strike Out the First Nine Men." The owner of pinpoint control, Paige would show his talent for precision by throwing the ball over the top of a Coke bottle. Durability was another Paige characteristic. He was a workhorse—pitching in 30 games over a 30-day span for the 1941 Kansas City Monarchs. In 1965, at age 59, he pitched the first three innings of a game for the Kansas City Athletics against the Boston Red Sox, yielding only a double to Carl Yastrzemski, Boston's top hitter.

Why were the Pittsburgh Crawfords believed to be the best of the Negro League teams?

During the 1930s, the Pittsburgh Crawfords owned five future Hall of Famers: Satchel Paige, Josh Gibson, Oscar Charleston, Judy Johnson, and Cool Papa Bell.

The Paige-Gibson battery was generally regarded as the best in the history of Negro League baseball, while Charleston was believed to be the premier hitter for average and a center fielder who was so agile that he was dubbed "the Greyhound of the Garden." If Gibson was the top power hitter in the Negro Leagues, Charleston was the best fundamental batsman.

Bell was regarded as the fastest man who ever wore a professional baseball uniform (it was said of him that he could turn the lights out, run for his bed, and be under the covers before the room got dark). Like Charleston, he was a standout defensive center fielder; Charleston played first for Pittsburgh when Bell was with the club.

Also in that infield was Johnson, generally regarded as the best third baseman in the Negro Leagues. A soft-spoken star with a reputation as a great clutch hitter, Johnson was manager of the Homestead Grays—another great Negro League team—before joining the Crawfords.

Why did Negro League teams fail to win more recognition?

Because Negro League teams played a mixture of league and exhibition games with little regard for opponents so long as they met expenses, the Major Leagues failed to pay them much attention. The big-league establishment charged frequently that the Negro Leagues were not organized, but the truth—historians say now—is that the Negro Leagues were relatively organized, but just not recognized.

The first successful Negro League, the Negro National League, was organized by the charismatic Rube Foster in 1920. Members were the Chicago American Giants, Chicago Giants, Cuban Stars, Dayton Marcos, Detroit Stars, Indianapolis ABCs, Kansas City Monarchs, and St. Louis Giants. No final standings were published but the American Giants were awarded the pennant.

The Negro National League lasted until 1931, was reformed by Pittsburgh Crawfords owner Gus Greenlee two years later, and was joined by a Negro American League in 1937. A new East-based Negro National League died in 1948, the year after Jackie Robinson integrated the majors (winning the instantaneous support of black baseball fans). The Negro American League played on until 1960.

A third major circuit in the Negro Leagues, the Eastern Colored League, lasted from 1923 to 1928.

Why was the Negro All-Star Game more important than the Negro World Series?

The black All-Star Game, or East-West game, like the midsummer classic of the white Major Leagues, began in 1933 and immediately became the most important black sporting event in the country. Fans voted in polls conducted by the *Chicago Defender* and *Pittsburgh Courier*, two black newspapers with national circulations, and thousands of returns were tabulated. The annual game drew some 30,000 fans—who paid big-league prices—and attracted attention from the white media as well as black sportswriters. Caliber of play was high and players considered it an honor to be picked for the Chicago-based game.

The Negro World Series did not have such luck. The season-closing series did not draw support from black fans because they couldn't afford to spend hard-earned money for a series that lasted from seven to nine games. Even with Negro World Series games in cities where black populations were large, the post-season series never received the attention of the East-West game.

Why is baseball the national game of Japan?

American missionary Horace Wilson taught baseball to his Japanese pupils in 1869 and Hiroshi Hiraoka brought back a translation of American rules in 1877. But it took a series of visits by American all-stars, starting in 1913, to fan developing Japanese interest in baseball.

Without competition from such American sports as football, basketball, or hockey, baseball became firmly emplanted as the Japanese national game. The island's first professional circuit was founded in 1936, two years after a crowd estimated at one million poured out to welcome an American all-star squad headed by Babe Ruth and Lou Gehrig. Ruth's popularity in Japan was so enormous—especially after his 13 homers helped the all-stars go 16-0 against college opposition—that traditionally shy Japanese fans dared to knock on his hotel room door for autographs. Even during World War II, Ruth's name remained on the lips of Japanese soldiers. They taunted their American adversaries with cries of, "To hell with Babe Ruth!"

Why was Sadaharu Oh called "the Japanese Babe Ruth"?

Like Babe Ruth, Sadaharu Oh was a lefthanded hitter with a penchant for hitting the long ball. Oh broke into Japan's pro ranks in 1959 and, in 1977, became the "world" home run champion when he socked No. 756 for the Yomiuri Giants, one of four clubs in Greater Tokyo. The 6-foot, 174-pound first baseman, who lost a televised home run derby to Hank Aaron in 1974, had a Mel Ott-like batting style that endeared him to his fans. As the ball approached, Oh lifted his front foot, adding momentum to his swing. Oh had numerous advantages in his quest to become the "world" home run leader; smaller Japanese stadiums (most 300 feet down the lines); no "brushback pitches," regarded as unsportsmanlike in Japan; umpires who favored the Yomiuri club by popular demand of the Japanese fans; and smaller pitchers who could not throw as hard as their American counterparts.

Why do Japanese teams use American players?

Because the level of play is better in the American Major Leagues than in the Japanese major leagues, Japanese teams actively seek American players. However, they are permitted to carry only two foreigners on their rosters. Among Americans who made good in Japan were infielder Dave Johnson, the first United States import to make a Japanese All-Star team, and outfielder Willie Davis, a one-time star with the Los Angeles Dodgers. Both Johnson and Davis eventually returned to the American big leagues after playing in Japan. Other Americans who did well in Japan were Roy White, Daryl Spencer, George Altman, Don Blasingame, Leron Lee, Clyde Wright, Don Buford, Jim Lefebvre, Adrian Garrett, Walter (No-Neck) Williams, Willie Kirkland, Roger Repoz, and Don Newcombe (a pitcher who made it big as a first baseman in the Orient).

Chapter 12

OFF THE FIELD

Introduction

If attendance figures can be used to gauge fan interest in baseball, the game has never been healthier. A record 45,530,856 fans attended major-league games in 1983; ten teams exceeded the two-million mark and one of them—the Los Angeles Dodgers—went over three million.

College teams also attracted record crowds. The magazine *Collegiate Baseball* reported that 1983 attendance was 12,896,497, led by the 139,843 fans drawn by the Miami (Florida) Hurricanes.

Good clubs, whether professional or amateur, usually have no trouble attracting crowds, though even the best teams stage promotions designed to add to the entertainment on the field. Most modern promotions (such as Bat Day, Jersey Day, Helmet Day, or Batting Glove Day) are simple giveaways with less imagination than the zany stunts pulled by Bill Veeck during his tenure with four clubs over four decades (beginning with the Cleveland Indians in the '40s). But Veeck's spirit survives with such ongoing minor-league promotions as cow-milking contests, auctions of radio announcers, animal giveaways, and giant ice cream sundae eat-a-thons.

Old-Timers Day, conceived by the New York Yankees in 1947, has become an extremely popular event in many ballparks. So has Fan Appreciation Day, when baseball gifts are given to those attending the games.

The boom in collectibles—sparked by the popularity of trivia and nostalgia—has also influenced team marketing departments and promotion people. Magazines, replica uniforms, pennants, buttons, and other items on sale at ballparks and novelty shops are sometimes featured on giveaway days. Fan magazines have sprung up to service the burgeoning baseball card hobby, which has become a full-time business for many collectors. Many of those collectors accidentally stumbled into hidden gold mines by postponing attic or garage cleanings that might have destroyed collectibles now considered to be valuable treasures.

Fans do not have to be baseball hobbyists to enjoy the game; nor do they have to attend games in person. Many avid baseball fans follow their favorite game through the media, which has been covering baseball almost since professional play began in the post-Civil War period.

Radio coverage was initiated in 1921 and television in 1939, giving the game a long and often colorful broadcast history. One of the men most adept at handling baseball re-creations (doing play-by-play through teletyped reports of distant action) was Ronald (Dutch) Reagan, who became President of the United States in 1980. Reagan spent five years at the microphone of Des Moines radio station WHO, where he re-created Chicago Cubs games for an audience that spanned several Midwestern states.

Broadcast coverage of baseball helped create the overwhelming popularity of baseball today. In 1984, three rival firms compete for the baseball card market, numerous newspapers and magazines carry lengthy articles on the game, and cable television stations bring faraway games into countless living rooms.

The traditional link between the fans and the game has been the daily newspaper. James T. Farrell's lifelong love of baseball influenced his novels, but Arthur Daley—who made baseball writing an art and elevated it to such a legitimate writing form that he won a Pulitzer Prize—probably reached more readers through his columns in *The New York Times.*

Red Smith, who concluded a brilliant career with the *Times,* also wrote baseball articles generally regarded to be classics. But few have been able to capture the flavor of an event like Dick Young, whose account of the almost no-hitter by Bill Bevens in the 1947 World Series is a portrait in prose of an unforgettable drama.

Many members of the media become as popular as the men they cover; Ford Frick went from sportswriter to Commissioner of Baseball (with a league presidency in between), while Mel Allen, Red Barber, and Russ Hodges—great play-by-play men of the past—established unforgettable images in the minds of the fans who heard them. Modern broadcast superstars Ernie Harwell, Harry Caray, and Vin Scully carry on that tradition.

This chapter discusses the fans and the media—the rooters and the writers—and their relevance to the stature of the game as America's national pastime. Many of the rooters and writers regard Marvin Miller, the one-time labor negotiator for the Major League Baseball Players Association, as a villain, but players look at him as a savior. His activities took place entirely off the field, with huge implications for the men in uniform, and are included in the pages that follow. Also included is the courtroom wrangling that created the era of free agency, million-dollar contracts, and the firm establishment of baseball as a business rather than a sport.

Too much happens off the field to be overlooked in any serious book on baseball. We choose to conclude our collection of "why" questions and answers with a probing look at some of those activities.

Why was the practice of selling season tickets inaugurated?

The season ticket concept was pioneered by Providence, an 1884 National League team which charged $15 for a season ticket purchased before March 15 and $20 before April 15. That same year, Boston of the National League charged $15 for a season ticket but lopped $5 off that price if the ticket was purchased by or for a woman. Modern major-league teams play 81 home games and can guarantee themselves a base attendance of 405,000 by selling 5,000 season tickets. The advantage of season tickets is obvious; money used to purchase such tickets is immediately available to the team.

Why do baseball tickets have rain checks attached?

Unlike football, baseball is subject to the vagaries of weather; games can be postponed when weather is inclement. Before the turn of the century, teams sold heavy cardboard tickets, collected them before each game, then used them again for future games. But when a game was shortened by rain one day in 1889, New Orleans owner Abner Powell saw fence-jumpers and complimentary guests join paying customers in the line for new tickets. He came up with the idea of a perforated rain-check stub, an innovation still in use today. The first major-league team to issue rain checks was the Detroit Baseball Association in 1890. Its tickets read: "In case rain interrupts game of this date before three innings are played, rain check will admit bearer to grounds for next league game only."

Why were Ladies' Days first held?

Because the presence of women is one way to bring more men to the ballpark, teams have always tried to entice the distaff side. New York of the National League used the idea of granting women free or reduced admission to the park on a one-time basis in 1883, but the practice of periodic

Ladies' Days was not adopted on a regular basis in the majors until 1889, when Cincinnati owner Aaron Stern decided to admit female fans free if they had a paid escort.

In the minor leagues, Abner Powell's New Orleans club had allowed female fans in "for a smile" one day per week as early as 1887. Ladies' Day (and later Ladies' Night) became such a popular promotion that the Chicago Cubs once reported 30,000 free females at Wrigley Field. (The Cubs subsequently decided to limit the number of free admissions for women to 20,000, giving the remainder top priority for the next Ladies' Day game.)

Why were "days" for players inaugurated?

Fans enjoy saying farewell to their heroes on special "days," as they did for Lou Gehrig in 1939 and Babe Ruth in 1947 at Yankee Stadium. Spectators also enjoy saluting popular players in their prime, as they did for Charlie Gehringer in Detroit in 1929 or Rabbit Maranville in Boston the following year. "Days" often feature the retirement of stars' uniform numbers—a tradition that began in 1939, when Gehrig's No. 4 was retired. Four-dozen others, including Hank Aaron and Casey Stengel twice each, have been honored since.

Why did an overflow crowd in Washington cost Walter Johnson a no-hitter?

Walter Johnson, opening the 1910 season for the Washington Senators, made a determined bid to become the first man to pitch a hitless game in the season's inaugural. He might have been successful if not for the huge crowd. In an effort to accommodate the fans, Washington management allowed the overflow to sit behind roped-off sections of the outfield—a common practice of the day. A child, seeking a better vantage point, squeezed under the ropes and inadvertently obstructed right fielder Doc Gessler on one play. When Gessler tripped over the youth, the ball—which had appeared to be a routine fly—dropped for a double. It was the only hit off Johnson that day. Thirty years later, in 1940, Bob Feller of the Cleveland Indians pitched the only Opening Day no-hitter, a 1-0 triumph over the Chicago White Sox.

Why did a player once race a horse around the bases?

In 1913, John (Hans) Lobert of the Philadelphia Phillies was reputed to be the fastest base runner in the National League. He had been timed at 13 4/5 seconds in circling the bases—exceptionally fast by any standard—and a teammate joked he could probably outrun a horse. That "joke" became a promotion when team officials decided to pit their man against a horse in a pregame race. Lobert lost by a nose—but only because the horse—crowding Lobert at third—violated an agreement to race on the outside of the base paths.

Why was the World Series not broadcast until 1921?

The World Series was not broadcast before 1921 because no baseball was broadcast before then. In that year, Pittsburgh's KDKA, founded a year earlier, aired the Pirates-Phillies game on August 5, with Harold Arlin at the mike. KDKA linked with two other Westinghouse affiliates—WJZ in New Jersey and WBZ in Springfield, Massachusetts—to air the Yankees-Giants World Series that fall. The announcer was sportswriter Grantland Rice. The first network broadcast of a World Series game occurred in 1923, when NBC radio aired another meeting of the Yankees and Giants. Announcers were Graham McNamee, Bill

McGeehan, Ford Frick, and Andrew White. Two years later, the Chicago Cubs became the first team to broadcast all home games. via radio station WMAQ.

Why don't teams employ field announcers anymore?

Before the advent of the public address system in 1929, teams employed field announcers, megaphone men who shouted the lineups and substitutions during games. Chicago's Pat Pieper, waiter by night and Wrigley Field megaphone man by day, remained active long after the PA system arrived. He was known for his long, drawn-out cry of "Play Ball!" delivered immediately after announcing the day's lineups.

Why was Lou Gehrig's four-homer performance overlooked the next day?

Although Lou Gehrig became the first American Leaguer (and the first player of the modern era) to hit four home runs in one game, his timing wasn't terrific. June 3, 1932—the date of Gehrig's greatest power show—was also the date John McGraw resigned after 30 years of managing the New York Giants. The New York press, in publicizing the McGraw resignation, virtually overlooked Gehrig's greatest day on the field.

Why did the baseball writers create the Most Valuable Player award?

Prior to 1931, top players in each league were recognized only sporadically. The Chalmers Automobile Company presented cars to the top performers in each circuit from 1911 to 1914, the American League honored its best athletes with league awards from 1922 to 1928, and the National did likewise from 1924 to 1929. The Baseball Writers Association of America—partly in an effort to promote the game by generating publicity—established the Most Valuable Player Award for each league in 1931. Except for a tie between Pittsburgh's Willie Stargell and St. Louis' Keith Hernandez for National League honors in 1979, one player in each league has been honored in the annual voting by a national panel of baseball writers.

Why was Jack Graney known as a trend-setter?

In 1932, Jack Graney started a continuing trend when he became the first former player to broadcast major-league games, jumping from left field to the radio booth of the Cleveland Indians. He lasted for many years and was particularly good at re-creating road games via ticker tape accounts of the play-by-play.

The idea behind using ex-athletes as announcers is to expose the listeners to perspectives that professional (non-player) announcers might not have. Hence, countless others have followed in his wake, including Phil Rizzuto, Ralph Kiner, Jerry Coleman, Don Drysdale, and Tony Kubek. Before his move to the broadcast booth, Graney had been the first player to bat against Babe Ruth, then a pitcher with the Boston Red Sox, in a major-league game (July 11, 1914).

Why did a girl once "bat" in the big leagues?

Kitty Burke was part of an overflow crowd that crammed Crosley Field, Cincinnati, when the Reds hosted St. Louis in one of the first major-league night games, on July 31, 1935. Fans literally spilled onto the field, causing mass confusion for umpires, ushers, and special police. While order was being restored, Ms. Burke dashed for home plate, grabbed a bat from Babe Herman, and took a swing in the batter's box. Although she was quickly escorted out, Kitty later went on the vaudeville circuit, where she was billed as "the girl who batted in the Major Leagues."

Why were games not broadcast in New York for so many years?

By 1936, baseball broadcasts were universally carried outside New York, but owners of the Yankees, Dodgers, and Giants—by handshake agreement—refused to accept radio as a valuable promotional tool. They believed airing the games would discourage fans from coming out to the park. After the close of the 1938 season, however, the thinking changed. The Giants sold exclusive radio rights to their 1939 games for $150,000 and the Dodgers got a contract for $77,000. Yankee games also went on the air that year.

Why did teams once "re-create" their games on the radio?

Better facilities at home studios, plus the high cost of sending announcers and engineers on the road, persuaded baseball teams to "re-create" road games in the studio using telegraphic reports. Broadcasters "re-created" the play-by-play as if they were at the ballpark. They worked with "canned" sound tracks of cheering fans, raising or lowering the volume in direct proportion to the excitement. They also used hollow blocks of wood to suggest the sound of bat hitting ball. Among the best re-creation men were Waite Hoyt, one-time pitching star of the Yankees before taking over microphone duties in Cincinnati, and Les Kieter, who re-created games of the San Francisco Giants for New York fans after the team transferred sites. Hoyt and Kieter both carried the art of re-creation well into the '50s.

Why was Mel Allen known as "the 26th Yankee"?

Mel Allen, the long-time voice of the New York Yankees, was called "the 26th Yankee" because he was as popular among fans as any of the 25 players carried on the Yankee roster. Allen could measure his popularity rating in the sales of Yankee sponsors' products.

Why is Old Timers' Day the best-known and usually the most popular baseball promotion?

For many years, the lone New York Yankee promotion was Old Timers' Day—a two-inning "game" involving stars of the past. Established by Yankee general manager George Weiss in 1947, Old Timers' Day has become a popular promotion for many clubs. Fans simply like to see their former favorites in action.

The idea for Old Timers' Day has its roots in the turn-of-the-century practice of activating retired players in meaningless end-of-season games. James (Orator) O'Rourke was 51 and 11 years gone from the majors when he caught a game for Joe (Iron Man) McGinnity of the New York Giants on September 22, 1904. Jimmy Austin, 46, doubled and stole home for the Browns in 1926. Johnny Evers, 47, played an inning for the 1929 Boston Braves and former pitcher Nick Altrock returned as a 53-year-old right fielder for the Washington Senators on October 6 of that same year.

In 1931, 49-year-old St. Louis Cardinal manager Gabby Street caught three innings in a September game for Sylvester Johnson. Three years later, on September 30, 1934, 52-year-old Charlie O'Leary returned to the majors after a 21-year hiatus to pinch-hit a single for the St. Louis Browns. Even Babe Ruth was used in end-of-season promotions during the '30s. The heavy-hitting right fielder of the New York Yankees reverted to his original position of pitcher on two separate occasions, beating his old Boston Red Sox teammates both times.

The most recent activation of an old-time star occurred in 1976, when the Chicago White Sox gave former hero Minnie Minoso six at-bats at the age of 53. Minoso, a long-time major-league outfielder, delivered one single in his six appearances.

Why was an announcer once traded for a catcher?

In 1948, Ernie Harwell was announcing minor-league baseball games for the Atlanta Crackers, then a top independent team. Dodger general manager Branch Rickey heard him while passing through town and filed his name away for future reference. When regular Brooklyn broadcaster Red Barber turned up ill in mid-season, Rickey asked Atlanta owner Earl Mann whether he would release Harwell from his contract. Mann declined, but said he would trade Harwell to Brooklyn for Cliff Dapper, a catcher who was on the Dodger farm at Montreal. Rickey agreed and the deal turned out well for all sides. Dapper became Atlanta manager in 1949.

Why was "Aunt Minnie" a key figure in Pittsburgh baseball?

When Ralph Kiner was crashing home runs for the Pirates in the late '40s and early '50s, the Pittsburgh radio voice was Rosey Rowswell. To keep fans entertained during those lean years (lean for all the Pirates but Kiner), Rowswell convinced fans to imagine a little old lady with an apartment window facing Forbes Field, then the home of the Buccos. When Kiner hit a long one, Rowswell yelled, "Open the window, Aunt Minnie, here it comes!" He then smashed a lightbulb near the microphone—letting his listeners know Kiner's blast had left the park and "smashed through Aunt Minnie's window."

Why did Brooklyn fans have such a zany reputation?

The reputation of Brooklyn fans stemmed from the exploits of the Brooklyn Dodgers, one of the game's most colorful teams. The Dodgers played in Ebbets Field, a bandbox ballpark which offered short fences and close fan proximity to players. Hilda Chester, one of the more vocal Dodger fans, liked to sit in the center field bleachers, ringing a four-pound cowbell (doctors had told her to exercise her rheumatic arm). The players responded, lending Hilda encouragement, and an Ebbets Field tradition was born. The Dodgers also had a volunteer five-piece band, named "the Dodger Sym-Phony" by broadcaster Red Barber. The band specialized in mocking the actions of rival players with music. Best known were the insulting strains which accompanied unsuspecting visiting batters on their long walks back to the dugout.

Why was Bat Day inaugurated as a promotion?

The idea of giving away bats to fans is a relatively recent one. It came about almost by accident. In 1952, Rudie Schaffer, business manager of the St. Louis Browns during the Bill Veeck regime, managed to purchase 12,000 bats from a supplier in a closeout sale. He then announced that bats would be given away at a doubleheader. More than 15,000 fans attended—a big crowd for the hapless Browns—and a new promotion was born. Such other giveaway days as Cap Day, Photo Album Day, and Seat Cushion Night were spawned by the success of Bat Day.

Why did Bill Veeck once stage a "day" for a fan?

During Bill Veeck's tenure as owner of the Cleveland Indians in the late '40s, a night watchman named Joe Early wrote a letter to the *Cleveland Press* asking why teams were always holding "days" for well-paid stars who didn't need the money instead of for loyal fans who did. Veeck, smelling a gimmick, got the watchman's address from the paper, invited him to the ballpark, but gave no indication of what was to come. The surprised Early first got a series of gag gifts, including an outhouse, a backfiring Model T, and assorted animals, then received a Ford convertible, a refrigerator, a washing machine, luggage, a watch, clothes, a stereo system, and cash.

Why did a midget once bat in the Major Leagues?

Bill Veeck, colorful owner of the St. Louis Browns, signed 3-foot, 7-inch Eddie Gaedel to a one-game contract during the 1951 season. On August 19, Gaedel popped out of a birthday cake marking the club's 50th anniversary in the American League. In the first inning of the second game that Sunday afternoon, Gaedel was sent up to bat for leadoff hitter Frank Saucier. Manager Zack Taylor had to produce his contract on the spot at the request of the umpires, but Gaedel got to bat after the arbiters inspected the documents (Veeck had anticipated such an eventuality and had the papers ready). Gaedel walked on four pitches, then left the game for a pinch-runner. He was ruled ineligible by the American League the next day.

Why is promotion critical in the minor leagues?

Even before competition from television, air-conditioning and other brands of entertainment threatened the survival of the minors, clever promotion was always important for operators who wanted to turn a profit. The lure of the game was just not enough. Joe Engel, whose Chattanooga franchise was one of the more enterprising in the minors, once auctioned off its radio announcer before thousands of cheering women. The winner used him to mow the lawn, wash the dishes, and do other household chores. The Miami team once gave away orchids, animals, and bicycles to entice fans.

Why is baseball card collecting so popular?

Baseball cards have been around since Old Judge Cigarettes made the very first cards in 1886 (players were photographed swinging at a ball on a string inside a studio). Cracker Jack issued a handsome set before 1920, and such gum companies as Big League Chewing Gum, Goudey, DeLong, and National Chicle were active during and after the Babe Ruth era. When the Topps Chewing Gum Company entered the field in 1951, Bowman and Fleer's were the chief competitors, but Topps quickly became the giant of the industry. By 1983, it was turning out more than 250 million cards per year and issuing awards to the top players. The Donruss Corporation joined Fleer's as major competitors for Topps in the early '80s.

The nostalgia wave of the early '70s caused a big boom in card collecting. Adults as well as youngsters got involved and some of them gave up their jobs to devote full attention to the lucrative business of buying, trading, and selling baseball cards.

Card prices vary, with mint condition, hard-to-get superstar cards commanding the highest prices. A 1910 Honus Wagner card issued by a tobacco company (Wagner disdained smoking and had his cards recalled) had a 1983 market value of $20,000—making it the most coveted baseball card of all time.

Why is score-keeping so essential in baseball?

On both the amateur and the professional levels, it is important to keep track of individual as well as team performance. In the Major Leagues, teams carry 25 players, allowing managers the privilege of using their best players as starters and the remainder as reserves. An English-born writer, Henry Chadwick, devised the first system of scoring and created the forerunner of the baseball box score, the compact game summary which yields such information as score by innings, home runs, errors, strikeouts and walks by pitchers, and attendance. Chadwick, long-time rules chairman of the National Baseball Association, began his baseball writing in 1858, two years before Abraham Lincoln got news of his nomination for President while playing in an amateur baseball game.

Why does baseball announce the name of each game's official scorer?

The Baseball Writers Association of America (BBWAA), which controls major-league press boxes, believes players, managers, and fans should know the scorer's identity in the interests of fairness. Revelation of the scorer's name is believed to promote objectivity because the scorer would not wish to be accused of bias, favoring the home club, or helping specific players by giving hits instead of errors on close calls.

Revealing the scorer has always been a controversial subject in baseball. In 1911, American League president Ban Johnson suggested the scorer's identity be kept secret so that players could not pressure him during or after the game. Chicago of the National League had employed a secret scorer—known only as E. G. Green—between 1882 and 1891. Only team president A. G. Spalding knew that Mrs. Elisa Green Williams, mother of team treasurer C. G. Williams, was scoring the games.

Modern scorers are usually BBWAA members except in cities where editors bar their writers from such assignments (not only to guarantee unbiased coverage but also because scorers are paid $50 per game). In some cities, retired or former BBWAA members hold scorers' jobs because they know the game well but have no other interest to protect—helping to promote objectivity.

Why was one person able to "play" for the New York Knicks, the New York Rangers, and the Brooklyn Dodgers?

Gladys Goodding, the organist at Ebbets Field (starting on May 9, 1942), also played for the New York Rangers hockey team and the New York Knickerbockers basketball team at Madison Square Garden—thus earning the rare distinction of "playing" for major-league teams in three sports. Gladys Goodding made a memorable debut in 1942 when she played "Three Blind Mice" as umpires Bill Stewart, Ziggy Sears, and Tom Dunn walked onto the field.

Why did Dodger fans bring radios to the ballpark when the team first moved to Los Angeles?

Cavernous Los Angeles Coliseum, where the Los Angeles Dodgers played before Dodger Stadium opened in Chavez Ravine in 1962, was so huge that fans could not be assured of seeing all the action. So they brought portable radios to the game. To test the number of radios in the ballpark, announcer Vin Scully once asked fans to shout "Happy Birthday" to umpire Frank Secory. Scully counted to three—the prearranged cue—and thousands of fans shouted their greetings to the surprised umpire.

Why did the Los Angeles Dodgers once draw 90,000 fans to an exhibition game?

When the Dodgers first moved from Brooklyn to Los Angeles, they played in the oversized Los Angeles Coliseum, a football field converted to baseball use. On May 7, 1959, when the New York Yankees came to town for an exhibition game, the team drew 93,103 fans, the largest crowd ever to watch a baseball game in the United States. Many came to honor Roy Campanella, the Dodger catcher whose career had been shortened by a winter auto mishap in New York. Three times during the 1959 World Series against the Chicago White Sox, Dodger crowds again exceeded the 90,000 mark.

Why did Curt Flood sue baseball?

After the St. Louis Cardinals traded Curt Flood to the Philadelphia Phillies in 1969, the fleet center fielder refused to report. Instead, he challenged the right of the Cardinals to trade him, filing a suit that challenged the antitrust exemption that baseball had enjoyed since a 1922 U.S. Supreme Court decision against the upstart Federal League. Although the Supreme Court denied Flood's challenge in 1972—exactly 50 years after the original landmark case— events were already in motion which would accomplish Flood's objective.

Why have labor-management problems created interruptions in the normal baseball routine?

Under the direction of former steelworkers' adviser Marvin Miller, a union called the Major League Baseball Player Associatior assumed tremendous power during the

'70s. On April 1, 1972, it staged a 12-day strike over retirement benefits and increased medical premiums. Four years later, with another strike brewing over the expired Basic Agreement between players and owners, teams decided to keep spring training camps closed rather than risk a strike during exhibition play or during the regular season. Commissioner Bowie Kuhn ordered the camps opened, with the players agreeing not to strike while negotiations proceeded. A new three-year agreement (creating free agency via the reentry system) was reached in July, 1976. Players staged a week-long walkout, cutting the last week of exhibition play, in Spring 1980 after an impasse developed over the issue of compensation to the teams losing free agents. That impasse eventually resulted in a seven-week strike that suspended play between June 12 and August 9, 1981.

When play resumed, baseball's hierarchy decided to recapture fan interest by dividing the season into two halves: pre- and post-strike. Winners of divisional races in each half met in pre-Championship Series playoffs (the Divisional Series). The unique format meant that teams did not play equal numbers of games and resulted in a mini-series berth for a sub-.500 team, the Kansas City Royals (50–53 overall), while denying postseason competition to the National League teams with the best records, the Cincinnati Reds and St. Louis Cardinals. (Neither the Reds nor the Cards finished first in either half of the season even though they compiled the best overall records in the league.)

Why do modern players regard Marvin Miller as their Messiah?

In his first 10 years as executive director of the Major League Baseball Players Association, Miller, formerly associated with the United Steelworkers, helped increase the average player salary from $32,500 to $170,000 per year, with top pay rising from $200,000 to $1.5 million per season. Daily meal money for players increased from $18 to $37.50 over the same span, and other player benefits also showed significant jumps.

Why did team mascots become so popular in the wake of free agency?

According to Bonnie Erickson of Harrison/Erickson, the New York commercial design firm which created the Phillie Phanatic, Youppi! (Expos), Dandy (Yankees), and Ribbie & Roobie (White Sox), mascots have become popular because they provide continuous team identification in an era where player movement between teams has increased. Mascots also give fans a rallying point at games and enable teams to stage aggressive off-field promotions. Explains Erickson: "Having a mascot who makes public appearances helps a team's public relations people who have a hard time getting players to make those appearances. Having a mascot available gives teams the chance to be in the public eye without being controversial—and so far none of them has been traded."

Why did an organization of historians almost cost Ty Cobb a batting title?

In 1981, researchers from the Society of American Baseball Research (SABR) discovered through a check of old boxscores that Napoleon Lajoie, and not Ty Cobb, was the winner of the 1910 American League batting crown. They pointed out that Lajoie had hit .383, a point higher than Cobb, thus breaking Cobb's string of nine straight batting titles (three straight crowns before 1910 and five straight after) in the middle.

The startling discovery by SABR resulted in a front-page story in *The Sporting News,* the baseball-oriented weekly, but didn't influence Commissioner Bowie Kuhn, who ruled

Cobb's crown would stand. Several baseball encyclopedias followed the SABR lead and changed the name of the 1910 American League batting champion from Cobb to Lajoie, but baseball officially resisted.

Why was the 1981 All-Star Game a barometer of fan interest in baseball?

The 1981 All-Star Game, originally scheduled for Cleveland on July 14, was cancelled because of the players' strike that began June 12. When the walkout ended, the All-Star Game was rescheduled for August 9 as the start of "the second season." With huge Municipal Stadium in Cleveland the site for the game, a record crowd of 72,086 turned out— a definite indication that the fans, upset over the strike, were glad to have the game back. The previous All-Star record crowd was 69,831, also at Cleveland, in 1935.

Index of Subjects

Doubleheaders
  decrease, 14
  origin of term, 216
  popularity of, 256

Earned run average (ERA)
  best gauge of pitcher, 158
  important statistic, 3
  qualifications for award, 158
  rules for, 43, 44
Eight-team format, 103
Emery ball, 29
Equipment, evolution of, 45-46
Expansion, 15

Fan Day, 295
Fans
  "Do not know rules," 17
  like offense, 29
  origin of term, 220
Farm teams, 228
"Father of Black Baseball," 277
Father of modern baseball, 1
Federal League, 266, 268, 269
Field announcers, 289
Five documents of baseball, 9
First basemen, lefthanded, 184
Forfeits, 31, 32
Foul balls
  batters adept at fouling pitchers, 27
  triple on foul ball, 31
Foul lines, avoiding, 246
Foul strikes, 27
Franchise shifts, 101
Free agency, 111, 159

Game never over, 187
Glasses, 58
Gloves
  first ones worn, 52
  first padded catcher's mitt, 53
  fish-net mitt, 53
  huge catcher's mitt, 53
  not left on field, 33
Gold glove awards, 265
Grand-slams
  major league record in one game, 37
  minor league record in one game, 37
  name, 226
"Grandstand Managers Day," 172

Hall of Fame
  in Cooperstown, 247
  enshrinement, 245
  enshrinement in two Halls, 24
  no relief pitcher in, 248
  no unanimous selection, 247
  opened in 1939, 1
  Orioles, original, in, 126
  requirements waived, 249
Helmet, batting, 55
Hidden-ball trick, 185
Hitting, difficulty of, 181. See also Batting.
Hitting streak
  American League record, 137, 270
  minor league record, 270
  National League record, 26
Holdout, 226
Home field advantage, 110
Home run
  challenge to record, 30
  "Chinese" home runs, 219
  credited with 3-run single, 38
  four home run performance overshadowed, 289
  gopher ball, 224
  inside the park, 69
  last American League pitcher to hit home run, 38
  last American League pitcher to hit home run in World Series, 38
  lost home run crown by blunder, 30-31
  lost home run crown by forfeit, 31
  previous career record, 30
  rule change regarding, 30
  seasonal record, 16, 210
"Homer in the Gloamin'," 197
Hot Corner, 224
Hot dog, associated with baseball, 263

Infield dragging, 260
Infielders, righthanded, 184
Injuries, 141, 149, 156
Inventor of Baseball, 1

Japanese baseball
  American players in, 282
  "Japanese Babe Ruth," 281
  national game, 280
  teams, 267

Index of Names